'Over the course of the 2016 anniversary celebrations, much will be said about Shakespeare's value. And yet, his very real cash value will remain for the most part the elephant in the room. Here at last is a book which owns up to it, and it's wide-ranging and insightful. Properly and refreshingly serious about Shakespeare's harder contributions to the cultural economy. And because of this honest worldliness, sometimes also funny.'

—Professor Ewan Fernie,
University of Birmingham, UK

'This wide-ranging and diverse set of essays demonstrate that, where Shakespeare is concerned, money matters. From the financial constraints and opportunities that shaped Shakespeare's own writing, to the ongoing exploitation of the Shakespeare brand to sell books, beers, dead kings and living actors, this book argues that Shakespeare's currency is inextricable from the worlds of big business, cultural imperialism, international diplomacy and corporate art. On the 400th anniversary of his death, *Shakespeare's Cultural Capital* makes a timely and important case for the ongoing value of Shakespeare's stock.'

—Dr Peter Kirwan,
University of Nottingham, UK

'A fascinating historical and thematic variety of Shakespeare branding, from his place in early modern commercial theatre and publishing, to his power to sell beer, and his importance in the current GREAT Britain government campaign to attract international investment in the UK. Its contributors raise awareness of our own responsibility as consumers of Shakespeare, as scholars, playgoers and members of the public.'

—Professor Alison Findlay,
Lancaster University, UK

Shakespeare's Cultural Capital

His Economic Impact from the Sixteenth to the Twenty-first Century

Edited by

Dominic Shellard
De Montfort University, Leicester

and

Siobhan Keenan
De Montfort University, Leicester

Editors
Dominic Shellard
De Montfort University
Leicester, UK

Siobhan Keenan
De Montfort University
Leicester, UK

ISBN 978-1-137-58314-7 (hardcover) ISBN 978-1-137-58316-1 (eBook)
ISBN 978-1-137-58315-4 (softcover)
DOI 10.1057/978-1-137-58316-1

Cover illustration: © Susana Guzman / Alamy Stock Photo

Printed on acid-free paper

This Palgrave Macmillan imprint is published by Springer Nature
The registered company is Macmillan Publishers Ltd. London.

Contents

List of Figures

Foreword

Culture and the market are often seen to be fundamental enemies. It has often been argued that culture can only flourish outside the market, and that works produced within the market necessarily are of low quality, or even that the outcome cannot be counted as art. This book therefore deals with a most relevant and topical issue. It is important to demonstrate that culture and the market can go well together, and in many cases reinforce each other. This does not mean that all cultural activities should be subjected to the market. Indeed, economic analysis has identified under which conditions the market fails with respect to culture, and when it works well.

Shakespeare's Cultural Capital makes interesting reading for everyone who is interested in knowing how the economic and cultural marketplace has worked and is working in the case of the greatest English author. It is fascinating to read how Shakespeare used the market to promote his texts and plays, and the extent to which he was influenced by the market in his writings and presentations of his plays. How Shakespeare is exploited today to promote tourism to Leicester due to the body of Richard III, or in connection to the London Olympics, is also noteworthy. Finally, many readers will be interested to see that Shakespeare has been used for national political purposes, in particular with regard to the quest for a GREAT Britain.

When reading the text I was struck that the relationship of great artists to the market is of considerable interest in many different countries. This is, for instance, true in the case of Germany, a country in which Goethe and Schiller have always played a huge role. Johann Wolfgang von Goethe was indeed quite aware of the conflicting relationship between culture and the market. In the 'Prelude on Stage' of his masterpiece *Faust Part I*, he sets a director of a theatre against a dramatist. As can be perceived from the following excerpts the two have quite opposing views of how to deal with customers:

Director: Say what success our undertaking
Will meet with, then, in Germany?
I'd rather like the crowd to enjoy it
...
I'd love to see a joyful crowd, that's certain,

When the waves drive them to our place

...

Dramatist: O, don't speak to me of that varied crew,
The sight of whom makes inspiration fade.
Veil, from me, the surging multitude,
Whose whirling will drives us everyway.
No, some heavenly silence lead me to,
Where for the poet alone pure joy's at play:
Where Love and Friendship too grace our hearts

...

What dazzles is a Momentary act:
What's true is left for posterity, intact.

...

Director: Make sure, above all, plenty's happening there!
They come to look, and then they want to stare

....

Each one, himself, will choose the bit he needs:
Who brings a lot, brings something that will pass:
And everyone goes home contentedly.
You'll give a piece, why then give it them in pieces!
With such a stew you're destined for success.

...

Dramatist: You don't see how badly such work will do!
How little it suits the genuine creator![1]

The text reveals how Goethe saw the tension between the goals of theatre directors who are acutely aware that they must attract a sufficient
number of customers in order to survive in their business, and the artists who fear to have to produce for the masses, losing their originality.

Goethe and Schiller, among many other German artists, were heavily
engaged in the economic, political and cultural marketplace. Especially
in the Romantic period they were used as symbols of German thinking
and culture, and to promote unification. But it comes immediately to
mind that the same has occurred for artists in other countries: Tolstoy
in Russia, Molière in France or Cervantes in Spain would be comparable.
The tension between culture and the marketplace is not restricted to
writers but also applies to composers such as Sibelius in Finland, Grieg
in Norway or Smetana in the Czech Republic.

Once a sufficient number of studies corresponding to Shakespeare
and the market have been undertaken, it is possible to compare the
fate of different artists and to gain insights into the exact conditions

under which there is indeed a conflict between culture and the market, as Goethe suggests in the 'Prelude' to *Faust* and in which they go well together, perhaps even reinforcing each other.

Shakespeare's Cultural Capital opens a welcome new area of research in cultural economics. It is to be hoped that similar works are written for artists in various cultural fields and in various countries. This would greatly enhance our knowledge about how artists feel about, and cope with, the market, and how the market copes with culture.

Bruno S. Frey
University of Basel, Switzerland

Note

1. Johann Wolfgang von Goethe (2003) 'Prelude on Stage', *Faust Part I* in *Faust Parts I & II*, translated by A. S. Kline, www.http://www.poetryintranslation. com, date accessed 27 October 2015, lines 35–7, 49–50, 59–65, 73–4, 89–90, 96–100, 104–5.

Acknowledgements

The editors would like to thank the following: Jerry Lewitt and the Warwickshire Beer Company (for permission to reproduce their 'Shakespeare's County' beer label, Figure 6.2); Tim Rees and Rees Bradley Hepburn Ltd (for permission to reproduce their 'Shakesbeer' Shakespeare 'Portraits' for Church End Brewery, Figure 6.4); James Snowling and Harry & Parker (for permission to reproduce their 'Shakesbeerd' label for Pheasantry Brewery, Figure 6.3); Bob Yates and Tunnel Brewery Ltd (for permission to reproduce their 'Quill 1' and 'Quill 2' beer labels, Figures 6.5 and 6.6); the British Council (for permission to reproduce Figures 8.1 and 8.2); the GREAT Britain campaign (for permission to reproduce Figure 8.3).

Notes on Contributors

Susan Bennett is University Professor in the Department of English at the University of Calgary, Canada. She has published widely in a variety of topics across theatre and performance studies, with a particular interest in contemporary productions of Shakespeare's plays. Her chapter in this volume is part of a new project about the instrumentalization of performance in contemporary culture. Co-edited with Mary Polito, her most recent book is *Performing Environments: New Directions in Medieval and Early Modern Drama*, published by Palgrave Macmillan (2014).

Conrad Bird CBE is Director of the GREAT Britain campaign, the UK Government's most ambitious international marketing campaign ever. Based in the Prime Minister's Office at 10 Downing Street, Conrad has been responsible for the global implementation and strategic development of GREAT since its launch in 2012. Prior to GREAT, Conrad was the head of Public Diplomacy and Strategic Campaigns at the Foreign & Commonwealth Office and, before joining Government, spent 18 years in the private sector working for leading advertising agencies and running his own award-winning communications consultancy.

Anna Blackwell is an honorary research fellow at De Montfort University in the Centre for Adaptations, where she also works on the recently acquired Andrew Davies archive and completed her doctoral thesis on the contemporary Shakespearean actor as the site of adaptive encounter. Anna has been published in *Adaptation, Critical Survey* and *The Shakespeare Institute Review*. She is working on chapters on Shakespeare and social media and prestige in adaptation.

Deborah Cartmell is Professor of English at De Montfort University and co-editor of the journals *Shakespeare* and *Adaptation*. She is the founder of the Association of Adaptation Studies and Director of the Centre for Adaptations at De Montfort University. Her most recent book is *Adaptations in the Sound Era: 1927–37* (2015). She is general editor of the Bloomsbury Adaptation Histories series and is working on a three-volume collection of adaptation criticism and a *Handbook to the Biopic*.

Gabriel Egan is General Editor of the New Oxford Shakespeare (2016) and Professor of Shakespeare Studies and Director of the Centre for Textual Studies at De Montfort University. He is the author of *Shakespeare and Ecocritical Theory* (2015) and *The Struggle for Shakespeare's Text* (2010). He co-edits the journals *Theatre Notebook* (for the Society for Theatre Research) and *Shakespeare* (for the British Shakespeare Association). His current research is on authorship attribution by computational stylistics.

Jason Eliadis and **Harvey Scriven** are the co-founders of Arcadian, a strategic evaluation consultancy established in 2003. With backgrounds in international blue chip consulting and marketing respectively, both Jason and Harvey each have over 23 years' experience of providing strategic evaluation advice to clients that range from global businesses to dynamic small companies and from international government institutions to local government agencies. Arcadian is the independent strategic evaluator of the GREAT Britain campaign.

Graham Holderness has published over 40 books, mostly on Shakespeare, and hundreds of chapters and articles of criticism, theory and theology. Recent publications include *Nine Lives of William Shakespeare* (2011); *Tales from Shakespeare: Creative Collisions* (2014); *Re-writing Jesus: Christ in 20th Century Fiction and Film* (2014); and *Black and Deep Desires: William Shakespeare Vampire Hunter* (2015).

Siobhan Keenan is Reader in Shakespeare and Renaissance Literature at De Montfort University, Leicester. She is the author of *Travelling Players in Shakespeare's England* (Palgrave Macmillan, 2002) and *Acting Companies and Their Plays in Shakespeare's London* (2014). She is completing an edition of a previously unpublished, seventeenth-century manuscript comedy, *The Twice Changed Friar* (forthcoming 2017). Her future research projects include a study of the progresses and royal entries of King Charles I.

Bryan Loughrey is an independent scholar who in his free time enjoys a decent pint and the convivial company of his local tavern. He is, with his long-term collaborator Graham Holderness, joint editor of the journal *Critical Survey*. His earlier professional roles included those of Professor of Literary Studies, Dean of Graduate School, Director of Research and international educational consultant. He has commissioned a number of significant literary series including *Shakespearean Originals* (again with Graham Holderness) and *Critical Studies*.

Dominic Shellard is Vice-Chancellor of De Montfort University in Leicester. He has written extensively on post-war British theatre, including biographies of the theatre critics Harold Hobson (*Harold Hobson: Witness and Judge*) and Kenneth Tynan (*Kenneth Tynan: A Life*). He has also undertaken a number of economic and social impact studies for Arts Council England and English regional theatres. This includes an *Economic Impact Study of UK Theatre* (2004).

1
Introduction

Siobhan Keenan and Dominic Shellard

'We were just in a financial position to afford Shakespeare
when he presented himself!'[1]

Subsequent research into the economic difficulties experienced by
late sixteenth-century England might have encouraged scholars such
as Melissa Aaron to reconsider John Maynard Keynes' famous remark
and to observe that 'England produced Shakespeare when she could
least afford him', but Keynes' comment usefully highlights the fact
that Shakespeare's work was financed and made possible by money and
the emergence of a professionalised theatrical market in late sixteenth-
century London.[2] It also reminds us that Shakespeare's 'value' and
impact in the UK and beyond has been economic as well as cultural.
Early twentieth-century scholars were quick to celebrate the cultural
importance of Shakespeare, but the world of Shakespeare studies has
been slower to acknowledge the economic importance of Shakespeare's
works and name, despite the fact that the scholarly Shakespeare
industry has itself been partly based on the ongoing marketability of
England's most famous playwright and his art.

Recent years have seen concerted efforts to address this apparent
'blind spot' in Shakespeare studies. Thus, there has been important
work on Shakespeare in relation to the theatre industry and economy
of his time by scholars such as Douglas Bruster and S. P. Cerasano.[3]
Much closer attention has been paid, likewise, to the business of playwriting and the commercial practices of early modern playwrights and
acting companies, including Shakespeare's main acting company, the
Lord Chamberlain's (later the King's) Men.[4] There have been a number
of studies which explore the use and appropriation of Shakespeare's
name and works, too, especially in modern culture, in spheres such as

the theatre, advertising and education.[5] Such studies have often been indebted to, and informed by, the research of contemporary cultural theorists, with Pierre Bourdieu's concept of 'cultural capital' proving especially important. Bourdieu used his famous phrase to describe the social status and esteem accrued by those members of society who possess 'the cultural competence' to interpret and understand works of art, such as literature.[6] It is a concept which this volume shall be returning to in a variety of ways, as our contributors contemplate the values associated with using and understanding Shakespeare.

The last thirty years have also witnessed fresh interest in Shakespeare's use of economic language, with a series of studies which document or explore his plays and poetry in relation to economic theories and/or their original economic context, borrowing since the 1990s from a new wave of literary criticism christened 'New Economic Criticism'. As two of its pioneers, Martha Woodmansee and Mark Osteen, explain, this can include investigating the 'social, cultural and economic contexts in which individual or related works have been produced', 'understanding texts as systems of exchange' and 'studying exchanges between characters and economic tropes in language', with a focus on 'issues such as the market forces at work in canonization' and the 'selling or publicising of art or literature'.[7] As this overview suggests, New Economic Criticism varies in its approaches to texts, although it is typically 'rooted in semiotic and historicist practices' and 'often employs formalist methods to discuss the interplay between literature and the economic'. The impact of this critical movement on Shakespeare studies was surveyed by Peter Grav in an important article published in the journal *Shakespeare* in 2012.[8] As Grav demonstrates, New Economic analyses of Shakespeare's plays and poetry have been very varied and have led to some fascinating new insights not only into Shakespeare's own overt concern with economic issues (such as usury) and forms of social exchange in plays such as *The Merchant of Venice* and the *Sonnets*, but have thrown fresh light on aspects of the economic context in which he and his peers lived and worked. This has included a growing awareness of the extent to which Shakespeare was an 'active participant in the construction of an economic world of theatre'.[9] There is, however, no existing study specifically focused on the marketing and economic (as well as cultural) impact of Shakespeare. In the year in which we mark the 400th anniversary of Shakespeare's death – an anniversary that will see a host of celebrations, publications and Shakespeare-related commerce – it is fitting that we now reflect more fully on Shakespeare's role in the economic as well as the artistic marketplace. It is with this aim that we invited the contributors to this volume to reflect on the 'cultural capital' and the direct and indirect economic impact associated with Shakespeare and his work since the early modern era. As an area that remains under-researched, we hope that the following essays will offer a timely and distinctive contribution to our understanding of Shakespeare and the Shakespeare industry, as well as a spur to further research in this important field.

The emergence of Shakespeare as cultural icon and brand

Today Shakespeare is a well-recognised cultural icon whose name, image and works circulate widely across the globe. As the world's most famous and arguably most esteemed playwright, Shakespeare has come to be associated internationally with 'high' culture, and yet his fame is not confined to the world of high art. As scholars such as Douglas Lanier have demonstrated, Shakespeare also features widely in modern popular culture: 'Movies, television, radio, pulp fiction, musicals, pop music, children's books, advertisements, comic books, toys, computer games, pornography: nearly every imaginable category of contemporary pop culture features examples of Shakespearian allusion or adaptation'.[10] Shakespeare's ongoing cultural importance would seem to confirm Ben Jonson's famous assertion that Shakespeare and his work were destined to be 'not of an age, but for all time'.[11] But Shakespeare's modern iconic status was neither inevitable nor immediately established.

Shakespeare did come to be recognised as the leading playwright of his day in his own lifetime (as will be discussed in Chapter 2), but drama itself was not held in high cultural esteem by many of his contemporaries. On the contrary, it was traditionally associated with popular culture. Shakespeare's success and the success of the professional stage more generally were to raise the profile and cultural position of drama, but only slowly. That the status of drama remained ambiguous is confirmed, indirectly, by responses to Ben Jonson's publication of a folio edition of his *Workes* in 1616, which included plays that he had written for the public playhouses, alongside his poems for elite patrons and his court masques. The edition faced considerable criticism. While some contemporaries mocked Jonson for his arrogance in publishing an edition of his works, others objected to the format Jonson had used. Folio editions were large and expensive and were traditionally associated with learned works, not plays. The Jonson *Workes* (which also celebrates its 400th anniversary in 2016) set an important precedent in treating plays with this seriousness, and its example was to inspire the posthumous publication of the First Folio edition of Shakespeare's plays in 1623. Indeed, in many respects it was the latter publication that marked the beginnings of Shakespeare's transformation from the most successful writer of his day into long-term cultural icon. As well as preserving approved copies of 36 of his plays, many of which had never been published before, the First Folio confirmed Shakespeare's growing literary reputation, and his importance as a writer to be read as well as performed. Over subsequent centuries, the popularity of Shakespeare's plays on stage was to wax and wane, as his plays were adapted and staged in accordance with changing theatrical practices and fashions, but his life in print was firmly established.

Shakespeare's wider significance as pre-eminent British cultural icon was to emerge more slowly, arguably taking firmest hold from the late eighteenth century in the wake of the Romantics' embracing and mythologising of Shakespeare as an original genius.[12] One sign of the growing importance of Shakespeare as an icon and a 'brand' – separate from his works – is the beginnings of the Shakespeare tourist industry in Stratford-upon-Avon. Often traced to David Garrick's inaugural Stratford Jubilee festival in 1769, the late eighteenth century saw growing numbers of people heading to Stratford-upon-Avon to visit the places where Shakespeare had grown up and the rise of what later scholars have christened 'bardolatry'. As Graham Holderness notes, 'bardolatry as an organised evangelical movement scarcely existed' before the Garrick Jubilee, but it was to thrive thereafter, as did the Stratford tourist industry.[13] Nicola J. Watson reports that visitor numbers steadily rose across the eighteenth and nineteenth centuries: 'in 1806, when records began to be kept, there were about 1,000 visitors a year; 2,200 came in 1851, but, after the opening of the railway line from Warwick in 1860, 6,000 came in 1862; in the tercentenary year of 1864 some 2,800 visitors came in the festival fortnight alone' and 'by 1900, there were some 30,000 visitors a year'.[14] As anyone who has visited modern Stratford will know, the local Shakespeare industry has continued to grow with 'well over a million visits … being paid annually' to the five properties owned by the Shakespeare Birthplace Trust, and many more visitors being drawn to the town in the last fifty years by the opportunity to see Shakespeare's plays performed in his home town by the Royal Shakespeare Company, the dedicated Shakespeare company set up in 1961 by Sir Peter Hall.[15] As the example of the Stratford tourist industry and the creation of the Royal Shakespeare Company indicates, the modern era has seen Shakespeare's increasing importance and deployment not only as a product (on stage and in print), but as a 'brand', with his name used to sell not just his plays and poetry but other products – some Shakespeare-related (such as Shakespeare memorabilia) and some not, such as beer and Britain (as is explored below in Chapters 6 and 8, respectively).

Recent years have seen some fascinating research on the emergence of Shakespeare as a 'brand' and his use in advertising and marketing. As this work has shown, the ways in which Shakespeare – and Shakespearean allusions and quotations or misquotations – have been used in advertising and other forms of popular culture have varied over time, but often businesses who draw on Shakespeare are relying either on the 'cultural capital' that has come to be associated with Shakespeare (to borrow Bourdieu's phrase) and/or the specific cultural associations that Shakespeare has accrued over time. These include his identification 'with "culture", quality, Britishness, tradition' and 'wisdom'.[16] As Douglas Holt explains, these kinds of symbolic associations are characteristic of cultural icons, such icons conventionally functioning as 'exemplary symbols that people accept as a shorthand to represent important ideas'.[17]

These same cultural associations, and the 'capital' associated with knowledge of Shakespeare, also help to explain how and why Shakespeare has come to occupy a key place in the educational systems of a number of countries in the last hundred years, mostly notably in the UK and North America. Despite a backlash against the study and teaching of canonical literature in schools and universities in the 1970s and 1980s, Shakespeare continues to occupy an important place in the UK education sector. Indeed, his place has become more firmly entrenched in the last 30 years, following the introduction of the National Curriculum. Currently, the study of Shakespeare is compulsory at Key Stages 3 and 4 (i.e. for 11–16-year-olds).[18] The widespread study of Shakespeare in schools in the UK and beyond has also stimulated and supported an expanding industry of Shakespeare textbooks, scholarly studies of his works and student editions of the plays, as well as feeding into theatre programming and outreach work at national and regional theatres. While defenders of the curriculum argue for Shakespeare's value in teaching students about the human condition as well as drama, the compulsory teaching of Shakespeare in schools has had its critics, with some arguing that Shakespeare is used to reinforce conservative views on issues such as class, race and gender.[19] In either case, what is clear from these debates is the perceived impact and continuing cultural significance of Shakespeare and his works. At the same time, the Shakespeare industry that has grown up around Shakespeare's place in the secondary and higher education sectors reminds us of Shakespeare's continuing economic, as well as cultural, impact and value.

Structure of the Book

In the following chapters, our contributors explore some of the different ways in which Shakespeare has had direct and indirect economic and cultural impacts, nationally and internationally, from the late sixteenth century to the twenty-first century. In the process they demonstrate how Shakespeare has been a part of economic and cultural markets from the beginning, but they also highlight some of the different ends to which he and his works have been put and alert us to some of the ways in which 'Shakespeare's cultural power has been reconceptualised' and redeployed 'over time'.[20]

In Chapter 2, 'Shakespeare and the Market in his Own Day', Siobhan Keenan looks at some of the earliest evidence of Shakespeare's place in the cultural and economic market, exploring Shakespeare's engagement with the world of commercial theatre in late sixteenth and early seventeenth-century London and the place of his plays and poetry in the burgeoning print marketplace. Keenan makes the case that Shakespeare's sustained commercial and artistic success was all but unique amongst the period's playwrights and was tied to the collective commercial strategy and business practices of Shakespeare and his fellow members of the Lord Chamberlain's Men from 1594 onwards. In her reading of Shakespeare's career, the Warwickshire playwright was exceptional not just in his talent as a writer, but in his ability to read the theatrical market and in his unusual financial position as a playwright, company shareholder and part playhouse owner. Keenan's chapter also makes clear that for Shakespeare and his peers, playwriting and playing were commercial as well as artistic pursuits. Shakespeare appears to have played a less active role in putting his plays into the print market, but the early success of his printed plays affords indirect testimony of his growing literary reputation, just as the increasing use of his name on his publications (and on other printed works that he did not write) affords an early example of the exploitation of the Shakespeare 'brand' to market non-Shakespearean, as well as Shakespearean, products.

In Chapter 3, 'Shakespeare and the Impact of Editing', Gabriel Egan extends this concern with the branding and marketing of Shakespeare's works to the present day, reflecting on the shaping and marketing of Shakespeare's plays and poems in print in recent times. Surveying some of the best-known modern editions of the plays, including the Oxford Shakespeare, the Norton Shakespeare and the Complete Works edition published by the Royal Shakespeare Company in collaboration with Palgrave Macmillan, Egan considers how the different editorial decisions on which these books are based inform readers' understanding of Shakespeare and ongoing debates about his work. He also makes the case that readers and playgoers are implicitly willing to pay more money for editions and performances informed by the latest scholarly work on Shakespeare, so that what might seem esoteric debates (e.g. about the authorship of Shakespeare's plays) have economic as well as cultural and scholarly significance.

In Chapter 4 Deborah Cartmell extends the discussion of Shakespeare's marketing to the world of cinema, exploring the advertising of Shakespeare on film. Focusing first on the history of Shakespeare on film in the early era of sound movies, Cartmell looks at the box-office failure of movies such as *The Taming of the Shrew* (1929) and *As You Like It* (1937) and the role played in this by ineffective marketing strategies. She contrasts this failure with the highly successful marketing of a number of late twentieth-century Shakespeare films, such as Baz Luhrmann's *William Shakespeare's Romeo + Juliet* (1996) and John Madden's *Shakespeare in Love* (1998), and makes the case that film companies and producers implicitly learned from the marketing strategies used earlier in the century. At the same time, Cartmell demonstrates the extent to which the ongoing 'life' of the Shakespeare 'brand' is partly attributable to its openness to commercial reinvention and to the marketability of 'Shakespeare' himself. As Douglas Lanier notes, unlike many corporate 'brands' the 'Shakespeare trademark' is not 'under the control of a single institution or cultural (re)producer. It thus remains ever a contested object of value, a body that, despite Shakespeare's warning about moving his bones, remains always in motion'.[21]

The values associated with Shakespeare and the Shakespeare 'brand' are also key to Anna Blackwell's chapter on 'Shakespearean Actors, Memes, Social Media and the Circulation of Shakespearean "Value"'. Paying particular attention to the careers of actors who have moved between Shakespearean work and more popular cultural forms (such as blockbuster movies), Blackwell considers the impact of contemporary Shakespearean actors on popular conceptions of Shakespeare and his cultural and economic value. As she shows, actors such as Tom Hiddleston and Benedict Cumberbatch potentially inflect contemporary understanding and views of Shakespeare, both through their performance of Shakespearean and popular roles and through their participation in digital cultural phenomenon, such as memes, and their engagement as 'Shakespeareans' with social media platforms such as Twitter.

Graham Holderness and Bryan Loughrey reflect on Shakespeare's place and use in a rather different cultural industry in their chapter on Shakespeare and brewing: 'Ales, Beers, Shakespeares'. As they note, the association of Shakespeare with the brewing industry has a long history and includes several supposedly biographical tales about the bard's taste for beer, but Holderness and Loughrey's focus is on the use of Shakespeare's name and image to promote and sell beer. Most famously, Shakespeare's image was adopted by the local Stratford-upon-Avon brewery, Flowers, to advertise its beers. Loughrey and Holderness show how Flowers and more recent brewers have implicitly sought to tap into Shakespeare's 'populist' reputation and his association with rural Stratford-upon-Avon, rather than his later associations with 'high' or metropolitan culture: another sign that the Shakespeare 'brand' has proved adaptable and a source of creativity in the hands of modern marketers.

Further evidence of the potential for a more localised branding of 'Shakespeare' is afforded by Dominic Shellard's chapter on 'A King Rediscovered: the Economic Impact of Richard III and *Richard III* on the City of Leicester'. Taking as its starting point the remarkable discovery of the body of the historical Richard III beneath a Leicester car park in 2012, Shellard looks at the fresh interest this prompted in Richard III, Leicester and Shakespeare's *Richard III* in the lead up to the celebrations organised to commemorate the reinterment of the Yorkist king (2015). In the process he considers how Shakespeare's *Richard III* and the real king were both used to promote tourism in Leicester, contributing to the local economy as well as Leicester's cultural life and reputation. In this respect, the chapter offers another example of the way in which Shakespeare has been used in the modern English tourist industry.

In Chapter 8, 'Shakespeare is "GREAT"' Conrad Bird, Jason Eliadis and Harvey Scriven extend this focus on Shakespeare and tourism to the international stage by looking at the use of Shakespeare in the government's GREAT Britain campaign. Launched to coincide with Britain's hosting of the 2012 Olympics and Paralympics and designed to promote the UK internationally as a great place to visit, study and do business, Shakespeare was – and continues to be – used in the campaign precisely because of his status as a national (and international) cultural icon and specifically because of the associations he has accrued with Britishness, tradition and quality, as mentioned above. Rather than using Shakespeare to sell a product, the British Government is implicitly using Shakespeare's name and reputation in order to promote British culture and excellence or 'Britishness' as a brand, in the hope of attracting more tourists and businesses to the UK and boosting the UK tourist industry and the broader economy. This chapter affords fascinating evidence of the economic, as well as cultural, benefits that this recent use of the Shakespeare 'brand' has brought to the UK.

In the final chapter ('Sponsoring Shakespeare'), Susan Bennett looks at a further, and arguably more troubling, example of Shakespeare's reputation being co-opted to bolster the reputation of another 'brand'. Paying particular attention to the controversial corporate sponsorship of a number of Shakespeare events during the 2012 Cultural Olympiad, including the British Museum's 'Shakespeare: Staging the World' exhibition, Bennett asks probing questions about the benefits that sponsors such as BP gain as a result of economic investment in a Shakespeare-branded experience. This includes the possible use of 'Shakespeare as a vehicle for corporate image-laundering', a phenomenon described by Douglas Lanier in his work on the Shakespeare brand.[22] As Bennett makes clear, her research invites us to question and reflect on whose interests are served by modern uses and appropriations of Shakespeare and his cultural authority. In other words, Bennett, like Alan Sinfield, invites us to think about how and why 'certain ways of thinking about the world may be promoted and others impeded' through modern uses of Shakespeare.[23] In this way, Bennett's research invites us all to consider the ways in which we engage with, borrow from and 'use' Shakespeare and his cultural authority and economic power today, as we celebrate the 400th anniversary of his death, including as scholars and editors contributing to a volume of this sort which reflects on the economic and cultural impact and place of Shakespeare, but which also co-opts his name and thereby implicitly adopts him as a sponsor of its contents and a symbolic guarantor of its quality and value. In this case, however, we hope that the reader and/or book-buyer is, at least, equipped to ask some of the right questions of us and our contributors, as we reflect collectively on Shakespeare's shifting cultural and economic impact and power over the last four hundred years.

Notes

1. John Maynard Keynes (1930) *A Treatise on Money*, 2 vols (New York: Harcourt, Brace & Co.), II, p. 154.
2. Melissa Aaron (2012) 'Theatre as Business' in Arthur F. Kinney (ed.) *The Oxford Handbook of Shakespeare* (Oxford: Oxford University Press), pp. 421–32 (p. 420).
3. See, for example, Douglas Bruster (1992) *Drama and the Market in the Age of Shakespeare* (Cambridge: Cambridge University Press); S. P. Cerasano (2009) 'Theatrical Entrepreneurs and Theatrical Economics' in Richard Dutton (ed.) *The Oxford Handbook of Early Modern Theatre* (Oxford: Oxford University Press), pp. 380–95.

4. See, for example, Andrew Gurr (2010) *The Shakespeare Company, 1594–1642* (Cambridge: Cambridge University Press); Grace Ioppolo (2006) *Dramatists and Their Manuscripts in the Age of Shakespeare, Jonson, Middleton and Heywood: Authority, Authorship and the Playhouse* (London: Routledge); Siobhan Keenan (2014) *Acting Companies and Their Plays in Shakespeare's London* (London: Bloomsbury Arden Shakespeare); Roslyn Lander Knutson (2001) *Playing Companies and Commerce in Shakespeare's Time* (Cambridge: Cambridge University Press); Bart van Es (2013) *Shakespeare in Company* (Oxford: Oxford University Press).

5. Such studies include the following: Barbara Hodgdon (1998) *The Shakespeare Trade: Performances and Appropriations* (Philadelphia: University of Pennsylvania Press); Graham Holderness (1988) *The Shakespeare Myth* (Manchester: Manchester University Press); Graham Holderness (2001) *Cultural Shakespeare: Essays in the Shakespeare Myth* (Hatfield: University of Hertfordshire Press); Douglas Lanier (2002) *Shakespeare and Modern Popular Culture* (Cambridge: Cambridge University Press); Douglas M. Lanier (2012) 'Marketing' in Arthur F. Kinney (ed.) *The Oxford Handbook of Shakespeare* (Oxford: Oxford University Press), pp. 498–514; Robert Shaughnessy (ed.) (2007) *The Cambridge Companion to Shakespeare and Popular Culture* (Cambridge: Cambridge University Press).

6. Pierre Bourdieu (2010) *Distinction: A Social Critique of the Judgement of Taste*, translated by Richard Nice and introduced by Tony Bennett (Abingdon: Routledge), p. xxv.

7. Mark Osteen and Martha Woodmansee (1999) 'Taking Account of the New Economic Criticism: An Historical Introduction' in Martha Woodmansee and Mark Osteen (eds) *The New Economic Criticism: Studies at the Intersection of Literature and Economics* (London: Routledge), pp. 3–50 (p. 35, p. 36, p. 37).

8. See Peter F. Grav (2012) 'Taking Stock of Shakespeare and the New Economic Criticism', *Shakespeare*, 8.1: 111–136 (p. 111). Examples of this emerging interest in economics and Shakespeare include works such as: Lars Engle (1993) *Shakespearean Pragmatism: Market of His Time* (Chicago: University of Chicago Press); Peter F. Grav (2008) *Shakespeare and The Economic Imperative: 'What's Aught But as 'tis Valued?'* (London: Routledge); David Hawkins (2015) *Shakespeare and Economic Theory* (London: Bloomsbury Arden Shakespeare); Vivian Thomas (2008) *Shakespeare's Political and Economic Language: A Dictionary* (London: Bloomsbury Arden Shakespeare); Frederick Turner (1999) *Shakespeare's 21st-Century Economics* (Oxford: Oxford University Press); Linda Woodbridge (ed.) (2003) *Money and the Age of Shakespeare: Essays in New Economic Criticism* (Basingstoke: Palgrave Macmillan).

9. Grav, p. 132.

10. Lanier, *Popular Culture*, p. 3.

11. Ben Jonson (1623) 'To the memory of my beloued, The Avthor Mr. William Shakespeare' in *Mr. William Shakespeare's Comedies, Histories, & Tragedies* (London: Isaac Jaggard and Ed. Blount), no page number.

12. On the rise of Shakespeare's reputation as British literary icon, see, for example, Michael Dobson (1995) *The Making of the National Poet: Shakespeare, Adaptation, and Authorship, 1660–1769* (Oxford: Clarendon Press).

13. Graham Holderness (1988) 'Bardolatry: or, the Cultural Materialist's Guide to Stratford-upon-Avon' in Holderness, *The Shakespeare Myth*, pp. 2–15 (p. 3).

14. Nicola J. Watson (2007) 'Shakespeare on the Tourist Trail' in Shaughnessy, pp. 199–226 (p. 213).

15. Watson, p. 213; David Addenbrooke (1974) *The Royal Shakespeare Company: The Peter Hall Years* (London: William Kimber), p. 47.
16. Douglas Lanier (2007) 'Shakespeare™: Myth and Biographical Fiction' in Shaughnessy, pp. 93–113 (p. 112); Lanier, *Popular Culture*, p. 9.
17. Douglas Holt (2004) *How Brands Become Icons: The Principles of Cultural Branding* (Boston: Harvard Business School), p. 1.
18. For more information on the history of teaching Shakespeare in English schools, see Tracy Irish, 'Teaching Shakespeare: A History of Teaching Shakespeare in England' (2008), available at http://www.rsc.org.uk, date accessed 28 September 2015.
19. See, for example, David Margolies (1988) 'Teaching the Handsaw to Fly: Shakespeare as a Hegemonic Instrument', in Holderness, *The Shakespeare Myth*, pp. 42–58.
20. Lanier, 'Marketing', p. 514.
21. Lanier, 'Shakespeare™', p. 112.
22. Lanier, 'Marketing', p. 509.
23. Alan Sinfield (1994) 'Heritage and the Market, Regulation and Desublimation' in Jonathan Dollimore and Alan Sinfield (eds) *Political Shakespeare: Essays in Cultural Materialism*, 2nd edn (Manchester: Manchester University Press), pp. 255–79 (p. 277).

Select Bibliography

Aaron, Melissa (2012) 'Theatre as Business' in Arthur F. Kinney (ed.) *The Oxford Handbook of Shakespeare* (Oxford: Oxford University Press), pp. 421–32.

Bourdieu, Pierre (2010) *Distinction: A Social Critique of the Judgement of Taste*, translated by Richard Nice and introduced by Tony Bennett (Abingdon: Routledge).

Bruster, Douglas (1992) *Drama and the Market in the Age of Shakespeare* (Cambridge: Cambridge University Press).

Cerasano, S. P. (2009) 'Theatrical Entrepreneurs and Theatrical Economics' in Richard Dutton (ed.) *The Oxford Handbook of Early Modern Theatre* (Oxford: Oxford University Press), pp. 380–95.

Grav, Peter F. (2012) 'Taking Stock of Shakespeare and the New Economic Criticism', *Shakespeare*, 8.1: 111–36.

Holderness, Graham (1988) *The Shakespeare Myth* (Manchester: Manchester University Press).

Holt, Douglas (2004) *How Brands Become Icons: The Principles of Cultural Branding* (Boston: Harvard Business School).

Keynes, John Maynard (1930) *A Treatise on Money*, 2 vols (New York: Harcourt, Brace & Co.), II.

Lanier, Douglas M. (2012) 'Marketing' in Arthur F. Kinney (ed.) *The Oxford Handbook of Shakespeare* (Oxford: Oxford University Press), pp. 498–514.

——— (2002) *Shakespeare and Modern Popular Culture* (Cambridge: Cambridge University Press).

——— (2007) 'Shakespeare™: Myth and Biographical Fiction' in Robert Shaughnessy (ed.) *The Cambridge Companion to Shakespeare and Popular Culture* (Cambridge: Cambridge University Press), pp. 93–113.

Sinfield, Alan (1994) 'Heritage and the Market, Regulation and Desublimation' in Jonathan Dollimore and Alan Sinfield (eds) *Political Shakespeare: Essays in Cultural Materialism*, 2nd edn (Manchester: Manchester University Press), pp. 255–79.

Watson, Nicola J. (2007) 'Shakespeare on the Tourist Trail' in Robert Shaughnessy (ed.) *The Cambridge Companion to Shakespeare and Popular Culture* (Cambridge: Cambridge University Press), pp. 199–226.

Woodmansee, Martha and Mark Osteen (1999) (eds) *The New Economic Criticism: Studies at the Intersection of Literature and Economics* (London: Routledge).

2
Shakespeare and the Market in His Own Day

Siobhan Keenan

> Did not *Will Summers* break his wind for thee?
> And *Shakespeare* therefore writ his comedy?
> All things acknowledge thy vast power divine,
> (Great God of Money) whose most powerfull shine
> Gives motion, life.[1]

Writing only shortly after Shakespeare's death, Thomas Randolph (and/or his reviser F. J.) claim that the world's most famous dramatist was motivated to write his plays by the 'Great God of Money'. It is an assertion which would have troubled many early Shakespeare scholars, most of whom were reluctant to see Shakespeare as a commercially driven artist. Indeed, as Douglas Bruster notes, 'for a long time, most commentators ignored the economic bases of Shakespeare's theatre' and when they did mention it 'they typically portrayed it as regrettable'.[2] However, as recent research on the early modern stage has made clear, the world of which Shakespeare was a part was a commercial – as well as a creative – industry; and Shakespeare's success within it is evidence not just of his artistic talent, but of the commercial 'nous' of himself and his fellow players in the company with whom he worked for most of his career: the Lord Chamberlain's (later the King's) players.

The late sixteenth century was a seminal time in the development of English theatre, witnessing the creation of the first purpose-built playhouses in London and the professionalisation of the theatre world, as the regular access that the playhouses afforded to large paying audiences opened up the possibility of making a living from the stage for would-be players. As William Ingram notes, 'prior to this time, stage playing in London had been largely a vocation, undertaken intermittently and in off-hours by people whose main source of income lay elsewhere', but now it became a full-time trade for at least some individuals.[3]

We have no detailed records of individual players' earnings, but Philip Henslowe's records at the Rose Theatre suggest that sharers in the Lord Admiral's Men earned between seven and 26 shillings a week in 1598, while the annual income for a sharer in Shakespeare's company is estimated to have been more than £60 in 1599.[4] This was much more than the £4–£9 that most 'workmen, journeymen' and 'hired servants' were expected to earn.[5] Some players even became rich by the standards of the day. When Richard Burbage, leading actor of the King's Men, died in 1619 he 'was reported to have left more than £300—a very large sum— in "land" (real estate)'.[6] His contemporary, Edward Alleyn, co-owner of the Fortune playhouse and famous as the leading actor of the rival Lord Admiral's Men, was even more successful, being able to afford 'the ten thousand pounds that founding Dulwich College is said to have cost him' in 1614.[7]

The thriving theatre industry created employment for a host of other people, too, including theatre owners, musicians, costume makers, and, significantly for Shakespeare, playwrights. The establishment of a repertory system whereby different plays were performed daily created a huge demand for new plays. Around 900 plays are thought to have been written for the stage between 1580 and 1642, of which 'just under 250' survive from the period 'roughly corresponding' to Shakespeare's career.[8] The position of playwrights was potentially more precarious than that of players, as they generally worked on a freelance basis, only receiving a one-off payment for the plays which they produced or to which they contributed. Nonetheless, it did become possible for some to make playwriting their profession. According to payments preserved in Henslowe's Diary from the Rose Theatre, Henry Chettle, for example, earned £123 17s 8d between 25 February 1598 and 9 May 1603, giving him an average income for his playwriting of 'about £25 a year', significantly higher than the average annual income of skilled artisans (as noted above).[9] Many of those who wrote for the commercial stage, including Shakespeare, were part of a new generation of grammar school-educated men for whom the theatre became an alternative career to the trades of their fathers, a trade in which they could exploit their knowledge of literature and rhetoric in new and exciting ways, and for profit.

The development of the professional theatre and the growing market for plays that it created was not without controversy. The late Elizabethan era witnessed the publication of a series of attacks on the stage. While some of the anti-theatricalists were concerned about the influence of plays on audiences, complaining that they taught people to be wicked, others argued that playing was not an acceptable trade. As William Ingram explains: 'Stage playing, because it could be neither weighed, measured, nor resold, was not a true commodity, and thus could have no just price affixed to it', or as contemporary critic William Prynne put it more starkly, plays 'in their best acceptation are but vanities or idle creations, which have no price, no worth or value in them: they cannot therefore be vendible because they are not valuable'.[10] As players did not make anything material and took working people's money in return for their performances, they also found themselves condemned as parasites by some contemporaries, such as the author of *A Second and Third Blast of Retrait from Plaies and Theaters*, who likened players 'which exhibit their games for lucre sake' to 'droanes, which wil not labor to bring in, but liue of the labors of the paineful gatherers'.[11] But concerns about the moral effects and legitimacy of playing did not prevent audiences from flocking to the Elizabethan playhouses. Despite the fact that the late sixteenth century was a time of economic difficulty in England, with 'the real incomes of many' people falling to their lowest levels for centuries, theatre audiences in London grew steadily.[12]

However, as with the English economy more generally, this flourishing industry had its losers as well as its winners. Playhouses and acting companies did not always last for long and many players and playwrights led uncertain, poverty-stricken lives.[13] In his landmark work *The Shakespearean Stage*, Andrew Gurr writes of the Lord Chamberlain's/King's Men company as one of the 'strong' companies of the day and thereby distinguishes Shakespeare's troupe from a number of other contemporary acting companies, which he, implicitly, deems 'weak'.[14] Shakespeare's company was, indeed, strong, in the sense that it enjoyed a long and comparatively stable career from 1594 until 1642, but it was also all but unique. Most other contemporary acting companies did not enjoy the same longevity or sustained success. Given this, it might be more accurate to distinguish between the period's acting troupes in terms of the 'usual' and the 'exceptional', with the career of Shakespeare and his company falling into the latter category. Traditionally, the 'exceptional' success of Shakespeare's company has been explained in terms of the quality of their resident playwright and its actors. But that is only part of the story; there are other more pragmatic ways in which Shakespeare and his troupe were exceptional and, thereby, successful. Key to this success, I shall argue, was the way in which Shakespeare and his peers engaged with the theatrical market, not just in terms of their repertory of plays, but in their business practices. It is this engagement that I shall be exploring in the following pages. In the process, I hope to show how Shakespeare's unique success – like the success of his company – had commercial, as well as artistic, roots.

Mastering the Elizabethan theatrical market

We do not know precisely how or when Shakespeare first came to write plays for the professional stage or whether he began his career as a writer and/or as an actor. One theory posits that Shakespeare joined the Queen's Men when they visited Stratford-upon-Avon in 1587.[15] Others have speculated that he started as a playwright, selling his plays to companies such as the Earl of Pembroke's Men.[16] The first direct evidence we have that Shakespeare was writing for the professional stage and beginning to gain a reputation as a playwright dates from 1592, when Robert Greene famously complained in his *Greenes Groats-worth of Witte* that

> there is an vpstart crow, beautified with our feathers, that with his Tygers hart wrapt in a Players hyde, supposes he is as well able to bombast out a blank verse as the best of you: and being an absolute *Iohannes factotum*, is in his owne conceit the onely Shake-scene in a countrey.

Although Shakespeare is not named directly, the adaptation of a line from his *Henry VI, Part III* ('O tiger's heart wrapped in a woman's hide! 1.4.138), and the apparent pun on Shakespeare's name has led most scholars to conclude that Greene was criticising the young Warwickshire playwright and actor.[17] The first record of one of Shakespeare's plays being performed in London may date from the same year, if the 'harey the vj' performed at the Rose Theatre on 3 March 1592 is Shakespeare's.[18]

Shakespeare's part in the professional theatre world is better documented after 1594, when he joined the new company of Lord Chamberlain's Men. The company was one of two new troupes set up in this year, apparently at the instigation of the Lord Chamberlain and the Lord Admiral (patron of the other company).[19] At this stage in his career, Shakespeare appears to have been working as a player and a playwright, becoming the new troupe's regular dramatist. It had not been unusual for earlier actors to write plays occasionally for their acting companies, but Shakespeare's role as a permanent in-house writer was new, initiating the 'phenomenon of the attached poetic playwright', as Bart van Es notes. For many years it was also a phenomenon unique to

Shakespeare's company.[20] Whether Shakespeare was paid separately for the plays that he produced and/or had a special contract (as did some later playwrights) is not known, but it is clear that it became usual for him to write roughly two plays per year in the 1590s, generally one serious play and one comedy.[21]

During the first phase of their career, the Lord Chamberlain's Men were based at the Theatre, the playhouse established in Shoreditch in 1576 by joiner-turned-player and theatrical entrepreneur James Burbage. The arrangement to use the Theatre was probably made with the assistance of Burbage's son (and Shakespeare's fellow Chamberlain's Man and leading actor) Richard Burbage. At this time the Lord Chamberlain's Men and the Lord Admiral's Men were the only officially licensed acting companies in London; and, like their rivals at the Rose Theatre, Shakespeare's company used this privileged position to their advantage, building up regular audiences and a large, diverse repertory of plays.

Although many of the plays performed in the 1590s by the two leading companies have been lost, we know from contemporary records and surviving titles and texts that there was considerable overlap between the two company's repertories in terms of the kinds of play genres and subjects covered. As well as reviving popular plays, the two leading companies commissioned sequels to 'hit' plays, and new plays that imitated those successful in their rival's repertory as well as their own.[22] Thus, in the 1590s there was a vogue for plays based on English history, which saw the Lord Admiral's and the Lord Chamberlain's Men performing plays on similar subjects, such as the reigns of England's medieval kings. The anonymous 'harey the v' performed at the Rose Theatre in 1595 was matched, for example, by Shakespeare's *Henry V* at the Globe Theatre in 1599; and Shakespeare's two *Henry IV* plays at the Globe (c.1596–97), featuring Sir John Falstaff (originally under the name of Protestant martyr, Sir John Oldcastle), were answered in 1601 at the Rose Theatre by the performance of the two parts of *Sir John Oldcastle*.[23]

At the same time, it is clear that the two leading companies sought to offer audiences novelty and to distinguish their repertories from each other on occasion as well, as when the Lord Admiral's Men bought George Chapman's *A Humorous Day's Mirth* (1597). This play pioneered a new sub-genre of comedy, known today as 'comedy of humours'. Such was the play's success that it was not long before Shakespeare's company responded by buying their own 'humours' comedy from Ben Jonson, *Every Man in His Humour* (1598) and its sequel, *Every Man out of his Humour* (1599). The two companies developed some distinctive specialities in their repertories, too. Thus, the Lord Admiral's Men became known for their London-based dramas, whereas Shakespeare and his company largely avoided London settings in their plays; and Shakespeare popularised romantic comedies in the 1590s, a genre that does not seem to have featured as significantly in the Lord Admiral's repertory at this time.[24] Making the most of the opportunity to work regularly with the same group of players, Shakespeare also appears to have started tailoring his plays for his fellow actors and their specific talents. This is perhaps particularly evident with regard to some of the comic roles that he was to create for company clown Will Kemp, including the parts of Bottom in *A Midsummer Night's Dream* (1595–96) and Dogberry in *Much Ado About Nothing* (1598). These are roles implicitly designed to exploit Kemp's established talent for playing down-to-earth figures and for physical comedy, improvisation, and amusing verbal play. Confirmation that Shakespeare had started to think about the actors who would play his roles could be found in the occasional use of performers' names in early printed editions of his plays. In the 1600 quarto edition of *Much Ado*, for example, the lines of Dogberry and Verges are assigned in one scene (4.2) not to the characters, but to their likely performers, (Will) Kemp and (Richard) Cowley, respectively.[25]

We do not have day-to-day records of the plays being performed by Shakespeare and the Lord Chamberlain's Men at the Theatre, but Henslowe's Diary of performances by the Lord Admiral's Men at the Rose playhouse gives us an idea of how intensive their theatrical schedule is likely to have been. The Admiral's Men 'performed at least 689 times at the Rose' during their first three and a half years there, staging 'eighty-three different plays' between 15 June 1594 and November 1597. The two companies were drawing large audiences, too, with estimates suggesting that in 1595 'the two acting companies were visited by about 15,000 people weekly'.[26] That Shakespeare and his fellow sharers in the Lord Chamberlain's Men were faring well in the late 1590s would seem to be confirmed by the investments we find Shakespeare making during this time. These included the purchase, on 4 May 1597, of New Place.[27] 'Reputedly the second largest house' in Shakespeare's home town, Stratford-upon-Avon, New Place had 'five gables, ten fireplaces, and a frontage of over 60 feet' as well as two barns and two gardens ('duob*us* horreis & duob*us* gardinis').[28] The exact price is 'unclear', as Peter Holland notes, but 'was probably in excess of £120'.[29]

Shakespeare was also in a position to contribute £100 to help Richard and Cuthbert Burbage when they decided to remove the timbers of the Theatre from Shoreditch and re-use them for a new theatre on the

Bankside in early 1599 – the Globe Theatre. The Burbages had been forced into this desperate piece of recycling after they failed to negotiate an extended lease on the ground-plot on which the Theatre stood. Short of funds to complete the rebuilding work they had turned to five of Richard Burbage's fellow sharers in the Lord Chamberlain's Men to become investors in the new playhouse.[30] It was to prove a key event in the career of Shakespeare and his company. The Lord Chamberlain's Men became the first playing company to become part-owners of the playhouse that they used. This unique arrangement guaranteed the company access to a London playing venue and meant that the sharers-turned-playhouse investors (or 'householders', as they were known) thereafter profited from their performances not only as players, but as landlords. We do not have financial records from the Globe, but Andrew Gurr's research suggests that the sharer-householders could have been earning more than £100 a year from their combined shares in the acting company and the Globe.[31] It was this combined income that was to make Shakespeare rich, rather than his playwriting.

Shakespeare's economic success in the 1590s was matched and underpinned by his growing literary reputation. He had yet to acquire his modern iconic status as a writer, but by the turn of the century Shakespeare was being recognised as one of England's best writers. In his 1598 discussion of English literature, for example, Francis Meres identified Shakespeare as the leading comic and tragic writer of his day, observing that: 'As *Plautus* and *Seneca* are accounted best for Comedy and Tragedy among the Latines: so Shakespeare among the English is most excellent in both kinds for the stage'.[32] As Andrew Murphy notes, we also find 'selections' from Shakespeare's poems becoming 'something of a staple of Renaissance anthologies' of verse.[33] That Shakespeare's acting troupe had come to be recognised, likewise, as the pre-eminent company of the day, would seem to be suggested by their selection to become the King's players in 1603, following the accession of King James I (VI of Scotland), while their rivals, the Lord Admiral's Men, became the Prince's Men.

The Jacobean market: consolidation and domination

The move to their own playhouse in 1599, followed by their acquisition of royal patronage in 1603, gave Shakespeare and his fellow sharers in the King's Men an unrivalled security as a playing company, but this new-found stability and protection did not lead Shakespeare or his company to become complacent. Shakespeare experimented artistically, turning his attention away from history to tragedy, producing his so-called 'great' tragedies in the first decade of the seventeenth century (*Hamlet, Othello, King Lear, Macbeth, Antony and Cleopatra*, and *Coriolanus*). Although he continued to write comedies, these also became darker, with plays such as *Troilus and Cressida* (1601–02), *Measure for Measure* (1603–04), and *All's Well That Ends Well* (1604–05) pushing at the boundary between tragedy and comedy, perhaps influenced by the turn of the century fashion for satirical poetry and by the tragicomic dramas performed by the boy companies that flourished briefly in the 1600s.[34]

While Shakespeare freshened up the company's repertory artistically, his fellow sharer Richard Burbage looked for ways of consolidating the company's position in London practically. In 1596, his father James had purchased a property in the ex-Blackfriars monastic precinct within the city walls and built within it an indoor playhouse. He had intended the playhouse for his son's acting company, in lieu of the Theatre (the lease of which was due to expire in 1597), but local opposition to the theatre prevented its opening. On his death in 1597, Burbage senior left his interest in the Blackfriars playhouse to his son Richard. In 1600 Burbage let the property to Henry Evans, who used it as a venue for performances by a boy company (the Children of the Chapel Royal), but in 1608 Evans gave up the lease.[35] A precedent had been set, however: the playhouse had been allowed to function without local protest and Burbage appears to have concluded that the King's Men would be able to use it for performances, likewise, without encountering the opposition originally faced by his father. This afforded the King's Men a second indoor playing venue, where the company might perform in the winter. However, rather than simply renting the venue to his company, as was usual of theatre owners, Richard Burbage and his brother Cuthbert chose to give the four surviving sharers in the lease on the Globe Theatre (including Shakespeare) similar shares in the lease of the Blackfriars playhouse. According to the later testimony of Cuthbert these shares were given to the players 'for nothing'.[36] Andrew Gurr notes that this may have been partly a way of compensating the Globe householders for the income they would lose from the Globe if the company started performing part of the time at the Blackfriars, but it also suggests that the Burbages had found the collective ownership model a good one. It was certainly to prove a durable model, lasting 'the company for the remaining forty-three years of its life'.[37]

Given the more comfortable playing conditions offered by the indoor playhouse and the higher charges it was customary to set for indoor performances, one might have expected Shakespeare and his fellows to give up the Globe Theatre at this point, but they did not. Instead, they chose to play at the Blackfriars playhouse in the winter and at the Globe in the summer. The retention of the Globe could have been a nostalgic gesture (as Andrew Gurr suggests) or a sign of the players' attachment to the open-air theatre and its diverse audiences, but it might, equally, be evidence of commercial caution and a sign that the players were hedging their bets.[38] Playing within the city walls had been suppressed in the past and there was no guarantee that the troupe would be allowed to perform consistently at the Blackfriars Theatre in the future. Retaining their outdoor playhouse beyond the city walls allowed the players to keep their options open and all but guaranteed them a place to play, whatever the vagaries of city rulings about theatre within its walls.

As well as strengthening the position of the King's Men in London and giving them a flexibility that no other company enjoyed, acquiring the Blackfriars Theatre consolidated the wealth of Shakespeare and his fellow players, as the indoor theatre yielded higher average takings than the Globe. Indeed, in 1612 Edward Kirkham claimed that the company 'took £1,000 a winter more at the Blackfriars than they had formerly taken at the Globe'.[39] In the case of the players who were 'householders' in both playhouses, as well as sharers in the acting company (including Shakespeare), the increase in income was even greater, as they received more money in both capacities from the Blackfriars Theatre. Andrew Gurr estimates that Shakespeare's combined income from the company and its two playhouses might have risen to around £200 annually.[40]

That Shakespeare was growing wealthy and was economically astute, like the Burbages, would seem to be confirmed by what we know of his ongoing financial activities in this period. Throughout the first decade of the seventeenth century we find him continuing to invest the profits of his theatrical career in property and land, mostly in Stratford-upon-Avon and its environs: on 28 September 1602 he bought a cottage in Dead Lane (today known as Chapel Lane) and paid £320 for 107 acres of land in the 'towne of Olde Stretford' (1 May); and in 1605 (24 July) he paid £440 for a share in the tithes of Stratford, 'Olde Stratforde welcombe & Bushopton'.[41] As Bart van Es notes, these 'were substantial investments' implicitly designed to convert 'immediate profit into ongoing security'. Shakespeare's investments were not confined to his home town, either. As late as 1613 he purchased the Blackfriars gatehouse in London. While this might have afforded him a new base in the city, it was as likely another property investment.[42]

The legal records relating to Shakespeare's financial investments are one of the few sources of information that we have about the playwright's private life. The careful concern with securing his financial legacy that they implicitly document has proved contentious, with some commentators prompted to characterise Shakespeare as mercenary.[43] The playwright's shrewd investment of his wealth certainly points to an individual who was financially strategic with the money that his creative work as a playwright and actor earned him, but the evidence we have of Shakespeare's care in his playwriting, including his implicit revision of plays such as *King Lear*, and the fact that he regularly wrote plays that were too long for the stage, indicate that he 'was not simply a practical man of the theater', as David Scott Kastan has noted, or wholly motivated by money, as is joked in *Hey for Honesty* in the epigraph to this chapter.[44] In this respect Shakespeare was not unique. For many Elizabethan and Jacobean playwrights and players the theatre was an artistic vocation as well as a business and a commercial pursuit.[45]

That Shakespeare and his fellows in the King's Men had developed a particularly profitable – as well as highly esteemed – theatrical business was not lost on their contemporaries and competitors. At least some other acting companies and entrepreneurs sought to imitate aspects of their business model. Edward Alleyn, for example, appears to have experimented with selling shares in the Fortune playhouse to the resident company (Palsgrave's Men) in 1618, but the Fortune burned down a few years later (10 December 1621) and the players lost 'all their apparel and play-bookes'. Alleyn rebuilt the playhouse, but, as Andrew Gurr reports, 'his backing now came from financiers, not the players', suggesting that the actors were not able to raise the necessary funds to reinvest in the theatre in the aftermath of the disaster.[46] Alleyn also became involved in a project to create a new indoor playhouse within the Blackfriars precinct (1615–16) that could be used as an alternative venue to the open-air Fortune Theatre, implicitly seeking to mimic the King's Men's dual ownership of, and alternating residency at, the Blackfriars and Globe Theatres. However, like the attempt to emulate the King's Men's stake in their playhouses, this scheme also failed to come to fruition after local opposition led to the almost immediate closure of the Porter's Hall playhouse.[47]

By the time that Shakespeare died in 1616, the King's Men's collective, actor-based business model had been diluted somewhat, as actors left or died and their shares in the company and its playhouses were inherited by relatives and new actors joined the troupe, but leading members such as Richard Burbage continued to enjoy a unique stake in the playhouses where the King's Men performed and an unequalled stability as a result. We do not know precisely when Shakespeare finally retired from the London theatre world, but he appears to have sold his shares in the company's two playhouses by 1613, when the remaining owners agreed to rebuild the Globe Theatre after it burned down in a fire, and his final known play (*The Two Noble Kinsmen*) was co-written in 1613–14 with his successor as resident playwright for the King's Men, John Fletcher.[48]

As well as involving several collaborations, it has long been recognised that the style of Shakespeare's late plays, many of which fall into the category of romance, is rather different from his earlier work. Shakespeare's turn towards romance can be seen as developing out of his growing interest in tragedy and tragicomedy in the early seventeenth century, but it also appears to have been influenced by the Jacobean fashion for tragicomedy, pioneered in part by John Fletcher and plays such as his *The Faithful Shepherdess* (1608). Some scholars have also linked aspects of the change in Shakespeare's playwriting style to the King's Men's use of the Blackfriars playhouse (after 1609), arguing that the more intimate setting and superior acoustics encouraged Shakespeare to experiment with a greater use of music and special effects, although it remained customary for Shakespeare's plays to be performed at the Globe Theatre, too, and there is no evidence to suggest that romances such as *Cymbeline* and *The Winter's Tale* were any less successful in staging or reception at the outdoor theatre.[49] Bart van Es argues that the late plays are also distinctive in being less tailored for individual actors and more indebted to, and engaged with, contemporary literary fashions. He links this to Shakespeare's gradual withdrawal from the acting company, along with changes in its membership, which meant that he did not enjoy the same intimacy with his fellow King's Men in later years.[50] Regardless of which explanation(s) is (are) correct, what is without doubt is the fact that when Shakespeare died in 1616 he was the English Renaissance stage's most famous *and* most financially successful playwright, having enjoyed a unique position as a player, theatre sharer, and playwright. As we know, his commercial and cultural importance was not to end there either. Today Shakespeare and his plays continue to be big business on and off stage, and he is even more famous than he was when Jonson celebrated him as 'not of an age, but for all time'.[51] Although his contemporaries might not have anticipated the scale of Shakespeare's commercial and artistic legacy, they were (like Jonson) alert to his theatrical importance and participated in the early consolidation of his reputation, for not only did Shakespeare's plays remain a staple part of the King's Men's repertory right up until the Civil War, but his plays continued to influence other playwrights in the late

Jacobean and Caroline eras, many alluding to, and imitating, his works long after his death.[52]

Shakespeare and the print market

The London theatre world was the chief market for Shakespeare's work in his lifetime, but it was not the only one. Shakespeare's plays and poetry were also to enjoy a significant place in the burgeoning print marketplace, even if this did not benefit him financially in the same way. Shakespeare's career in print began with the publication of *Venus and Adonis* (1593) and *The Rape of Lucrece* (1594). Both poems, which are dedicated to Henry Wriothesley, the young Earl of Southampton, are thought to have been written and prepared for the press by Shakespeare during the long plague-induced closure of the playhouses in 1593, when he may have been seeking an alternative career as a professional writer through 'print and court patronage'.[53] Whether he gained much financially from the sale of his poems (or from his patron) is not known, but their publication did contribute to his emerging artistic reputation. In 1598 Gabriel Harvey noted that the 'younger sort takes much delight in Shakespeares Venus, & Adonis', adding that 'his Lucrece, & his trage-die of Hamlet, Prince of Denmark, haue it in them, to please the wiser sort' (1598).[54]

Shakespeare's first play to appear in print was *Titus Andronicus* in 1594, although the title page did not name him, presenting it instead as a text 'Plaide by the Right Honourable the Earle of *Darbie*, Earl of *Pembrooke*, and Earle of *Sussex* their Servants'.[55] This was not unusual. Most Elizabethan plays that appeared in print were identified by the playing company (or companies) that had performed them and/or the playing venue(s) where they were staged, rather than by their author. This reflects the fact that acting companies were the owners of the plays (once purchased from their writers) and that the Elizabethan stage was essentially an actors' theatre in which greater importance was placed upon the performers than the writers who supplied them with their plays. But in Shakespeare's case this situation was to change.

In the late 1590s Shakespeare's name began to appear for the first time on the title pages of several of his printed plays, including on the first quarto edition of *Love's Labour's Lost* (1598) and the second editions of *Richard II* and *Richard III* published in the same year. In 1599 Shakespeare was named, likewise, on the title page of *Henry V*; and in 1600 his name appeared on the title pages of editions of *The Merchant of Venice*, *Much Ado About Nothing*, *A Midsummer Night's Dream*, and

Henry IV, Part II.[56] At a time when naming playwrights in printed plays remained the exception rather than the rule, the use of Shakespeare's name in each of these cases is indicative of his growing reputation as a dramatist and a sign that 'Shakespeare' was becoming a recognised and saleable 'brand' off-stage as well as on. Indeed, this would seem to be confirmed by the fact that some publishers started to attribute other non-Shakespearean plays to Shakespeare, including *Thomas, Lord Cromwell* (1602), *The London Prodigal* (1605), *The Puritan* (1607), and *A Yorkshire Tragedy* (1609).[57] Implicitly, the expectation was that his name would help to sell these works, an early example of the economic capital associated with 'Shakespeare', the brand, and rather like the use of Shakespeare's name in book titles or film titles today, as Deborah Cartmell explores in Chapter 4.

This expectation is borne out by the publication history of Shakespeare's plays and poems. Shakespeare's most popular printed work in his lifetime was *Venus and Adonis*, going into ten editions before his death, but a number of Shakespeare's plays sold well, too.[58] The three most popular, each of which feature in the list of the top ten best-selling English Renaissance plays compiled by Peter Blayney, were *Henry IV, Part I* (1598) which went through seven editions in 25 years, and *Richard III* (1597) and *Richard II* (1597), both of which went through five editions over the same period.[59] Further proof of Shakespeare's success as a printed playwright is afforded by Brian Vickers' research: he records that Shakespeare's name appears 'on a total of forty-nine quarto and octavo editions of plays and poems published between 1598 and 1622, far more frequently than any other poet or dramatist, indeed, more often than most professional writers'.[60]

The extent to which Shakespeare did or did not write his plays with an eye to publication as well as performance has been a matter of modern debate, with the editors of the pioneering Oxford *Complete Works* of Shakespeare emphasising the plays' primary status as performance texts, while, more recently, Lukas Erne has made the case for seeing Shakespeare as a literary dramatist as well.[61] Whether or not Shakespeare was interested in readers as well as theatre audiences, he was to become the first bestselling dramatist of the English Renaissance stage, and, in the view of Alan B. Farmer and Zachary Lesser, helped 'to establish the playbook market itself'.[62]

Confirmation of the marketability of Shakespeare's name is arguably afforded by the posthumous publication of the First Folio edition of his plays by his one-time colleagues in the King's Men, John Heminges and Henry Condell in 1623. The volume contained 36 plays, almost half of which had not been printed before. Traditionally, plays were published individually in cheap quarto or octavo editions, formats in keeping with their conventionally low-brow associations. The much larger, more expensive, folio format was generally reserved for editions of learned or religious works (such as the Bible). Ben Jonson's publication of his *Workes* (including plays that he had written for the professional stage) in a folio edition in 1616 had set a precedent for treating plays more seriously, but the decision to publish the First Folio of Shakespeare's plays was still a bold gesture and a commercial gamble. Not everyone approved either. The famous contemporary anti-theatricalist William Prynne was later to bemoan the fact that 'Shackspeers Plaies are printed in the best Crowne paper, far better than most Bibles'.[63] The high quality of the volume was reflected in its price. According to Grace Ioppolo, copies of the Folio cost 15 shillings unbound, 16 to 18 shillings with a plain binding, and £1 if leather bound.[64] This contrasted greatly with the cost of individual quarto and octavo editions which ranged in price from the five pence that the 1600 Quarto of *Henry IV, Part II* is reported to have cost to the eight pence charged for the 1595 Octavo of *The True Tragedy of Richard Duke of York* (*Henry VI, Part III*).[65] That the publishers considered the First Folio a worthwhile investment is arguably a testimony to the artistic and commercial reputation that Shakespeare's plays had earned by this time. Implicitly, the gamble paid off: the publication of a Second Folio in 1632 suggests, as Anthony West notes, 'that demand for the First Folio was such that it sold out in less than a decade'.[66]

Those who bought the First Folio were implicitly buying the plays in order to read them, but the market for Shakespeare's printed plays was not confined to readers. At least some of those who purchased quarto editions of individual plays may have done so with a view to using them for performance. This appears to have been true of a group of provincial players led by Catholic shoemakers Robert and Christopher Simpson in Jacobean Yorkshire. In early 1610, the Simpson players are reported to have performed *Pericles* and *Lear* at Gowthwaite Hall in Nidderdale.[67] It is likely that *Pericles* was Shakespeare's *Pericles* (pr. 1609) and possible that *Lear* was his *King Lear* (pr. 1608). We do not know how the players acquired the plays, but it is possible that they bought them from one of the bookshops in nearby York, where at least one bookseller sold plays and works by Shakespeare.[68] As this example suggests, the market for Shakespeare's works in print was not confined to London, any more than performances of his plays were, even in his own lifetime.

Conclusion

Shakespeare was the most famous and most successful playwright in his own day, culturally and commercially, off-stage as well as on. Shakespeare's exceptional talent and the talent of the playing company with which he worked so closely for most of his career were clearly important to this achievement, but their mutual success and the wealth it brought were also rooted in their collective commercial strategy and business practices. Thus, Shakespeare's success as a writer derived not just from his own imaginative and artistic talent, but from his ability to read and respond to the dramatic marketplace as he pioneered new theatrical fashions (such as the vogue for romantic comedies in the 1590s) and responded to the theatrical 'hits' of his competitors (as in the case of his romances). Likewise, the sustained success of Shakespeare's acting company was made possible by the unique stability that they enjoyed. The King's players were easily the most successful and enduring company in Renaissance London, but they – and Shakespeare – did not succeed just because of Shakespeare's genius, but because members of the acting company owned the theatres that they used and thus could guarantee the use of those spaces and a regular playing income. At the same time, their part ownership of their places in which they performed meant that the leading players benefited more fully from the profits of their performances than most other actors, while Shakespeare's multiple roles as player-sharer and theatre-householder, as well as playwright, meant that he enjoyed an income and control over his plays that no other playwright of the day was to emulate. For the majority of Elizabethan and Jacobean acting companies, life was far less certain. Shakespeare and his acting company were exceptional not just in their talents, but because they mastered the business, as well as the art, of the early modern theatrical marketplace.

Notes

1. Thomas Randolph and F. J. (1651) *A Pleasant Comedie, Entitled Hey for Honesty, Down with Knavery* (London: F. J.), 1.2., p. 6.
2. Douglas Bruster (2003) 'On a Certain Tendency in Economic Criticism of Shakespeare' in Linda Woodbridge (ed.) *Money and the Age of Shakespeare: Essays in New Economic Criticism* (Basingstoke: Palgrave Macmillan), pp. 67–77 (p. 67).
3. William Ingram (2004) 'The Economics of Playing' in Arthur F. Kinney (ed.) *A Companion to Renaissance Drama* (Oxford: Oxford University Press), pp. 313–27 (p. 313).
4. Andrew Gurr (1996) *The Shakespearian Playing Companies* (Oxford: Clarendon Press), p. 99; Andrew Gurr (2004) *The Shakespeare Company, 1594–1642* (Cambridge: Cambridge University Press), p. 108.

5. See Paul L. Hughes and James F. Larkin (1996) (eds) *Tudor Royal Proclamations: The Later Tudors (1588–1603)* (New Haven: Yale University Press), III, pp. 22–5.

6. Mary Edmond (2008) 'Burbage, Richard (1568–1619)' in *Oxford Dictionary of National Biography*, Oxford University Press, online edn, http://www.oxforddnb.com, date accessed 21 July 2015.

7. Andrew Gurr (2012) *Shakespeare's Opposites: The Admiral's Company, 1594–1625* (Cambridge: Cambridge University Press), p. 20.

8. Gerald Eades Bentley (1971) *The Profession of Dramatist in Shakespeare's Time* (Princeton: Princeton University Press), p. 25; Martin Wiggins (2000) *Shakespeare and the Drama of His Time* (Oxford: Oxford University Press), p. 1.

9. Bentley, *The Profession of Dramatist*, p. 100.

10. Ingram, p. 319; William Prynne, cited in David Mann (1991) *The Elizabethan Player* (London: Routledge), p. 97.

11. Anonymous (1580) *A Second and Third Blast of Retrait from Plaies and Theaters* (London: Henrie Denham), p. 121.

12. See Douglas Bruster (1992) *Drama and the Market in the Age of Shakespeare* (Cambridge: Cambridge University Press), p. 18; Andrew Gurr (2005) *The Shakespearean Stage, 1574–1642*, 3rd edn (Cambridge: Cambridge University Press), p. 213.

13. Philip Henslowe's Diary includes evidence of several playwrights finding themselves in debt and turning to him for help, including Henry Chettle. See R. A. Foakes (2002) (ed.) *Henslowe's Diary*, 2nd edn (Cambridge: Cambridge University Press), p. 119.

14. Gurr, *The Shakespearean Stage*, pp. 41–9.

15. Peter Holland (2013) 'Shakespeare, William (1564–1616)' in *Oxford Dictionary of National Biography*, Oxford University Press, online edn, http://www.oxforddnb.com, date accessed 21 July 2015.

16. See, for example, Bart van Es (2010) '"Johannes fac Totum"?: Shakespeare's First Contact with the Acting Companies', *Shakespeare Quarterly*, 61.4: 551–77 (p. 551); Bart van Es (2013) *Shakespeare in Company* (Oxford: Oxford University Press), pp. 51–2.

17. Robert Greene (1592) *Greenes Groats-worth of Witte* (London: William Wright), sig. Fv; William Shakespeare, *The True Tragedy of Richard, Duke of York* (*3 Henry VI*) in Stephen Greenblatt et al. (1997) (eds) *The Norton Shakespeare* (London: Norton), pp. 291–369.

18. See Foakes, p. 16.

19. See Gurr, *The Shakespearian Playing Companies*, p. 65.

20. van Es, *Shakespeare in Company*, p. 80.

21. Gurr, *The Shakespeare Company*, p. 129.

22. On this point and the importance of imitation and duplication as commercial strategies, see Roslyn Lander Knutson (2001) *Playing Companies and Commerce in Shakespeare's Time* (Cambridge: Cambridge University Press), p. 149.

23. Foakes, p. 33, p. 125, p. 129.

24. Gurr, *The Shakespeare Company*, p. 134, p. 133, p. 135.

25. See William Shakespeare (1600) *Much Adoe About Nothing* (London: Andrew Wise and William Aspley), sig. G3v–G4v.

26. Gurr, *Shakespeare's Opposites*, p. 36; Gurr, *The Shakespearean Stage*, p. 213.

27. See Stratford-upon-Avon, Shakespeare Birthplace Trust, MS 27/4a.

28. Holland, 'Shakespeare, William'; Shakespeare Birthplace Trust, MS 27/4a.
29. Holland, 'Shakespeare, William'.
30. Gurr, *The Shakespeare Company*, p. 33.
31. Gurr, *The Shakespeare Company*, p. 97.
32. Francis Meres (1598) *Palladis Tamia. Wits Treasury Being the Second Part of Wits Commonwealth* (London: Cuthbert Burbie), p. 282.
33. Andrew Murphy (2003) *Shakespeare in Print: A History and Chronology of Shakespeare Publishing* (Cambridge: Cambridge University Press), p. 19.
34. See Diana E. Henderson (2007) 'From Popular Entertainment to Literature' in Robert Shaughnessy (ed.) *The Cambridge Companion to Shakespeare and Popular Culture* (Cambridge: Cambridge University Press), pp. 6–25 (p. 15); Mary Bly (2011) 'The Boy Companies, 1599–1613' in Richard Dutton (ed.) *The Oxford Handbook of Early Modern Theatre* (Oxford: Oxford University Press), pp. 136–50 (p. 138).
35. See Siobhan Keenan (2014) *Acting Companies and Their Plays in Shakespeare's London* (London: Arden Shakespeare), p. 96.
36. Gurr, *The Shakespeare Company*, p. 35.
37. Gurr, *The Shakespeare Company*, p. 31.
38. Gurr, *The Shakespearian Playing Companies*, p. 117.
39. Cited in Gerald Eades Bentley (1948) 'Shakespeare and the Blackfriars Theatre', *Shakespeare Survey*, 1: 38–50 (p. 47).
40. Gurr, *The Shakespeare Company*, p. 115.
41. See Shakespeare Birthplace Trust, MSS ER 28/1, ER 27/1, and ER 27/2. For transcriptions of the relevant manuscripts, see E. K. Chambers (1930) *William Shakespeare: A Study of Facts and Problems* (Oxford: Clarendon Press), II, pp. 111–12, pp. 107–8 and pp. 120–2.
42. van Es, *Shakespeare in Company*, p. 161, p. 261. See Chambers, pp. 154–7 for a transcription of the relevant document.
43. See, for example. Edward Bond (1974) *Bingo: Scenes of Money and Death* (London: Eyre Methuen). This play, based on the later years of Shakespeare's life, characterises the playwright as selfish and mercenary, focusing on the story of the playwright's part in the enclosure of common land in Welcombe near Stratford-upon-Avon.
44. David Scott Kastan (2008) '"To Think These Trifles Some-Thing": Shakespearean Playbooks and the Claims of Authorship', *Shakespeare Studies*, 36: 37–48 (p. 46).
45. See, for example, Keenan, p. 59.
46. Gurr, *Shakespeare's Opposites*, pp. 46–7.
47. See S. P. Cerasano (1989) 'Competition for the King's Men? Alleyn's Blackfriars Venture', *Medieval and Renaissance Drama in England*, 4: 173–86.
48. Gurr, *Shakespeare Company*, p. 30.
49. See, for example, Bentley, 'Shakespeare', 47–8.
50. van Es, *Shakespeare in Company*, p. 259, p. 263, p. 277.
51. Ben Jonson (1623) 'To the Memory of My Beloued, the Avthor Mr. William Shakespeare' in *Mr. William Shakespeare's Comedies, Histories, & Tragedies* (London: Isaac Jaggard and Ed. Blount), no page number.
52. See Wiggins, pp. 125–31.
53. van Es, *Shakespeare in Company*, p. 17.
54. Gabriel Harvey, cited in Murphy, p. 31.

55. Anonymous (1594) *The Most Lamentable Romaine Tragedie of Titus Andronicus* (London: John Danter).
56. Gurr, *The Shakespeare Company*, p. 124.
57. Jonathan Hope (1994) *The Authorship of Shakespeare's Plays: A Socio-Linguistic Study* (Cambridge: Cambridge University Press), p. 116, p. 114, p. 121, p. 124.
58. Murphy, p. 19.
59. Peter W. M. Blayney (1997) 'The Publication of Playbooks' in John D. Cox and David Scott Kastan (eds) *A New History of Early English Drama* (New York: Columbia University Press), pp. 383–422 (p. 388).
60. Brian Vickers (2002) *Shakespeare, Co-Author* (Oxford: Clarendon Press), p. 6.
61. See John Jowett et al. (2005) (eds) *The Oxford Shakespeare: The Complete Works*, 2nd edn (Oxford: Clarendon Press), p. xv; Lukas Erne (2003) *Shakespeare as Literary Dramatist* (Cambridge: Cambridge University Press).
62. Alan B. Farmer and Zachary Lesser (2005) 'The Popularity of Playbooks Revisited', *Shakespeare Quarterly*, 56.1: 1–32 (p. 11).
63. Cited in Anthony James West (2001) *The Shakespeare First Folio* (Oxford: Oxford University Press), p. 7.
64. Grace Ioppolo (2004) 'The Transmission of an English Renaissance Play-Text' in Arthur F. Kinney (ed.) *A Companion to Renaissance Drama* (Oxford: Blackwell), pp. 163–79 (p. 176).
65. Blayney, p. 422.
66. West, p. 7.
67. See London, The National Archives, Star Chamber MS 8/19/10, mb. 30.
68. See John Barnard and Maureen Bell (1994) (eds) *The Early Seventeenth-Century York Book Trade and John Foster's Inventory of 1616* (Leeds: Leeds Philosophical and Literary Society), p. 93, p. 28, p. 85.

Select bibliography

Bentley, Gerald Eades (1971) *The Profession of Dramatist in Shakespeare's Time* (Princeton: Princeton University Press).

Blayney, Peter W. M. (1997) 'The Publication of Playbooks' in John D. Cox and David Scott Kastan (eds) *A New History of Early English Drama* (New York: Columbia University Press), pp. 383–422.

Bruster, Douglas (2003) 'On a Certain Tendency in Economic Criticism of Shakespeare' in Linda Woodbridge (ed.) *Money and the Age of Shakespeare: Essays in New Economic Criticism* (Basingstoke: Palgrave Macmillan), pp. 67–77.

Erne, Lukas (2003) *Shakespeare as Literary Dramatist* (Cambridge: Cambridge University Press).

Farmer, Alan B., and Zachary Lesser (2005) 'The Popularity of Playbooks Revisited', *Shakespeare Quarterly*, 56: 1–32.

Foakes, R. A. (2002) (ed.) *Henslowe's Diary*, 2nd edn (Cambridge: Cambridge University Press).

Gurr, Andrew (2004) *The Shakespeare Company, 1594–1642* (Cambridge: Cambridge University Press).

—— (2012) *Shakespeare's Opposites: The Admiral's Company, 1594–1625* (Cambridge: Cambridge University Press).

—— (1996) *The Shakespearian Playing Companies* (Oxford: Clarendon Press).

———— (2005) *The Shakespearean Stage, 1574–1642*, 3rd edn (Cambridge: Cambridge University Press).

Holland, Peter Holland (2013) 'Shakespeare, William (1564–1616)', *Oxford Dictionary of National Biography*, Oxford University Press, online edn, http://www.oxforddnb.com.

Ingram, William (2004) 'The Economics of Playing' in Arthur F. Kinney (ed.) *A Companion to Renaissance Drama* (Oxford: Oxford University Press), pp. 313–27.

Ioppolo, Grace (2004) 'The Transmission of an English Renaissance Play-Text' in Arthur F. Kinney (ed.) *A Companion to Renaissance Drama* (Oxford: Blackwell), pp. 163–79.

Kastan, David Scott (2008) '"To Think These Trifles Some-Thing": Shakespearean Playbooks and the Claims of Authorship', *Shakespeare Studies*, 36: 37–48.

Keenan, Siobhan (2014) *Acting Companies and Their Plays in Shakespeare's London* (London: Arden Shakespeare).

Knutson, Roslyn Lander (2001) *Playing Companies and Commerce in Shakespeare's Time* (Cambridge: Cambridge University Press).

Murphy, Andrew (2003) *Shakespeare in Print: A History and Chronology of Shakespeare Publishing* (Cambridge: Cambridge University Press).

van Es, Bart (2013) *Shakespeare in Company* (Oxford: Oxford University Press).

Vickers, Brian (2002) *Shakespeare, Co-Author* (Oxford: Clarendon Press).

West, Anthony James (2001) *The Shakespeare First Folio* (Oxford: Oxford University Press).

Wiggins, Martin (2000) *Shakespeare and the Drama of His Time* (Oxford: Oxford University Press).

3
Shakespeare and the Impact of Editing

Gabriel Egan

As readers, almost all of us first encounter Shakespeare in a modern printed edition of his works rather than something resembling the forms in which his first readers encountered him. The conventions of spelling in Shakespeare's time present a barrier that modern editors feel obliged to remove. It is hard enough to understand what Caesar means when he says 'What touches us ourself shall be last served' (*Julius Caesar*, 3.1.8) without having to read it in the original spelling and punctuation as 'What touches vs our felfe, shall be last feru'd'.[1] The old-fashioned long *s*, the appearance of *u* where we would expect *v* and vice versa, the abbreviation of preterite verb endings ('*d*), and the use of punctuation to show pauses for breathing rather than to mark off grammatical clauses – if indeed that is why a comma here obtrudes between a verb and its subject – convey nothing we really need to know. These features merely distance Shakespeare's writing from modern readers.

A great part of the labour of modern editors, and indeed the one thing that they almost all agree they should be doing, is modernising the letter-forms, spelling and punctuation of Shakespeare's works. When asked by non-specialists just what editors of Shakespeare do, these activities come readily to mind as benefactions likely to be granted approval by all but those purists who delight in alienation from the author. But once we get beyond these merely superficial activities, the need for editors of Shakespeare becomes rather more difficult to explain. To appreciate the impact of their work – to understand why one modern edition of a play may be quite unlike another – we must return to the origins of Shakespeare's writing and consider how it has come down to us. Modern editions based on the same raw materials – Shakespeare's work – are constructed by differing principles and offer distinctly different texts once we look beyond the superficial similarities.

The first readers of his plays would have been Shakespeare's fellow actors in the playing company called the Lord Chamberlain's Men (renamed the King's Men in 1603) in which Shakespeare spent almost his entire professional career. To this company of actors Shakespeare would have passed one or more copies of the script as he completed each play he wrote for them. Necessarily, such a script would have been handwritten in ink on paper, taking the material form of a 'manuscript', from the Latin words *manus* for 'hand' and *scriptus* for 'written'. With the exception of a small part of one play to which Shakespeare contributed a scene-and-a-bit some time in 1600–3, called *Sir Thomas More*, none of these manuscripts in Shakespeare's handwriting survives. But we can get an idea of what they probably looked like by considering the few remaining authorial manuscripts of other playwrights and by considering Shakespeare's likely working practices.

Things that we consider important to convey to a modern reader might well have been omitted by Shakespeare when writing for his fellow actors, and certainly were omitted by other professional dramatists. For example, certain kinds of stage business implied by dialogue ('I'll stop your mouth' or 'Here is my purse') are generally not supported by stage directions. One reason for such omissions is that in most cases the dramatists could attend rehearsals and other pre-performance discussions to simply tell the actors what they had in mind. Just as importantly, some things probably did not need saying at all. Being among his fellow professional actors, Shakespeare quite likely felt that certain decisions were rightly their prerogatives as performers, not his as the writer, and other details were most likely covered by the routine practices of theatre. A special case of omitted detail in playscripts from this period is that when a single actor is to 'Enter' it is not usually specified which door he (actors were always male) should use. But where two actors must enter using different doors this is often recorded, as with '*Enter a Fairy at one door and Robin Goodfellow, a puck, at another*' (*A Midsummer Night's Dream*, 1.2.0). These characters are to be imagined coming from different directions and meeting in the forest outside Athens, so entering through different doors is somewhat more realistic than entering through the same one, although modern notions of realism are no sure guide when making sense of a script that refers to a pair of doors in a forest.

Exits are more tricky, since surviving scripts from the period frequently omit these entirely, leaving the actor to figure out when he is no longer needed on stage and should leave. This seems a striking omission from our modern point of view, but begins to make sense when we start to think of the purposes for which playscripts were created in Shakespeare's time. If a script were constructed for the purpose of managing the backstage activities of a performance-in-progress then the omission of 'Exit' is understandable, since 'Enter' marks when the actor should be sent out onto the stage, but after that he is on his own: no one backstage can bring him off again. Considered in the light of the practicalities of the theatre in Shakespeare's time, the omission of a great many things that we would like to find explicitly addressed is unsurprising because the agreed customs and practices of the theatre rendered it superfluous to record them. One of the areas of expertise required of the modern editor, then, is knowledge of early modern theatrical practices from which to make reasonable guesses about what words to invent for a modern edition, and where to put them, in order to cover details omitted in the original documents.

Texts in motion

It is possible that the script Shakespeare gave his actors went through various transformations before the play was first performed. The only means of making extra copies of a script was to have someone write it out by hand (the process called transcription), and since paper and a scribe's time were expensive it was not possible to give each actor a full copy of the script made this way. Instead, each actor received only the lines he was to speak, preceded by a few 'cue' words, the last ones spoken by the previous speaker.[2] These 'parts', as they were called, collectively formed a copy of the whole script, but it would not be a linear reading text that we would recognise. It is possible that another complete transcript of the author's papers was made in order to provide a reading copy for the state censor, the Master of the Revels, who had to grant a performance licence before the play could be acted in public. For all we know, other complete transcripts might have been made for other necessary purposes, such as the provision of properties and the casting of the play, or, later, to give an important aristocratic patron a clean reading copy.

A great deal of the debate amongst twentieth-century editors of Shakespeare was focused on determining how many copies of the author's original papers might have been created as part of the routine procedures for getting a new play into performance, and what kinds of information might have been contained in each one. Since none of these manuscript documents survive in Shakespeare's case, why would this even matter? Why would editors waste time debating what might have appeared in documents that no longer exist and might not, in some cases, ever have existed at all? The answer is that what do survive are the first printed editions of Shakespeare, and by definition each of these was made by the typesetters using as their 'copy' – that is, the authoritative document whose words they were setting in type – one or more of these preceding (now lost) manuscripts. Since all we have are these early printed editions, they give us our only access to what Shakespeare wrote and it is to those that editors must turn to make a modern edition of Shakespeare.

Why then – as a purist might enquire – do we bother making modern editions at all, rather than just reading the earliest printed editions? What are editors for, again, besides modernising the spelling and inventing missing stage directions? The answer to this question takes us back to those now-lost and perhaps in some cases only hypothetical manuscripts on which the first printed editions were based. When we examine the early printings, they contain puzzling flaws that seem only explicable in terms of those manuscripts. Sometimes the flaws are simple printing errors (typos) that are easily detected and fixed. But others are particular words (or 'readings' in the editors' parlance) that we suspect may be corrupted but which might on the other hand be quite correct and merely strange to us. Sometimes we find in the early editions features that are not quite errors exactly, but which do not conform to modern expectations of readability in a playscript. How editors respond to these puzzling cases varies considerably between modern editions.

Take, for example, the edition of *Romeo and Juliet* printed in 1599, in which Juliet's mother has speech prefixes that call her '*Wife*', '*Old La[dy]*' and '*Mo[ther]*' depending on who she is talking to.[3] Once R. B. McKerrow pointed it out, the explanation for this seemed blindingly obvious: Shakespeare thought of the character not in fixed but in relational terms, so his own label for her varied as she fulfilled these different social roles at different moments in the play.[4] This early edition, it seemed, was printed from Shakespeare's own manuscript in which such name variation would naturally be present, and other early editions in which the speech prefixes are more consistent might reflect a process of tidying up of the script during rehearsal and other preparations for first performance.

If one believed that the play manuscripts that they received from dramatists were seldom recopied by theatre companies – because scribes' time and paper were expensive and the proliferation of copies of a valuable property was not generally desirable – then one might well suppose that the 1599 edition of *Romeo and Juliet* reflects the variations in speech prefixes for Juliet's mother because its printer held

Shakespeare's own handwritten manuscript as his guide while he set the type. If that were true, this 1599 edition brings us as close as we can get to – just one remove from – Shakespeare's lost manuscript of the play. *Romeo and Juliet* was printed again in 1609, but the new edition seems to have been based on the 1599 edition rather than on Shakespeare's manuscript, and when the play was printed in the 1623 Folio it seems that the 1609 edition, itself a reprint of the 1599 edition, was used for the typesetting. Whenever a book is simply reprinted the inevitable printing errors begin to accumulate. Believing all the hypotheses that I have just sketched, many twentieth-century editors argued that the 1599 edition of *Romeo and Juliet* was indeed printed directly from Shakespeare's own manuscript and hence should be the basis of any modern edition in preference to an earlier edition published in 1597 and any later edition, including the 1623 Folio.

For most of the twentieth century editors thrashed out these principles of textual authenticity and understood as their first obligation the laborious task of figuring out just which early edition of Shakespeare was a reprint of which other preceding edition, which were based on authorial manuscripts, and which on other kinds of manuscript.[5] With this knowledge, an editor could find the early edition that stands at the root of the genealogical tree of textual transmission that began with the author's first complete manuscript and could base the modern edition on that. Indeed, this process (called recension) of arranging the editions into a family tree came to be considered the essential groundwork for any serious (that is, 'critical') edition of a play, such as the second series of the Arden Shakespeare that appeared between 1951 and 1982.

Once recension had established which early printed editions were merely reprints of other existing printed editions, the remaining editions that were not reprints must, by definition, have been set from manuscripts. According to standard twentieth-century editorial theory, known as New Bibliography, the next task was to determine in each case whether the manuscript was the author's own papers or merely a transcript of these (or a transcript of a transcript) used for such purposes as managing a performance of the play as it happened. The latter kinds of manuscript would be distanced from Shakespeare's own writing by all manner of secondary interference: the adding of sound and property cues, the tidying up of speech prefixes and stage directions, and (most damagingly) the alteration or even excision of lines resulting from decisions made in rehearsal. Philip Edwards summed up the idea in his edition of *Hamlet*: 'it is sadly true that the nearer we get to the stage, the further we are getting from Shakespeare'.[6]

Just as Edwards was making this remark, a team of editors was putting the finishing touches to an edition of Shakespeare for Oxford University Press that took entirely the opposite approach.[7] Rather than seeing the theatre as a place where Shakespeare's plays were damaged by others' interference, they saw the work of these many hands as a collaborative endeavour that fulfilled the potential that was only latent in Shakespeare's original script. Shakespeare, they argued, was fully engaged in the work of his theatre company, sharing in its risks and profits, and would have seen the processes of readying a play for performance, including rehearsal, as opportunities for collective refinement of the script, not a debasing of it.

Where it appeared that an early edition of one of his plays reflected changes made in the readying of the play for performance, the Oxford *Complete Works* editors preferred to show their readers how the play looked after such changes rather than before them. This extended even to cases where whole speeches were apparently cut in rehearsal, so that their edition of *Hamlet* excluded from the main body of the play the soliloquy beginning 'How all occasions do inform against me' – present in the edition of 1604–05 but not the 1623 Folio – and put it into an appendix that they print after the end of the play to hold speeches cut during rehearsal.

Many reviewers of the Oxford *Complete Works* thought that in doing this the editors had gone too far, and had exercised too much editorial power by relegating well-loved speeches to an appendix. But when one considers the principles on which these decisions were made, they cannot logically be faulted. If one thinks that Shakespeare's plays achieve their apotheosis in performance then the state of the script for the first performances – ones that Shakespeare himself could most readily influence and probably oversaw – are especially important moments in the life of the ever-evolving text and something quite reasonable for the editors to try to reflect in their modern editions. These first performances are not the only possible moments in the life of the play that one might choose to base a modern edition upon, and other kinds of modern edition that privilege the version of the play as it left the author's pen – before entering the collaborative phase of readying and rehearsal – are equally defensible. But privileging the author's pre-social script over the socialised version arising from collective preparation would be incompatible with the conviction that Shakespeare was primarily a man of the theatre for whom the first complete draft of a play was only the beginning of its fullest realisation in performance.

Since the Oxford *Complete Works* edition appeared in 1986, four major shifts in editorial thinking have changed how we go about making a modern edition. The first is the collapse of the consensus sketched above about the ways that we determine for each early printed edition the question of whether its underlying copy was an authorial manuscript or one reflecting subsequent readying for performance. This consensus was fundamental to the New Bibliography, and in the 1980s and 1990s it was subject to a series of criticisms arising from its overly specific characterisation of the differences between authorial papers and those used to run a play in performance.[8] More generally, the editorial confidence that led New Bibliographers to interfere extensively in the texts they were editing, especially in correcting what they perceived as errors, has come to be seen as editorial hubris.

The second change is that, partly as a consequence of the Oxford Shakespeare editors pressing this point, it has become generally accepted that as well as accommodating others' changes to his plays Shakespeare revised them himself so that differences between early editions might simply reflect authorial second thoughts. The third major change in the past 30 years is that much has been learnt about Shakespeare's habits of collaborative writing, and we now know that perhaps a third of all his plays were co-authored.[9] The fourth major change is that our image of Shakespeare as essentially a man of the theatre who took little or no interest in how his plays reached a print readership has been challenged, and many commentators now accept that he also sought and achieved success as a published writer, as is discussed by Siobhan Keenan in Chapter 2.[10] Some of what we find in the early editions may never have been intended to be performed in the theatre at all and was written by Shakespeare with his readers, not his audiences, in mind. This theory has the considerable merit of helping to explain why Shakespeare wrote plays that are considerably longer than most other plays of his time.[11]

Present problems in editing

Let us take these developments in reverse order. The new idea that Shakespeare wanted to be, and succeeded in becoming, a published author has not yet had a substantial impact on what editors do, but it surely must. Editing *As You Like It* for the third Arden Shakespeare series, Juliet Dusinberre declared herself convinced by this new idea about Shakespeare and so paid more attention to its literary qualities than previous recent editors did.[12] But because *As You Like It* survives only in the 1623 Folio edition, Dusinberre could not exercise her conviction by choosing a more readerly over a more theatrical early edition to base hers upon.

Our new knowledge about Shakespeare's habits of collaborative writing present a series of special problems for editors. We can no longer assume that we even know the boundaries of the Shakespeare canon that we are trying to edit. New admissions to the recently expanded canon are *Edward III* (co-written with a person or persons unknown), *Sir Thomas More* (with Anthony Munday, Henry Chettle, Thomas Dekker, Thomas Heywood and one other person unknown), *Arden of Faversham* (with a person or persons unknown) and *The Spanish Tragedy* (added to by Shakespeare after Thomas Kyd's death).[13] At the same time as expanding in these directions, the canon is contracting in other directions as we ascribe to other writers parts of plays we thought wholly Shakespeare's because they appear in the 1623 Folio. This affects *Henry VI Parts I, II,* and *III* (co-written with Christopher Marlowe and others), *Titus Andronicus* (with George Peele), *Timon of Athens* (with Thomas Middleton), *Henry VIII* (with John Fletcher), and *Measure for Measure* and *Macbeth* (now known to be adaptations of lost Shakespearean originals made by Middleton after Shakespeare's death); see again footnote 9 for the references to the vast body of scholarship supporting these attributions. *Pericles* (with George Wilkins) and *The Two Noble Kinsmen* (with John Fletcher) have long been acknowledged as collaborations.

The reshaping of the Shakespeare canon has practical implications for an editor working on problematic moments in a single play. When deciding whether a certain word or phrase is an error or a Shakespeareanism, it is usual to look for parallels and analogues in other Shakespeare plays. No longer can this be done on the assumption that every play in the 1623 Folio provides evidence for Shakespeare's habits of writing: one must look to only those parts of the collaborative plays that are his, and must look beyond the 1623 Folio at his contributions to other plays. More complicatedly still, when editing plays that are now known to be Shakespeare's collaborations there can no longer be assumed (if ever there could) a singular authorial intention, as Suzanne Gossett has pointed out.[14] An editor must ask whether each author confined his intention to the part he wrote, or hoped to influence the other's work. This raises the awkward question of whether an editor should treat the entire play as if it were an homogenous artistic unity by effacing any discontinuities arising from co-authorship, or should instead highlight these discontinuities to make plain the composite nature of the play.

The now-general acceptance that Shakespeare revised his plays presents a special problem for the printed edition because it is inherently singular, although some attempts have been made to represent how a play looked 'before' and 'after' alteration. The Oxford Collected Middleton included Shakespeare's *Macbeth* and *Measure for Measure* because we now know that the 1623 Folio texts of those plays (our only authorities for them) reflect the effects of adaptation by Middleton. Both plays were presented as 'Genetic Texts' in the collection, meaning that the editors attempted to convey as far as possible their genesis towards their final state in the 1623 Folio.[15] The primary means for this was typographical: lines added or rewritten by Middleton were presented in boldface type, lines deleted by Middleton (or meant to be deleted) were printed in grey, and lines moved by Middleton appeared in grey where they originally stood and in boldface where they ended up. Thus to apprehend Shakespeare's original version one should read the regular type and the grey and to apprehend Middleton's version one should read the regular type and the boldface. This innovation has not become a widespread solution to the problem of conveying how texts change over time and would be unsuitable for less well-known plays. That is, this kind of disorienting innovation is suitable only where it does not distract from the important editorial duty of conveying unfamiliar works to new readers. What Gary Taylor wrote of *Macbeth* in this regard applies equally to *Measure for Measure*: the plays are 'already available in more editions than any other work in this Collected Works; readers who want a more comfortable text can find it easily enough elsewhere'.[16]

The first of the four substantial changes in editorial thinking since the 1980s, the collapse of the consensus known as the New Bibliography, has had the most profound impact on editors' behaviour because it has reduced confidence in their own ability to spot and correct errors. Most editors no longer think that they can tell from an early printed edition what kind of manuscript – authorial or theatrical – it was based upon. Without this foundational knowledge, they feel unable to explain the differences between early printed editions because there exist more possible causes than there are effects to be accounted for, and the competing causes overlap in their consequences. That is to say, authorial revision can easily produce effects that are difficult to tell apart from non-authorial revision. (In the case of *Macbeth* and *Measure for Measure* the editors were fortuitously enabled to make this distinction by the 1623 Folio texts containing material, including a popular song and topical references, that was most likely composed after Shakespeare's death, eliminating him as the creator.) Textual corruption in scribal copying and in the printshop can easily produce effects that are difficult to tell apart from non-authorial revision. For example, the letter *u* or *n* may be accidentally inverted in the printing press to produce a false but poetically meaningful variant that is not obviously an error: in Shakespeare an unhappy woman may be both *louely* (= lovely) and *lonely*.

The term 'over-determination' from psychology has come to be used generally where there are more possible causes than are needed to explain any particular effect and where several of them may be operating at once. Over-determination is a significant philosophical obstacle to editorial work. Since texts are almost always to some degree corrupted in transcription and printing, we can be sure that differences between the various early printed editions of Shakespeare are in part due to such corruption. But with authorial and non-authorial revision also highly likely to be present it becomes difficult to decide the cause of particular variants. Once editors stop believing that they can distinguish the signs of authorial papers from those of post-rehearsal papers their ability to make such distinctions is significantly weakened.

If one is sure that a particular early edition was based solely on authorial papers, then by definition one can exclude non-authorial revision as the cause for a particular puzzling feature: it must be a Shakespeareanism or else a corruption in transmission. Equally, if one is sure that a particular early edition was based on papers that had been annotated by someone in the theatre to show sound cues (such as a flourish of trumpets for each royal entrance) and a full set of stage directions, then one can explain the apparent misplacing of such features as merely errors made during annotation and not authorial peculiarities to be understood and explained. Without such guiding principles, editors are apt to give up on using the early printed editions in an attempt to reconstruct the play as it was first written or as it was first performed, and instead they aim for the less ambitious target of simply reproducing a particular early edition, cured of its obvious textual corruptions. This intellectually modest practice of 'single text' editing, aiming to reproduce not the artistic work as an ideal but only its instantiation in a particular early edition, is now what most editors do. Its danger is that in removing only the obvious textual corruptions they leave behind the merely likely corruptions that previous, more confident editors, cleared away.

The impact of three major editions

To illustrate how the above changes in the theoretical underpinnings of editions of Shakespeare have played out in practice over the past three decades, let us take three illustrative cases: the first edition of *The Norton Shakespeare* published in 1997 (based on the Oxford edition of 1986) and edited by Stephen Greenblatt and others, the *Royal Shakespeare Company (RSC) Complete Works* published in 2007 and edited by Jonathan Bate and Eric Rasmussen, and the third edition of *The Norton Shakespeare* published in 2015 and edited by Greenblatt and others.

The Norton Shakespeare first edition (1997)

After decades of false starts, progress on the Oxford *Complete Works* that eventually appeared in 1986 began in earnest in 1978 and its editors were full-time employees of the press rather than being academics making time for the work between other obligations.[17] This ability to focus solely on the task enabled them to undertake the most thorough survey of the textual foundations of Shakespeare ever attempted, and the edition's *Textual Companion* remains the single most useful resource on this topic.[18] Although it was originally intended to have explanatory notes, the Oxford *Complete Works* appeared without them, making it unattractive to the large American undergraduate student market.[19] (In American universities, unlike British ones, it is common for students not studying English Literature as their main topic to nonetheless take at least one course in it, and these courses often feature Shakespeare's works.) Via a deal with Oxford University Press, the American publisher W. W. Norton released in 1997 a Complete Works of Shakespeare 'based on' the 1986 Oxford *Complete Works*. What does 'based on' mean? The general editor Greenblatt characterised his team's job as 'to prepare the necessary teaching materials around the existing Oxford text' in order to make it suitable for classroom use.[20] The Norton editors were able to use the unpublished commentaries of the Oxford *Complete Works* and supplied many more materials to help the undergraduate student make sense of Shakespeare, including genealogies of historical figures, explanations of how early modern theatres operated and transcriptions of key historical documents. Regarding the most radical innovations of the Oxford *Complete Works*, Greenblatt listed a series of Norton differences that can fairly be characterised as a combination of some advances and much backsliding.[21]

The Oxford *Complete Works* offered two fully edited texts of *King Lear*: one reflecting the play as originally composed in 1605 and represented in the 1608 edition and one reflecting the script after Shakespeare's extensive revision of it in 1610 and represented in the 1623 Folio.

Where the Oxford printed these two scripts in different parts of its chronologically ordered edition, the Norton – which was also chronologically ordered for everything else – printed them on the facing pages of each opening in succession. This has the advantage of showing most clearly where one version has something that the other lacks, made visible by as much as half a page being blank. At one point there is an entire blank page-and-a-half for where the 1623 Folio lacks the scene (17) in which Kent receives news of Cordelia and the King of France from the First Gentleman.

The facing-page format also allowed ready comparison of lines that are variant between the two versions, such as Regan's 'Sir, I am made/ Of the self-same mettle that my sister is' (1608 edition, 1.60–61) and 'I am made of that self mettle as my sister' (1623 Folio, 1.1.67). To see how well this facing-page solution presented the phenomenon of minor textual variation, compare it with the Arden3 edition of the play published the same year, in which R. A. Foakes elected to use superscripted 'Q . . . Q' (for 'quarto', the book format) and 'F . . . F' (for 'Folio') to show words appearing only in one or other edition: 'QSirQ I am made of that self mettle as my sister'.[22] To avoid littering the line with too many markers, Foakes treated whole phrases – *selfe same* versus *self-* and *sister is* versus *sister* – not as alternatives but as equivalents for which he could prefer the 1623 Folio wording without marking it. Thus readers of the Arden3 *King Lear* might easily gain the impression that the 1608 and 1623 editions differ only regarding the first word in this line, while the Norton fully disclosed the variation.

The Norton edition's admirably clear use of facing pages to help readers apprehend the complex textual variations between the two early editions of *King Lear* was followed by something of a collapse in confidence: a third, conflated text that tried to combine the 1608 and 1623 editions. This is necessarily an intellectually compromised solution to the problem that readers want one version, not two, of a play and yet do not want to miss anything that Shakespeare wrote. The trouble, of course, is that something being present in the first version and absent in the second might well be compensated for by something else absent in the first version and present in the second. That is, a revising author might cut here and add there to execute a single artistic change. In conflating the two versions we end up with duplication, offering both of two pieces of material that the author never intended should appear together because they were meant to be alternative, not complementary, ways to handle a dramatic point.

Stanley Wells understood the pressure to give readers what they want in this regard, but was memorably picturesque in conveying the artistic incoherence of acceding to it:

It is perhaps understandable that they [editors] should therefore base a text on the one that they regard as closest to Shakespeare's final version while adding to it bits that are present only in the other version. It is, I say, understandable, even though its effect might resemble that which would be achieved by an art expert faced with two versions of a portrait who decided that the best way to represent them would be by superimposing one upon the other, even if in the process he made the sitter appear to possess four eyes.[23]

The problem is not quite so great for other plays as for *King Lear* – the one for which we have the clearest evidence of substantial authorial revision – but it does also affect *Hamlet*, which appeared in an edition of 1604–05 that seems to reflect the play as first written and before refinement in preparation for performance, and appeared in the edition of 1623 that seems to reflect the play after such refinement. Mostly this refinement consisted of the cutting of various speeches, which the Oxford *Complete Works*, based on the 1623 edition, published as a series of 16 Additional Passages – present in the 1604–05 edition, absent in the 1623 edition – that they printed at the end of the play. *The Norton Shakespeare* put these Additional Passages back into the main body of the play but, aware of the logical incoherence of conflation, they indented them and rendered them in a different typeface to make apparent their different provenance. As Greenblatt remarked, readers wanting to read the 1623 version 'can simply skip over the indented ... passages'.[24] This typographic innovation was meant to serve the same function as the more sophisticated use of three weights of typeface (normal, grey, bold) in the Oxford Collected Middleton, as we have seen. The same expedient was used to a lesser extent in *The Norton Shakespeare* for other plays where conflation is undesirable.

This typographic expedient is only a partial solution to the problem. As Paul Werstine pointed out,[25] there are in the 1604–05 and 1623 editions of *Hamlet* two distinctly different explanations for why, before their duel in the final scene, Hamlet apologises to Laertes about his behaviour at Ophelia's graveside. In the 1604–05 edition but not the 1623 edition – and thus reproduced in the Norton indented and in a distinct typeface – there is a passage in which an anonymous lord tells Hamlet that 'The Queen desires you to use some gentle entertainment

to Laertes before you fall to play'.[26] In the 1623 edition but not the
1604–05 edition, Hamlet says to Laertes 'I am very sorry ... That to
Laertes I forgot myself;/For by the image of my cause I see/The por-
traiture of his'.[27] These are competing, alternative exclusive explanations for Hamlet's apology: in revision (most likely by Shakespeare),
one explanation replaced the other. Although the typography of *The
Norton Shakespeare* indicates which lines are unique to the 1604–05
edition – by indenting and styling them – it has no means for showing
what is unique to the 1623 edition, so the reader cannot readily see
that the 1623 explanation for Hamlet's behaviour is an alternative to
the 1604–05 explanation. Indeed, the reader of the Norton who duti-
fully digests rather than skipping over the passages that are indented
and styled hears both explanations and will quite possibly assume that
Shakespeare wanted Hamlet to have two reasons to apologise when in
fact Shakespeare wanted only one and changed his mind about what it
should be. It is hard to see how misleading the reader in this way can be
justified as arising from the needs of students and their teachers.

As we shall see, when Shakespeare first wrote *Henry IV, Part I* the fat
knight Sir John was originally surnamed Oldcastle (rather than Falstaff),
and for this play the Oxford *Complete Works* used this name and the
original names of his companions Russell and Harvey. In deference to
the needs of teachers and 'the centuries of enthusiastic criticism' of the
play, the Norton edition changed these names to the more familiar (but
historically belated) Falstaff, Bardolph and Peto.[28] It is not at all clear that
pedagogical expediency requires readers to be given not the character
names that Shakespeare originally chose but instead the alternative names
that he was forced to invent because powerful persons at court objected to
the original names as insulting to their own ancestors. This is nothing but
censorship, and we should teach students to resist and undo such abuses
of power rather than accepting them as inevitable artistic compromises.

One aspect of the Oxford *Complete Works* that its editors soon came to
see as a mistake was the use of broken brackets to indicate their 'debate-
able editorial intervention' in stage directions. That is, the Oxford editors freely rewrote Shakespeare's stage directions where they thought
that their changes were essential to the action of the play or the reader's
comprehension of it, providing necessary exits where the early editions
lack them, correcting errors in names, and so on. But where such interventions were not certain – say, giving a character a property to hold
because she refers to it, or indicating that a speech is spoken to be heard
only by certain other characters – the Oxford editors placed the words
they added inside broken brackets.

The trouble is, of course, in distinguishing between certain and debatable interventions, and the Oxford editors came to believe that they should have emended stage directions without making any such distinction since 'Our edition, like all others, is thoroughly mediated, and it is both useless and dishonest to pretend otherwise'.[29] The brackets give the false impression that words outside of brackets were from Shakespeare's own stage directions, but in fact here too editors had altered the wording, but left no signs of it because they were certain of the need for those changes. Better to have no brackets and tell the reader that stage directions had been emended where necessary, just as the dialogue had been. The Norton edition moved in the opposite direction, deciding that wherever its stage directions used words that cannot be found the 1623 Folio or one of the preceding editions, these should be placed in square brackets.[30] This approach suggests a greater respect for – perhaps undue deference to – the authority of the early editions than the editors of the Oxford *Complete Works* showed in their radical rethinking of the bases for modern editions.

The Royal Shakespeare Company (RSC) *Complete Works* (2007)

For 16 of the 36 plays in the 1623 Folio of Shakespeare, that edition was not the first: there exist earlier single-play editions, usually more than one for each play. (Of these, *Henry IV, Part I* was the most popular in print, reaching seven editions by 1622; the average across all 16 plays was 2.75 editions before the Folio.) For a further four plays in the 1623 Folio there had been earlier publication of a play somewhat similar in title and/or plot and/or language: before *The Taming of the Shrew* there had been *The Taming of a Shrew* (1594), before *King John* there had been the two-part *Troublesome Reign of King John* (1591), before *Henry VI, Part II* there had been *The Contention of York and Lancaster* (1594), and before *Henry VI, Part III* there had been *The True Tragedy of Richard Duke of York* (1595). For these four plays, the relationship between the 1623 Folio text and the earlier edition is uncertain, and scholars have long debated whether some might be early versions of the same plays, or sources for the same plays, or perhaps – although this explanation is largely out of favour now – the early editions might be more-or-less pirated texts put together by minor actors collectively recalling and writing down the lines that they spoke in order to cobble together a saleable manuscript for a publisher.

Thus for 20 plays, more than half of those in the 1623 Folio, there exists a preceding edition that an editor would want to consider as perhaps an alternate witness to what Shakespeare wrote. When this consideration was first systematically undertaken in the nineteenth and twentieth centuries, it was found that in most cases the 1623 Folio text was essentially a reprint of one of the existing editions.[31] For just five of the plays for which an earlier edition existed – *The Merry Wives of Windsor, Henry IV, Part II, Henry V, Hamlet* and *Othello* – did the 1623 Folio publishers eschew reprinting that earlier edition and instead freshly set their text from a manuscript.[32] For the rest, a copy of an existing print edition was reprinted in the 1623 Folio, but only after it was first annotated by comparison with an authoritative manuscript supplied by the acting company.

This process of annotation was sometimes thorough (making the 1623 Folio text markedly different from the earlier edition on which it was based) and sometimes careless (leaving the 1623 Folio text much the same as the earlier edition on which it was based). Because the manuscripts used for this process of annotation appear to be authoritative – coming from the theatrical company and thus being independent witnesses of how Shakespeare's plays were first performed – the resulting 1623 Folio texts have a kind of mixed authority. Because the 1623 Folio texts of such plays are primarily reprints of existing earlier editions an editor ought to prefer that earlier edition as the basis for a modern one (since inevitable corruptions in transmission mean that originals are always to be preferred over copies) but, having what John Jowett and Gary Taylor memorably and aptly called 'sprinklings of authority', each of the 1623 Folio text's individual differences from the edition it reprints (differences created by the process of annotation) commands special attention as possibly a correct reading derived from the authoritative manuscript and not present in that earlier edition.[33] This gives editors of some plays a lot of difficult work to do.

One might expect that a specially commissioned Complete Works edition by the Royal Shakespeare Company that on its half-title declared itself to be 'based on the 1623 First Folio' would be the place for this painstaking editorial work to find its fullest expression. Careful readers' alarm bells sounded, however, when the half-title described the 1623 Folio as 'the first and original Complete Works' of Shakespeare, when of course it was at best a complete plays edition – strictly speaking a collected plays edition, since some plays were missing – and not a complete works at all: Shakespeare's extensive output of non-dramatic poetry is absent from the 1623 Folio.

In fact, the half-title's claim that the RSC *Complete Works* was 'based on' the 1623 Folio meant simply 'reprinted from': for each play the edition merely modernised the spelling and punctuation of the 1623

Folio, corrected its most obvious printing errors, and provided the kinds of regularised apparatus that modern readers expect. An example of the last of these features is that where the 1623 Folio text of *Romeo and Juliet* retains the earlier editions' variability in the speech prefixes for Juliet's mother – calling her '*Wife*' and '*Old La[dy]*' and '*Mo[ther]*'– the RSC edition regularised the name as 'LADY CAPULET'.[34] (Just why the editors gave her the title 'LADY' is unclear: then as now, to describe someone as an old lady is not to imply that she has an aristocratic title, and nothing in the play suggests this about the Capulets.) The irregularity of the 1623 Folio is thus smoothed for the modern reader, but it remains the sole authority for the dialogue of each play.

For the plays first printed in the 1623 Folio this editorial principle is entirely just and has no ill effects. But for plays for which there exists an earlier edition, the RSC *Complete Works*'s preference for the 1623 Folio in every case is merely dogma: we have no reason to assume that the 1623 Folio will in each case take us closest to what Shakespeare wrote. And in a few particular cases, we can be certain that the 1623 Folio takes us further from what Shakespeare wrote than would be case if we read the preceding edition. Two examples of this may stand for several. Shakespeare's *Richard II* was first printed in 1597 and reprinted (each time from the previous edition) in 1598 (twice), 1608 and 1615. The 1623 Folio text was for the most part printed from a copy of one of the 1598 editions that was first annotated by reference to an authoritative manuscript from the playing company.[35] At the play's climax, Sir Piers Exton presents Henry IV with the body of his predecessor King Richard II, hoping for royal approval of, and reward for, the murder. In the 1597 edition, Henry IV's response is:

> *king* Exton, I thanke thee not, for thou has wrought
> A deed of slaunder with thy fatall hand,
> Vpon my head and all this famous Land.[36]

This accusation of slander is no small point, since the play makes much of the role of poor public relations in Richard's downfall. The new king's first concerns are to shore up the reputation of the monarchy that he weakened as an institution by overthrowing his cousin Richard. Henry is himself in considerable danger of being overthrown in turn and needs to stop the social turmoil he has set in motion, as the next two plays in the cycle will illustrate. In the closing moments of *Richard II*, Henry forgives his implacable enemy, the Bishop of Carlisle, who spoke eloquently against the sin of overthrowing an appointed monarch. The shoe, we might say, is now on the other foot.

Leaving the deposed Richard in prison for the rest of his life was much the safest policy, and by murdering him Exton has brought upon Henry the same public relations disaster – an accusation of murder – that began the action of *Richard II* when Henry and Thomas Mowbray fell out over Richard's responsibility for the Duke of Gloucester's death. The killing of Richard not only slanders Henry, says the king, but also the entire country ('all this famous Land') because it earns England the reputation as a place of savagery. The RSC edition of *Richard II*, however, obscures all of this because it follows the 1623 Folio instead of the 1597 edition for the above lines, rendering them as:

BULLINGBROOK Exton, I thank thee not, for thou hast wrought
A deed of slaughter with thy fatal hand
Upon my head and all this famous land.[37]

The idea that a deed of slaughter (instead of slander) could apply to the whole of England is barely meaningful. Moreover, Henry has shown no compunction about slaughtering his enemies, and indeed as his public support grew he openly vowed this intention towards 'The caterpillars of the commonwealth', meaning Richard's favourites Bushy, Bagot and Green, 'Which I have sworn to weed and pluck away' (*Richard II*, 2.3.165–66). Bushy and Bagot were duly dispatched by Henry at Bristol after a brief show trial at which Henry explicitly declared that for their slaughter he should incur no public displeasure: 'to wash your blood/ From off my hands, here in the view of men/I will unfold some causes of your deaths' (*Richard II*, 3.1.5–7). Considered in this context of intense concern for public reputations, it is then virtually impossible that Henry should call Exton's killing of Richard a deed of slaughter rather than a deed of slander. The RSC *Complete Works* is forced to corrupt Shakespeare's meaning here – and in many hundreds of similar cases across the canon – because of a dogmatic adherence to the 1623 Folio as the basis for every play it contains, even where its textual corruption in transmission clearly takes us further from what Shakespeare wrote.

One further example will show how large an impact this dogma has upon the way readers apprehend Shakespeare's dramatic creations. In the sequel to *Richard II*, Shakespeare introduced his comic creation of fat Sir John, originally surnamed Oldcastle, but renamed shortly after the first performances as Falstaff.[38] This sequel ended up being two plays, *Henry IV, Parts I and II*, in which Sir John displays at length his self-indulgence, cowardice and foul language. At least, he does if editors base their modern texts on the early editions printed shortly after these plays premiered in the 1590s. But for *Henry IV, Part II* the 1623 Folio publishers appear to have used a theatrical manuscript of the play that reflected expurgations made to bring it in line with a law passed in May 1606 called the 'Act to Restrain Abuses of Players'. The law prohibited the use of the name of God, Jesus Christ, the Holy Ghost or the Trinity of all three in any stage play.

Sir John's dialogue was written 8–10 years before this censorship law was passed and is full of swear-words that fall foul of such a prohibition, including oaths such as *'sblood* (from 'God's blood') and *swounds* (from 'God's wounds'). This visceral language is a considerable part of the pleasure and interest of this character, and it appears unexpurgated in the first edition of the play, published in 1600. But in the manuscript used to print the 1623 Folio someone had softened Sir John's idiolect. Instead of answering the Lord Chief Justice's 'Well, God send the prince a better companion' with a witty 'God send the companion a better prince',[39] the *RSC Complete Works* follows the Folio to give 'Well, heaven send the prince a better companion!' and 'Heaven send the companion a better prince!'.[40] The joke is intact, but weakened by the expurgation.

Instead of Sir John saying of the conscript Peter Bullcalf 'Fore God a likely fellow'[41] he says, in the RSC *Complete Works*, 'Trust me, a likely Fellow!'.[42] Instead of taking his leave with a characteristically vigorous 'God keep you M. Scilens', Sir John in the RSC Shakespeare edition offers only a limp 'Farewell, Master Silence', and in response to Shallow's promise to come to court Sir John's 'Fore God would you would' becomes 'I would you would, Master Shallow'.[43] Instead of swearing 'by the Lord',[44] Sir John simply says 'I swear'.[45] And his crucial welcoming cries to the new king Henry V are changed from 'God saue thy grace King Hall' and 'God saue thee, my sweet boy' to 'Save thy Grace, King Hal' and 'Save thee, my sweet boy!'.[46] The ending of *Henry IV, Part II* depends on Sir John remaining the unregenerate figure we met in *Henry IV, Part I* and believing, vainly, that the world has finally turned his way because Prince Hal will remain unregenerate as king. By depriving Sir John of the full vigour of his language the RSC *Complete Works* gives the impression, quite unintended by Shakespeare, of a man who no longer speaks as forcefully as he did in *Henry IV, Part I*, as if he were reforming in anticipation of the new reign. Its only reason for doing this is an entirely unreasonable devotion to the Folio text, even where, as here, it is manifestly inferior.[47]

The Norton Shakespeare third edition (2015)

The second edition of *The Norton Shakespeare* (2008) essentially reprinted the first. For its third edition, *The Norton Shakespeare* broke from the

Oxford *Complete Works* of 1986 and re-edited all the works afresh from the original documents. The primary editorial principle was 'single-text editing – that is, where more than one early authoritative text of a given play has survived, rather than merging them into one (as has traditionally been done), we have edited each text in its own right'.[48] The point of doing this was not to represent the plays as first performed – the goal of the 1986 Oxford Shakespeare – but rather to render them 'as close as possible to the original versions read by Shakespeare's contemporaries'.[49] This readerly rather than theatrical Shakespeare addressed at once two of the main changes in editorial thinking since the 1980s: we no longer believe that we can see beyond the early editions to their antecedent underlying manuscripts and the mainly performative purposes for which they were created, and we now think that Shakespeare himself was interested in how his plays were read by his contemporaries.

The Norton's approach to authorial revision changed too, so that instead of a conflated *King Lear* this edition applied to that play the solution used for *Hamlet* in the preceding Norton editions: the 1623 Folio text was made primary and the lines found only in the 1608 edition were grafted into it but with typographical distinctions so that the reader who wished to could skip over them. As should be clear from the above discussion, this does not quite solve the problem of alterations where Shakespeare removed one piece of writing from the play and added something elsewhere in compensation for it, for which only a two-text solution is satisfactory. For *Hamlet* itself this 'scars-and-stitches' typographical approach was again used, but instead of making the 1623 Folio the base text and grafting into it the passages it lacks that appeared in the 1604–05 edition, *The Norton Shakespeare* now made the 1604–05 edition basic and grafted into it the passages found only in the Folio. Again, the weaknesses of such a procedure described above significantly impact upon the reader's experience of the play.

The most conspicuous matter on which the Norton third edition did not reflect the impact of recent thinking is Shakespeare's collaborative writing. The prefatory essay by Greenblatt mentioned collaboration in 'the late plays *Pericles, Henry VIII, The Two Noble Kinsmen*, the lost *Cardenio*, and – more debatably – such works as *Henry VI, Part I, Titus Andronicus*, and *Timon of Athens*',[50] but this is only a partial list. Each of these allegedly debatable cases is in fact attested by multiple independent studies that put the case for co-authorship beyond dispute, and the Norton simply ignored the growing evidence of the co-authorship of *Henry VI, Parts II and III* and the clear evidence for Shakespeare's hand in *Arden of Faversham* and the revised *Spanish Tragedy* (see again the essay cited in footnote 9); those last two plays were simply left out of *The Norton Shakespeare*. The 'General Textual Introduction' to the edition mentioned Shakespeare's practice of co-authorship just once and only to liken it to the work of editing – risking the charge of self-aggrandisement – and the Table of Contents gave no indication that many of the plays are not by Shakespeare but by Shakespeare and one or more others.[51] The individual introductions to the plays frequently made no mention that what follows is not simply Shakespeare but, for whole stretches of many plays, someone else's writing. For *Titus Andronicus*, the Textual Introduction itself – where these matters are discussed for other plays – made no mention of the hundreds of lines of Peele's writing in it.

Conclusion

Editors' views on how to turn the surviving documents that contain Shakespeare's works into readable modern editions change over time. Modern editions from the major publishers reflect these changing ideas and are themselves periodically rethought, making a Complete Works of Shakespeare purchased now significantly different from one purchased 50 years ago and highly different from one purchased 100 years ago. The most readily apparent difference over the past 50 years has been the universal acceptance of thorough-going modernisation of spelling in place of the incomplete modernisation practised before Wells's small book *Modernizing Shakespeare's Spelling* convinced virtually everybody of its necessity.[52]

Other changes in the intellectual bases of editing take longer to have an impact on what readers receive, but in general there is distinct evidence of steady progress: theory leads practice, and once a new idea – such as Shakespeare being essentially a man of the theatre, or being also a literary author, or being inclined to revise his plays – takes hold amongst scholars the major editions of his works begin to reflect this new thinking. There are, of course, moments of regression, and the RSC *Complete Works*, based on the Folio, is a signal example of an incoherent editorial policy producing an incoherent edition. We might lament that some ideas take longer to affect editorial practice than they should, the obvious example here being the well-attested case for Shakespeare's extensive co-authorship, but even conservative editions cannot hold back the rising tide of evidence on this topic. The impact of these matters on what readers read goes beyond the choice of words on the page, since – contrary to literary theories dominant since the 1960s – authorship really does matter. Once we re-attribute a work, or part of it, we have changed the conditions and contexts in which it must be read. We are only just starting to make sense of the impact of these changes in the case of Shakespeare.

Notes

1. William Shakespeare (1623) *Comedies, Histories and Tragedies*, STC 22273 (F1) (London: Isaac and William Jaggard for Edward Blount, John Smethwick, Isaac Jaggard and William Aspley), sig. kk5v.
2. See Simon Palfrey and Tiffany Stern (2007) *Shakespeare in Parts* (Oxford: Oxford University Press).
3. William Shakespeare (1599) *[Romeo and Juliet] The Most Excellent and Lamentable Tragedie, of Romeo and Juliet*, STC 22323 BEPD 143b (Q2) (London: Thomas Creede for Cuthbert Burby), sig. B4r-C1r.
4. R. B. McKerrow (1935) 'A Suggestion Regarding Shakespeare's Manuscripts', *Review of English Studies*, 11: 459–65.
5. Gabriel Egan (2010) *The Struggle for Shakespeare's Text: Twentieth-century Editorial Theory and Practice* (Cambridge: Cambridge University Press), pp. 12–99.
6. William Shakespeare (1985) *Hamlet*, ed. Philip Edwards, The New Cambridge Shakespeare (Cambridge: Cambridge University Press), p. 32.
7. See William Shakespeare (1986) *The Complete Works*, ed. Stanley Wells, Gary Taylor, John Jowett, and William Montgomery (Oxford: Oxford University Press); Stanley Wells, Gary Taylor, John Jowett and William Montgomery (1987) *William Shakespeare: A Textual Companion* (Oxford: Oxford University Press).
8. See Paul Werstine (2013) *Early Modern Playhouse Manuscripts and the Editing of Shakespeare* (Cambridge: Cambridge University Press).
9. See Gary Taylor (2014) 'Why Did Shakespeare Collaborate', *Shakespeare Survey*, 67: 1–17.
10. See Lukas Erne (2003) *Shakespeare as Literary Dramatist* (Cambridge: Cambridge University Press); Lukas Erne (2013) *Shakespeare and the Book Trade* (Cambridge: Cambridge University Press).
11. A[lfred] Hart (1932) 'The Time Allotted for Representation of Elizabethan and Jacobean Plays', *Review of English Studies*, 8: 395–413; A[lfred] Hart (1932) 'The Length of Elizabethan and Jacobean Plays', *Review of English Studies*, 8: 139–54.
12. William Shakespeare (2006) *As You Like It*, ed. Juliet Dusinberre, The Arden Shakespeare (London: Thomson Learning), pp. 113–20.
13. The essay cited in note 9 above contains a full set of references of all the recent scholarship underpinning the new attributions.
14. Suzanne Gossett (2006) 'Editing Collaborative Drama', *Shakespeare Survey*, 59: 213–24.
15. Thomas Middleton (2007) *The Collected Works*, ed. Gary Taylor and John Lavagnino (Oxford: Clarendon Press), pp. 1165–201, 1542–85.
16. Gary Taylor and John Lavagnino (eds) (2007) *Thomas Middleton and Early Modern Textual Culture: A Companion to the Collected Works* (Oxford: Clarendon Press), p. 692.
17. Andrew Murphy (2003) *Shakespeare in Print: A History and Chronology of Shakespeare Publishing* (Cambridge: Cambridge University Press), pp. 221–29, 247–60.

18. See Wells et al., *William Shakespeare: A Textual Companion*.
19. Stanley Wells and Gary Taylor (1990) 'The Oxford Shakespeare Re-Viewed', *Analytical and Enumerative Bibliography*, 4: 8–14.
20. William Shakespeare (1997) *The Norton Shakespeare Based on the Oxford Shakespeare*, ed. Stephen Greenblatt, Walter Cohen, Jean E. Howard, and Katharine Eisaman Maus (New York: W. W. Norton), p. xi.
21. Shakespeare, *The Norton Shakespeare*, pp. xii–xiii.
22. William Shakespeare (1997) *King Lear*, ed. R. A. Foakes, The Arden Shakespeare (Walton-on-Thames: Thomas Nelson), 1.1.69.
23. Stanley Wells (1988) 'The Unstable Image of Shakespeare's Text' in Werner Habicht, D. J. Palmer and Roger Pringle (eds) *Images of Shakespeare: Proceedings of the Third Congress of the International Shakespeare Association in Berlin, 1–6 April 1986* (Newark DE: University of Delaware Press), p. 312.
24. Shakespeare, *The Norton Shakespeare*, p. xii.
25. Paul Werstine (1988) 'The Textual Mystery of *Hamlet*', *Shakespeare Quarterly*, 39: 3–4.
26. Shakespeare, *Hamlet* in *The Norton Shakespeare*, 5.2.146.11–12.
27. Shakespeare, *Hamlet* in *The Norton Shakespeare*, 5.2.76–79.
28. Shakespeare, *The Norton Shakespeare*, p. xiii.
29. Wells & Taylor, 'The Oxford Shakespeare Re-viewed', 15.
30. Shakespeare, *The Norton Shakespeare*, p. 75.
31. William Shakespeare (1863) *The Works*, ed. William George Clark and John Glover, vol. 1: *The Tempest, The Two Gentlemen of Verona, The Merry Wives of Windsor, Measure for Measure, The Comedy of Errors*, 9 vols (Cambridge: Macmillan), pp. xxv–xxvi; Wells et al., *William Shakespeare: A Textual Companion*.
32. Gabriel Egan (forthcoming) 'Folio Provenance', in Emma Smith (ed.) *The Cambridge Companion to Shakespeare's First Folio (1623)* (Cambridge: Cambridge University Press).
33. John Jowett and Gary Taylor (1985) 'Sprinklings of Authority: The Folio Text of *Richard II*', *Studies in Bibliography*, 38: 151–200.
34. Shakespeare, *Comedies, Histories and Tragedies*, sig. ee4r–ee4v.
35. Jowett & Taylor, 'Sprinklings of Authority: The Folio Text of *Richard II*'; Wells et al., *William Shakespeare: A Textual Companion*, pp. 306–307.
36. William Shakespeare (1597) *[Richard II] The Tragedie of King Richard the Second*, STC 22307 BEPD 141a (Q1) (London: Valentine Simmes for Andrew Wise), sig. K1v–K2r.
37. William Shakespeare (2007) *Richard II* in The *Complete Works (=The Royal Shakespeare Company Complete Works)*, ed. Jonathan Bate and Eric Rasmussen (Basingstoke: Macmillan), 5.6.34–36.
38. Gary Taylor (1985) 'The Fortunes of Oldcastle', *Shakespeare Survey*, 38: 85–100; David Scott Kastan (1998), 'Killed with Hard Opinions: Oldcastle, Falstaff, and the Reformed Text of *1 Henry IV*', in Laurie E. Maguire and Thomas L. Berger (eds) *Textual Formations and Reformations* (Newark DE: University of Delaware Press), pp. 211–27.
39. William Shakespeare (1600) *[Henry IV, Part II] The Second Part of Henrie the Fourth*, STC 22288 BEPD 167a(i) (Q) (London: V[alentine] S[immes] for Andrew Wise and William Aspley), sig. B3v.
40. Shakespeare, *Henry IV, Part II* in *The Complete Works (=The Royal Shakespeare Company Complete Works)*, 1.2.141–42.

41. Shakespeare, *[Henry IV, Part II] The Second Part of Henrie the Fourth*, sig. F1v.
42. Shakespeare, *Henry IV, Part II* in *The Complete Works (=The Royal Shakespeare Company Complete Works)*, 3.2.129.
43. Shakespeare, *[Henry IV, Part II] The Second Part of Henrie the Fourth*, F3r; Shakespeare, *Henry IV, Part II* in *The Complete Works (=The Royal Shakespeare Company Complete Works)*, 3.2.208, 14.
44. Shakespeare, *[Henry IV, Part II] The Second Part of Henrie the Fourth*, sig. G4v.
45. Shakespeare, *Henry IV, Part II* in *The Complete Works (=The Royal Shakespeare Company Complete Works)*, 4.1.395.
46. Shakespeare, *[Henry IV, Part II] The Second Part of Henrie the Fourth*, sig. K4v; Shakespeare, *Henry IV, Part II*, in *The Complete Works (=The Royal Shakespeare Company Complete Works)*, 5.5.35, 37.
47. For a while after its publication in 2007 the *RSC Shakespeare Complete Works* was used by the acting company to provide the scripts for its productions. The author was fortunate to witness a performance in which this Folio-centricity had significant unintended consequences. David Warner, who usually played Sir John in Michael Boyd's *Henry IV, Part II* of 2007–8, was one evening indisposed and so was his understudy. A series of role exchanges left Julius D'Silva (normally Bardolph) essaying the fat knight, a role for which he was unprepared and would need to read from a book. Rather than the unwieldy RSC *Complete Works*, D'Silva was given a small single-play edition, which from the Courtyard Theatre's first gallery could just be made out to be the Arden2 edition by A. R. Humphreys, based on the 1600 edition. From Sir John's first scene it was clear that no one in the company had anticipated that Humphreys' edition would make Sir John say things that the rest of the cast were not expecting. The cast were hearing and visibly responding to a Sir John who was not only unaccountably restored to the rhetorical vigour they had not witnessed since Part One, but who was also giving cues they were not expecting and expecting cues they had not practised to give. D'Silva earned a standing ovation for overcoming formidable difficulties in his performance, a great many of which no one on stage had anticipated.
48. William Shakespeare (2015) *The Norton Shakespeare*, Third edition, ed. Stephen Greenblatt, Walter Cohen, Suzanne Gossett, Jean E. Howard, Katharine Eisaman Maus and Gordon McMullan (New York: W. W. Norton), p. xxv.
49. Shakespeare, *The Norton Shakespeare*, Third edition, p. xxv.
50. Shakespeare, *The Norton Shakespeare*, Third edition, p. xxvii.
51. Shakespeare, *The Norton Shakespeare*, Third edition, p. 91.
52. Stanley Wells and Gary Taylor (1979) *Modernizing Shakespeare's Spelling, with Three Studies in the Text of Henry V* (Oxford: Clarendon Press).

Select Bibliography

Egan, Gabriel (forthcoming) 'Folio Provenance' in Emma Smith (ed.) *The Cambridge Companion to Shakespeare's First Folio (1623)* (Cambridge: Cambridge University Press).
Egan, Gabriel (2010) *The Struggle for Shakespeare's Text: Twentieth-Century Editorial Theory and Practice* (Cambridge: Cambridge University Press).

Erne, Lukas (2013) *Shakespeare and the Book Trade* (Cambridge: Cambridge University Press).

Erne, Lukas (2003) *Shakespeare as Literary Dramatist* (Cambridge: Cambridge University Press).

Wells, Stanley and Gary Taylor (1979) *Modernizing Shakespeare's Spelling, with Three Studies in the Text of Henry V* (Oxford: Clarendon Press).

Wells, Stanley, Gary Taylor, John Jowett and William Montgomery (1987) *William Shakespeare: A Textual Companion* (Oxford: Oxford University Press).

Werstine, Paul (2013) *Early Modern Playhouse Manuscripts and the Editing of Shakespeare* (Cambridge: Cambridge University Press).

4

Marketing Shakespeare Films: From Tragedy to Biopic

Deborah Cartmell

In the sound era, the so-called heyday of film adaptations, Shakespeare and film became identified, as Louis B. Mayer famously declared, with Hollywood tragedy, or more precisely as box office poison.[1] Indeed the so-called 'Prestige' productions of the film studios, United Artists' *Taming of the Shrew*, directed by Sam Taylor, 1929, Warner Brothers' *A Midsummer Night's Dream*, directed by Max Reinhardt and William Dieterle, 1935, MGM's *Romeo and Juliet*, directed by George Cukor, 1936, and the British (Inter-Allied) adaptation, *As You Like It*, directed by Paul Czinner, 1936 (best known today for Laurence Olivier's first appearance on screen in a Shakespeare film), were box office flops, in spite of their frantic and multi-angled marketing campaigns. Their only achievements at the time of their releases were dubious prestige for the film companies during a period in which Hollywood was besieged by complaints about the shallow, violent and lascivious content of the movies. This chapter considers the marketing of Shakespeare films in the early sound period, which, whilst failing to convince moviegoers of the cinematic qualities of the Shakespeare films that were being promoted, contained many of the ingredients contributing to the most financially successful Shakespeare film to date: John Madden's biopic of 1998, *Shakespeare in Love*.

Shakespeare and the movies

It was not until Olivier's *Henry V* (1944) that Shakespeare and sound film were applauded critically and commercially. Olivier became the first 'Shakespeare auteur', with film successes *Hamlet* (1948) and *Richard III* (1955) following his hugely successful directorial debut. Musicals, such as *Kiss Me Kate* (based on *The Taming of the Shrew*, directed by George Sidney,

57

1953, and adapted from the 1948 Cole Porter Broadway musical) and *West Side Story* (based on *Romeo and Juliet*, 1961, directed by Robert Wise and Jerome Robbins and adapted from the 1957 Leonard Bernstein and Stephen Sondheim Broadway musical) were popular mid-century, and following Olivier more 'Shakespeare auteurs' emerged, such as Orson Welles (*Macbeth*, 1948; *Othello*, 1952; *Chimes at Midnight*, 1965) Akira Kurosawa (with adaptations of *Macbeth*, *Throne of Blood*, 1957; *Hamlet*, *The Bad Sleep Well*, 1960; *King Lear*, *Ran*, 1985), Grigori Kozintsev (*Hamlet*, 1964; *King Lear*, 1971), Franco Zeffirelli (*The Taming of the Shrew*, 1967; *Romeo and Juliet*, 1968; *Otello*, 1986; *Hamlet*, 1990) and Kenneth Branagh (*Henry V*, 1989; *Much Ado About Nothing*, 1993; a loose adaptation of *Hamlet* in the 'let's put on a show' genre, *In the Bleak Midwinter*, 1995; *Hamlet*, 1996; *Love's Labour's Lost*, 2000; *As You Like It*, 2006). Following in Olivier's footsteps, Branagh's *Henry V* seemed to inspire a renewed interest in Shakespeare films in the last decade of the twentieth century, among them *Othello* (Oliver Parker, 1995), *William Shakespeare's Romeo + Juliet* (Baz Luhrmann, 1996), *A Midsummer Night's Dream* (Michael Hoffman, 1999) and *10 Things I Hate About You* (*The Taming of the Shrew*, Gil Junger, 1999). A comparison of the profits generated by these films (with the acknowledgement that figures will vary) is revealing of Shakespeare's marketability:

Shakespeare in Love (John Madden, 1998): Approximately $300 million worldwide
William Shakespeare's Romeo + Juliet (Baz Luhrmann, 1996): Approximately $150 million worldwide
10 Things I Hate about You (*The Taming of the Shrew*, Gil Junger, 1999): Approximately $55 million worldwide.[2]

In spite of huge strides to market Shakespeare adaptations, from the early sound era to the end of the twentieth century, the most popular Shakespeare film in this period is, significantly, not by Shakespeare, but about Shakespeare. Although roughly based on events in *Romeo and Juliet* and *Twelfth Night*, it is astounding that Shakespeare flourishes most on screen, not in comedy, tragedy, pastoral or romance, but in the genre of the biopic, easily the most despised of all film genres.[3] Possible reasons for the historic low regard of the biopic are that the form is seen, by film critics, historians and literary scholars, as formulaic, misleading and money grabbing in its embracement of celebrity culture: in other words, it is despised for its blatant commercialism (and its consequent popularity).

Shakespeare's relatively modest box office success is mirrored in Academy Award recognition. Major Oscars were given to Shakespeare films on a few notable occasions. Laurence Olivier won best film and best actor for *Hamlet* (1948). A loose adaptation of *Othello, A Double Life,* directed by George Cukor, won a best actor award for Ronald Colman in the previous year. *West Side Story,* the musical rewriting of *Romeo and Juliet,* won the Oscar for best film in 1961. But, in terms of Academy Awards, the most triumphant of all Shakespeare films was not a film adapted from one of Shakespeare's plays, but the biopic *Shakespeare in Love,* nominated for 13 Academy Awards, winning best film, best actress for Gwyneth Paltrow and best supporting actress for Judi Dench. Significantly, the most successful Shakespearean film of the twentieth century, in both financial returns and in Academy Awards, is not a film based on a Shakespeare play, but one based on Shakespeare's life. It seems that the 'presence' of Shakespeare, or rather Shakespeare as movie star, rather than Shakespearean content, seems to be what sells Shakespeare on screen.

Shakespeare as would-be filmmaker: marketing screen adaptations of Shakespeare

The cliché almost always reiterated by adaptors of Shakespeare, that if the playwright were alive now he would be working for Warner Brothers, can be traced to approaches to pitching Shakespeare to a range of audiences in the early sound period (when Shakespeare's words were introduced to filmgoers for the first time), from audiences unfamiliar with Shakespeare, to those prejudiced against highbrow culture and to those with a scholarly interest in the dramatist. While marketing campaigns of this period can be described as hit and miss, there were sustained efforts to market film adaptations of Shakespeare through the presence of the dramatist himself. The first Shakespeare talkie, Sam Taylor's *Taming of the Shrew,* 1929, starring (for the first time together), Douglas Fairbanks and Mary Pickford (whose marriage, unbeknown to audiences at the time, was on the decline), markets the film through ignoring Shakespeare's authorship and, conversely, through jokingly insisting that the playwright was fully consulted in the production process. An article in *Photoplay* in 1930 informs readers that: United Artists' 'sales force was mortally afraid of Will Shakespeare's name from the moment the picture was planned. Who'd go to see Shakespeare?'.[4] It quotes from an advert that appeared in 'a daily paper in a city of 100,000 people':

'GLORIOUS FUN! CYCLONIC ACTION!'
'DOUG GIVES THIS LITTLE GIRL A HAND! SOCK!

RIGHT ON THE NOSE! 'CAUSE OUR MARY'S A MEAN
MAMA, AND DOUG'S TAMING HER! IT'S A RIOT OF FUN –
ENDING WITH TENDER ROMANCE'.[5]

In direct opposition to this advert, the playwright is far from ignored
but repeatedly mentioned in the pressbook, with 'Shakespeare' himself
endorsing the movie. An illustrated article in the 1929 pressbook features the ghost of Shakespeare taking tea with stars Mary Pickford and
Douglas Fairbanks where he receives reassurance that he 'may know
first hand that thou [Pickford and Fairbanks] hast preserved the laughs
and ribald spirit' of *The Taming of the Shrew* (see Figure 4.1). Fairbanks
replies 'Gadzooks, egad and a couple of ha ha's, I should say we never
lost the ribald spirit', a speech which completely satisfies Shakespeare
that the film is more than worthy of him.[6]

Later films don't go down this route of audaciously claiming
Shakespeare's unqualified approval, but the later promotional materials
reflect the film companies' desperation and bewilderment regarding how
to promote Shakespeare, with attempts to sell the movies from every
conceivable angle, first of all marketing the films as prestige entertainment, employing academics to endorse the movies or provide 'scholarly
articles' in the pressbooks and to act as consultants on the films. For
instance, to the horror of literary critic Harley Granville-Barker, the
'Literary Consultant' Professor William Strunk, Jr., of Cornell University,
is featured in the opening credits of George Cukor's 1936 *Romeo and Juliet*,
in an effort to validate the movie's cultural worth.[7] At the same time,
promoters produced tie-in products, unsuccessfully attempting to bring
in school audiences with the promise of introducing and converting

Figure 4.1   Images of Douglas Fairbanks, Mary Pickford and William Shakespeare
from *The Taming of the Shrew* Pressbook, 1929
Source: From the British Film Institute Collection.

the young to Shakespeare. In contrast to claiming the films' educational worth, there were also doomed attempts to draw in audiences by claiming that Shakespeare was not obscure and purely educational, but 'fun'. The 1929 *Taming of the Shrew* (Figure 4.2), for example, tries both strategies, attracting pure pleasure seekers and those searching for cultural capital: the pressbook includes a cartoon serial for local newspapers, illustrated with Pickford and Fairbanks in the title roles, which makes Shakespeare 'easy', and a 'scholarly' article in which 'Research Expert Gives Graphic Account of Stage Premiere in Shakespeare's Day' ('Opening in 1600') in which Shakespeare himself appears as the Prologue:

Behind the filmy curtain stands the Prologue, with dry lips and trembling hands. With a quick movement he pulls aside the curtain, advances with a quiet smile, and bows to the crowd. 'It is Shakespeare! Look, it is Shakespeare!' The name spreads through the house... With a grace and dignity of his own, Shakespeare recites the introductory verses and retires slowly, followed by the applause of his friends.[8]

The pressbook of what I would rank as the worst of all of the Shakespeare films of the early sound period, *As You Like It* (starring Elisabeth Bergner and the upcoming star Laurence Olivier), and significantly the last film to be made in this period, betrays numerous anxieties about the film's reception (see Figure 4.3). Seemingly petrified by the prospect of failure, the promoters of the movie, in even more desperation than their predecessors, attempt every trick in the book to entice the widest range of cinemagoers. The pressbook, presumably much to the chagrin of 'real' scholars, insists upon its Shakespearean credentials. Paul Czinner, the director of the film, is praised as 'one of the foremost authorities' on Shakespeare and the academic benefits of the film are stressed in the study guides accompanying the movie. The film's fidelity to Shakespeare (and the director's affinity with the dramatist) is alluded to in a letter from the Managing Director of Radio City Music Hall, New York, prominently featured on the first page of the pressbook, which claims 'Had Shakespeare been alive today, working in motion pictures, he probably would have presented his play much in the manner of this new picture'.[9] The pressbook also features a series of cartoon drawings with a tattooed workman extolling the film's comic exploits, a mother and young son rushing to the picture and two young women in twin beds talking dreamily about the film: 'BUT DID YOU EVER SEE A MAN LIKE THAT ORLANDO BEFORE? HO-HUM! PLEASANT DREAMS!'.[10] One of the promotional suggestions is to place

Figure 4.2 From *The Taming of the Shrew* Pressbook, 1929.
Source: From the British Film Institute Collection.

Figure 4.3 From *As You Like It* Pressbook, 1937
Source: From the British Film Institute Collection.

a 'GIANT BOOK IN LOBBY' and 'As patrons open cover, stills and copy on picture are revealed to them'.[11]

The film is promoted as educational, authentic and full of jokes and romance. (In watching it today, it is none of these things. Laurence Olivier looks sulky and uncomfortable beside his co-star, Elisabeth Bergner, who shouts out all her lines as if that will make them easier to understand.) These pressbooks are treasure troves of Shakespeare marketing in the early sound period, and reading them today it is possible to conclude that with this vintage of Shakespeare adaptations the pitch is better than the product.

In spite of the frenzied attempts to promote these movies, the films themselves were box office failures; but the trailers, the advertising campaigns and the accompanying short films, were, in my view, minor masterpieces which have fallen into obscurity due to the failures of the films they sought to advance. Warner Brothers' *Shake, Mr Shakespeare* (Roy Mack, 1936) and MGM's *Master Will Shakespeare* (Jacques Tourneur, 1936) were short Shakespeare films released to promote the 1935 *A Midsummer Night's Dream* and 1936 *Romeo and Juliet*. *Shake, Mr Shakespeare* is the unacknowledged first Shakespeare musical, adapting Shakespeare to the sounds of Hollywood. It begins with an assistant production manager receiving a cable from a film producer, following the imagined overnight success of Warner Brothers' *Midsummer Night's Dream*, displayed by a montage of fake newspaper reviews. The cable reads: 'I want you to read all Shakespeare's plays tonight and let me know tomorrow what they are all about'. A dream sequence follows in which Shakespearean characters emerge from books, each performing song and dance numbers based on their stories, explicitly influenced by Hollywood cinema. The songs in this spoof adaptation are brilliantly conceived, such as, 'We're going to Hollywood' ('The play was the thing they used to say'), 'Romeo, Where the Heck are You?' ('Why don't you come up and see me sometime?'), 'Friends, Romans and Countrymen' ('lend me thy feet/To the tune we love, the rhythm of 42nd Street'), Cleopatra's song 'You Can Be Kissed' ('because you're a snooty little cutie') and 'Shake, Mr. Shakespeare' ('When you start to swing/You'll be king'). The film features Henry VIII as a stand-up comedian, a dancing Hamlet and an acrobatic Cleopatra, prophetic of the popularity of musical Shakespeare films to come, such as *Kiss Me Kate* (1953) and *West Side Story* (1961). Shakespeare is the last character to arrive in this short film, emerging from the book *The Man Shakespeare*, by Frank Harris (1909), possibly suggesting that the future for Shakespeare films is not in Shakespeare's plays and characters but in Shakespeare's biography.

The MGM short, *Master Will Shakespeare*, is the second Shakespeare biographical film of the sound era, following a forgotten British film, *The Immortal Gentleman* (1935), described in Luke McKernan and Olwen Terris's *Walking Shadows: Shakespeare in the National Film Archive* as being as 'dreadful a film as has ever been made, meanly produced, ill-lit, ill-staged, scarcely directed at all, with some howlingly bad excerpts from the plays', 'the nadir of filmed Shakespeare'.[12] Essentially, the film features Shakespeare observing customers in a Southwark pub who resemble characters from his play.[13] This is not the first attempt to present Shakespeare on screen, however. The first biographical film was Georges Méliès' *Le Mort de Jules César*, 1907, in which Shakespeare (played by the director) falls asleep and 'dreams up' the play. The 1936 MGM talkie follows young Will Shakespeare as he makes his way from Stratford to London, carrying his scripts, hobo-like, in a sack. The journey is explicitly linked to the plight of Hollywood hopefuls as the narrator reaches out to an audience, keen to make the big time. Will's journey from the dull and obscure town of Stratford-upon-Avon, likened by the narrator to the numerous aspiring stars making their way to Hollywood ('you've heard that call, little stage-struck Sally, haven't you?') brings him to London where he encounters Manager Burbage, a sixteenth-century version of a Hollywood mogul. Will works his way up as a prompter and gets his big break when an actor forgets his lines and he substitutes extemporaneous lines of his own, much to the amazement and delight of the audience. We follow his path to success, which includes his frustrations with the limitations of the stage (implying that film would be the answer to his dreams) and the film ends with a reflective and romantic Shakespeare, separated from his cronies, Ben Jonson and Thomas Dekker, where he recalls what is identified as his favourite play, *Romeo and Juliet*, the film that the 'documentary' was designed to promote. Accompanying Will's recitation of Romeo's last speech, as Stephen M. Buhler has noted, is the music from Tchaikovsky's ballet, used throughout Cukor's film, the introduction of which turns what we think is a documentary into an advert, suggesting that Shakespeare's vision will finally be realized: his 'favourite' play will achieve perfection on screen.[14] The short film, like Georges Méliès' silent film, *Le Mort de Jules César*, makes a connection between playwright and filmmaker, one which has stuck in the popular imagination and which is repeated frequently in Shakespeare and film publicity, such as Laurence Olivier's assertion in the preface to the screenplay of *Henry V*: 'Shakespeare, in a way, "wrote for the films"',[15] rephrased by screenwriter Marc Norman in the documentary made for *Shakespeare in Love*: 'If Shakespeare were alive today he'd have a three picture deal with Warner Brothers, he'd be driving a Porsche and he'd be living in Bel Air'.[16]

The merging of filmmaker and early modern playwright is persistent in the marketing of Shakespeare films. Olivier's *Hamlet* is advertised in 1948 with the words from a *Life Magazine* review, 'A WORK OF GENIUS', making it unclear as to whether the compliment is referring to Shakespeare or to Laurence Olivier. The advert features Oliver surrounded by a golden glow, as if electrified with the presence of Shakespeare. The publicity images for the film almost always include a shadow looming behind Olivier, a reference to the ghost of Hamlet's father, but also to the presence of Shakespeare, the ghost behind the actor. The connection between actor, director and playwright is expressed throughout the reviews and publicity for the film. A short review in *Screenland* declares 'This second attempt of Olivier's to bring Shakespeare to movie audiences should make the Bard of Avon everlastingly grateful for making three-quarters of the dialog as understandable as today's English'.[17] Olivier set a pattern for the Shakespeare auteurs to follow, by implicitly linking director and playwright. The connection between filmmaking and Shakespeare is taken to its logical conclusion in *Shakespeare in Love*, demonstrating a will to resurrect William Shakespeare, playwright, as William Shakespeare, film writer and movie star, combined with a desire to read the dramas as concealed autobiography. The film achieves what the promotional literature of the late 1920s and 30s attempted to do: it makes Shakespeare into a genuinely marketable commodity.

Shakespeare in the marketplace: *Shakespeare in Love*

Uncannily resembling the marketing material of the early sound period, such as the placement of Mary Pickford, Douglas Fairbanks and William Shakespeare, side by side, *Shakespeare in Love* presents Shakespeare as would-be filmmaker and Hollywood heartthrob. It not only adapts other film versions of Shakespeare's works, most notably Zeffirelli's and Luhrmann's films of *Romeo and Juliet*, it also shows the influence of the failed (but brilliant in themselves) earlier attempts to market Shakespeare on screen, explicitly commercialising the Shakespeare product. One of the trailers announces the award-winning film 'Shakespeare in Love', then closes in on the film itself with Shakespeare replying to Christopher Marlowe (played by Rupert Everett) with the words 'good title', referring now to the movie, *Shakespeare in Love*, rather than Marlowe's play (as the line appears in the film). The trailer is very much in the spirit of the film, attempting a seamless connection between Shakespeare as dramatist and Shakespeare as moviemaker. The decision to include Shakespeare's name in the title, against executive producer Harvey Weinstein's objection (echoing that of Louis B. Mayer), who reputedly hated the title and claimed that going to a Shakespeare movie was like going to the dentist, proved, counter-intuitively, to be an astute marketing decision.[18]

Shakespeare in Love mixes advertising with 'high culture' and the promotion of Shakespeare with Shakespeare himself, a combination long resisted by scholars of English. Writers Marc Norman and Tom Stoppard and director John Madden (who graduated with a degree in English Literature from Sidney Sussex College, Cambridge, in 1970) would have been well aware of the legacy of F. R. Leavis and his identification of advertising as the enemy of art, as far removed from Shakespeare as it is possible to be. F. R. Leavis and Q. D. Leavis, writing at the beginning of the talkies, were outspokenly horrified by the employment of market-driven tactics by contemporary writers, such as Hugh Walpole (who also worked as a screenwriter) and Edgar Rice Burroughs (best known for his Tarzan novels), who, they claim, in the manner of advertisers, stoop to appeal to the lowest possible denominator. Like F. R. Leavis in his bleak re-evaluation of Matthew Arnold's *Culture and Anarchy*, Q. D. Leavis is keen to distinguish between 'mass civilisation' and 'minority culture' and writes about the herd mentality that characterizes advertising, popular writing and film: it 'is more than difficult, it is next to impossible, for the ordinary uncritical man to resist, when whichever way he looks in the street, from poster and hoarding, and advertisement in bus and tramcar, whichever paper or novel he picks up, whatever play or film he attends for amusement, the pressure of the herd is brought to bear on him'.[19] The belief that money and art cannot mix is still felt today and the heady and self-conscious mixture of advertising and Shakespeare in this film seems designed to provoke the Shakespeareans in the audience through the blatant commercialising of the playwright. Richard Burt has argued that the breakdown of the boundary between mass culture and academia (an argument that recalls the Leavises' outrage at popular entertainments' threat to cultural authority) as it is manifested in this film marks what he calls 'the end of the Shakespearean'.[20] The explicit commodification of Shakespeare may be the reason why *Shakespeare in Love* has received relatively little critical attention. Samuel Crowl explains that it is absent from his survey, *Shakespeare and Film* (2008), because 'spin-off films are never included in the standard Shakespeare survey course'.[21] In major studies of Shakespeare adaptations, such as Christy Desmet and Robert Sawyer's collection, *Shakespeare and Appropriation* (1999), Russell Jackson's collection, *The Cambridge Companion to Shakespeare on Film* (2000) and Russell Jackson's *Shakespeare & the English Speaking Cinema* (2014), *Shakespeare in Love* is given only a few pages, while other studies, such as Judith Buchanan's *Shakespeare on Film* (2005), fail to mention it at all. It is not even considered in Charles Gant's list of the highest grossing Shakespeare movies, published in *Sight and Sound* in 2015.[22] The absence of literature on the film may be due to the fact that it is a biopic, and therefore not of interest to Shakespeareans. However, in spite of its numerous awards and its subject matter, it is also conspicuously missing from the major study of the biopic genre, Dennis Bingham's *Whose Lives are they Anyway?: The Biopic as Contemporary Film Genre* (2010).

As Michael Anderegg has noted, like *Romeo + Juliet, Shakespeare in Love* seems defiantly to relish in its commercialism, perhaps accounting for a resistance in Shakespeare scholarship to take it seriously. In considering Hugh Fennyman's deliberations about the potential gains of putting on a play, Anderegg observes that the film is 'in one sense, as much a movie about money as it is about Shakespeare'.[23] For Anderegg, Hugh Fennyman's economic advice to Philip Henslowe is at the heart of the film:

> FENNYMAN
> A play takes time. Find actors ... rehearsals ... let's say open in three weeks. That's – what – five hundred groundlings at tuppence each, in addition four hundred backsides at three pence – a penny extra for a cushion, call it two hundred cushions, say two performances for safety – how much is that Mr. Frees?
>
> FREES
> Twenty pounds to the penny, Mr. Fennyman.
> HENSLOWE
> But I have to pay the actors and the author.
> FENNYMAN
> A share of the profits.
> HENSLOWE
> There's never any ...
> FENNYMAN
> Of course not!
> HENSLOWE
> *(impressed)*
> Mr. Fennyman, I think you may have hit on something.[24]

From another perspective, it is a film as much about advertising as it is about Shakespeare. The movie follows in the footsteps of Baz Luhrmann's *William Shakespeare's Romeo + Juliet*, which, as Douglas M. Lanier notes, packs its *mise en scène* with Shakespeare adverts, such as a billboard advertising a recliner with the caption from *The Tempest*, 'such stuff as dreams are made on', to suggest: 'how thoroughly Shakespeare's language has been appropriated and corrupted to serve the ends of the two corporate giants, Montague and Capulet, who tower over Verona Beach'.[25] But, like Luhrmann's film itself, the adverts reflect a mixture of high and low culture, F. R. Leavis's ultimate nightmare, popularising and debunking the cultural status of Shakespeare by reducing both the writer and his works to the level of marketing. The adverts call attention to the film's (or that of Shakespeare films in general) exploitation of Shakespeare, which, on a cynical level, can be seen to actively and greedily transform culture into capital.

Adverts also form part of *Shakespeare in Love*'s *mise en scène* (Figure 4.4). The opening sequence closes in on an Elizabethan version of a flyer, 'The Lamentable Tragedie of the Moneylender Reveng'd' (and a nod to Olivier's *Henry V*, which begins with a crinkled handbill), and as is almost always commented on in every account of the film, Shakespeare is first seen throwing his rejected paper into a mug with the inscription 'A Present from Stratford upon Avon', a nod to the commercial exploitation of Shakespeare which has transformed Shakespeare's birthplace into another Shakespearean marketplace.

Why this causes reviewers to pause is worth considering here. The merging of Shakespeare, the romantic individual writer, with the mass

Figure 4.4   Screenshot from *Shakespeare in Love*, directed by John Madden
Source: Miramax (1998).

cultural industry that has grown up in his name in many respects epitomizes the film's strategy as a whole, which embraces and celebrates the commercialization of Shakespeare. Marketing comes to the fore in the Elizabethan version of a 'shrink', with Dr Moth's signs proclaiming his many services: 'Apothecary Alchemist Astrologer', 'Priest of Psyche' and 'Interpreter of Dreams'. The final play, performed at Burbage's Curtain Theatre, is introduced by another leaflet, announcing 'Mr. Henslowe's Presentation of The Admirall's Men in Performance of The excellent and Lamentable Tragedie of Romeo and Juliet' (which makes no mention of Shakespeare's authorship), that flies in the face of Wessex (played by Colin Firth) immediately following his wedding. The film begins and ends with advertising campaigns.

On the 2004 DVD director's commentary John Madden makes no mention of the genre of the film (the biopic) and fails to mention Arthur Brooke's poem of 1562, *The Tragicall Historye of Romeus and Juliet*, which Shakespeare adapts into *Romeo and Juliet*. These two omissions – the concealment of the source that invalidates the film's narrative and the resistance to talk about a genre that traditionally fabricates the myth that art is based on a life – are key to the film's success. The film becomes not a Shakespearean adaptation, but a story based on a formative and fictional experience in the life of Shakespeare. The biopic is among the most formulaic of all film genres (what Q. D. Leavis would condemn as the worst sort of 'standardization', which can be translated as 'commercialization') and it is hard to imagine a more self-consciously formulaic biopic than *Shakespeare in Love*, in which art is seen unequivocally to imitate life. Biopics of authors tend to involve a conflict between an individual and the establishment (Shakespeare versus Hugh Fennyman), a trial scene or performance in which the central figure proves their worth (the final performance of *Romeo and Juliet*), the moral that success comes at a price (the separation of Viola and Will) and, as stated above, the notion that art imitates the life of the author. The life of Will and Viola echoes that of Romeo and Juliet, and fiction and 'fact' are increasingly interwoven in the film to the extent that it is often difficult to determine when Will and Viola speak in their own voices and when they are reciting lines from the play. *Shakespeare in Love* indulges in the well-trodden biopic formula, a form despised by critics of film, literature and history, but loved by fans and a well-trodden route to Academy Award success. Andrew Higson includes *Shakespeare in Love* in the 'Brit-lit biopic' category,[26] and for Higson these films seek historical and cultural validation while they 'personalize and individualize the historical project, organizing the representation of the past around desire and romance'.[27] Essential to their success is the name of the author, used in numerous films to claim ownership of the literary works (for example, Francis Ford Coppola's *Bram Stoker's Dracula*, 1992; Kenneth Branagh's *Mary Shelley's Frankenstein*, 1994; and Baz Luhrmann's *William Shakespeare's Romeo + Juliet*, 1996), and the involvement of a literary figure – in this case Tom Stoppard, a distinguished playwright known most of all for his adaptation of *Hamlet*, *Rosencrantz and Guildenstern are Dead*, first staged in 1966. Stoppard came to Marc Norman's script later in the process, perhaps to add his cultural cachet to the product, and clearly proved a better choice than MGM's academic advisor, Professor William Strunk Jr, in 1937. In the 2004 DVD commentary, Marc Norman also relates that in preparing the screenplay, he also sought academic advice, holding regular meetings with Shakespeare scholar Stephen Greenblatt, who he claims agreed that the film was a totally legitimate project.

Rick Altman has argued that 'Britishness' is a key selling point in the early biographical film, citing the first example of this as *Disraeli* in 1929, directed by Alfred E. Green and starring George Arliss.[28] Shortly after Green's film, Alexander Korda's *The Private Life of Henry VIII* (1933) capitalized on the appeal of British subjects to American audiences, winning Charles Laughton the first Academy Award to be given to a British actor. The film catered for an American audience fascinated by the British, in particular British landmarks, but also a fan-obsessed audience intrigued with the private lives of the stars and what goes on behind closed doors. The film begins with an external shot of Hampton Court and immediately follows with the maids of court gathered around Henry's still warm bed as they prepare the room for the next female occupant, Jane Seymour. The biopic literally opens the door onto Henry, taking audiences to his most private spaces. Laughton's performance ultimately exposes Henry as a somewhat pathetic and ordinary man, presumably much to the delight of the American audience, but one who also resembles a Hollywood mogul and the stars of the period, whose many divorces were a frequent topic of fan magazines.[29]

Shakespeare in Love employs a similar opening strategy, as we first see Shakespeare alone in his attic room, frustrated by an inability to write. The film's sumptuous exteriors and interiors locate it within the British Heritage genre of films, with filming locations that include Broughton Castle, Holkham Hall, Eton College, Hatfield House and Whitehall. Shakespeare is played by an actor of English, Irish and Scottish, origins, Joseph Fiennes (born Joseph Alberic Iscariot Twisleton-Wykeham-Fiennes) and his love interest, Lady Viola De Lesseps, by American actress, Gwyneth Paltrow, known for playing British literary characters, such as Austen's Emma in 1996 and Dickens's Estella in 1998, just prior to the release of *Shakespeare in Love*. The importance of Paltrow (although the film was initially linked to Julia Roberts and Winona Ryder) is hard to overestimate – allegedly when Harvey Weinstein read the script, he refused to make the picture if Paltrow was not in it.[30] In keeping with the genre of the biopic, the film was conceived as a star vehicle – interestingly not for the actor playing Shakespeare, but for the actress playing Shakespeare's love interest. The mixing of British and American actors in the casting is nothing new, but the casting of an American star and a lesser-known Irish/British actor in the title parts intimates that Shakespeare needs America (what Viola calls 'a new world' following her first sexual encounter with Shakespeare) in order to write.[31] Of course, the film begins with Shakespeare unable to write in London and ends with him inspired by his vision of the new world, a dreamscape that turns out to be America itself. Like Korda's *Private Life of Henry VIII*, the film takes a quintessentially British subject and Americanizes it, appealing to American Anglophilia while flattering the American audience by hinting at their significant contribution to British culture.

The poster advertising the film loudly proclaims its biopic credentials. The tagline 'LOVE IS THE ONLY INSPIRATION' implicitly gives credit to the face, in profile, occupying the most central location of the poster: Paltrow as Viola De Lesseps. Will's face is positioned in profile in the top left, Viola's in the middle to bottom right, forming a diagonal line in which they are about to embrace. In between the couple is the much smaller figure of Shakespeare, seen in silhouette with his back to the viewer, symbolically representing 'art' standing between 'love'. The poster suggests that 'love' is the most significant of all things (as Viola says in the film, 'there is something even better than a play. Even your play') and the artist, a lonely figure who will sacrifice life for art, is nonetheless empowered by it.[32] Like Olivier in the 1948 promotions of *Hamlet*, the little figure of Shakespeare is encircled by a warm orange glow, presumably the after-effect of his relationship with Viola, a glow that inspires him to write.

Perhaps the worst 'crime' of all in *Shakespeare in Love* for traditional lovers of Shakespeare is the presentation of Shakespeare as opportunistic, unscrupulously stealing good lines wherever he finds them and essentially, like the 'typical' screenwriter, selling out by writing for money. This certainly was the view of academics, poets and novelists, for most of the twentieth century, on the subject of writers who worked in Hollywood: writing for the films is regarded, as seen by the Leavises and even those who succumbed to the lure of Hollywood themselves, as a devaluation of writing. Nonetheless, the ultimate accolade for a play (perhaps with the exception of Shakespeare's plays), throughout the twentieth century is to become a film. Among the many examples that could be cited of film adaptations of plays are *The Barretts of Wimpole Street* (1934, adapted from the play by Rudolf Besier, written in 1930), *Arsenic and Old Lace* (1944, the screen version of the 1939 play by Joseph Kesselring), *Cat on a Hot Tin Roof* (1958, adapted from Tennessee Williams' Pulitzer winning play, first performed in 1955) and *My Fair Lady* (1964, an adaptation of the 1956 stage musical by Alan Jay Lerner and Frederick Loewe, based on George Bernard Shaw's *Pygmalion*), films that have possibly usurped their sources in popular and critical regard. In line with numerous film to play conversions of the 21st century, such as *Billy Elliot*, 2005 (adapted from Stephen Daldry's 2000 film), *Brief Encounter*, 2008 (adapted from David Lean's 1946 film) and *Fatal Attraction*, 2014 (adapted from Adrian Lyne's 1987 film), which serve to validate the canonicity of the films, *Shakespeare in Love* is now a play too. The play of the film, adapted by Lee Hall, opened in the Nöel Coward Theatre, London, in July 2014 and there is planned a production at the Stratford Ontario 2016 season, as part of the festivities commemorating the 400th anniversary of the dramatist's death. It is without doubt that this non-Shakespearean Shakespeare product is Shakespeare's most successful media venture, a venture which is the product of a long and successful history of selling Shakespeare the man over the far less successful mass marketing of Shakespeare's writings.

Shakespeare in Love is a film that is unashamedly commercial, and it is the most commercial (in terms of box office takings) of all 'Shakespeare films' to date. The now famous beginning of *Shakespeare in Love*, in which Shakespeare's signature is fetishized in close-ups, a signature that he rehearses with different spellings and which he ultimately discards into the souvenir mug, sums up the appeal of the movie as a whole. It is a film, like so much of the early twentieth-century marketing approaches to Shakespeare that the film perhaps unintentionally emulates, that simultaneously stresses and ignores the name 'Shakespeare': the film announces itself through the use of the name, while at the same time throwing away the writing. The film demonstrates what most of us would suspect (and contrary to Juliet's, 'What's in a name?'): that the dramatist's economic capital is first and foremost not in the plays and poetry, but in the name 'Shakespeare'.

Notes

1. Quoted in Robert F. Willson Jr. (2000) *Shakespeare in Hollywood 1929–1956* (Cranbury, NJ, London, Mississauga, Ontario: Associated University Presses, 2000), p. 7.
2. These figures are taken from Daniel Fischlin, Tom Magill and Jessica Riley (2014) 'Transgression and Transformation: *Mickey B* and the Dramaturgy of Adaptation' in Daniel Fischlin (ed.) *OuterSpeares: Shakespeare, Intermedia and the Limits of Adaptation* (Toronto, Buffalo and London: University of Toronto Press), pp. 153–97 (pp. 196–7).
3. For a discussion of the critical disregard for the genre of the biopic, see Steve Neale (2000) *Genre and Hollywood* (London and New York: Routledge), p. 60.
4. *Photoplay* (1930), February, p. 49, https://archive.org/details/photoplay 3738movi, date accessed 19 August 2015.
5. *Photoplay* (1930), February, p. 49.
6. *Taming of the Shrew* (1929) Pressbook (British Film Institute Collection) (np). The pressbooks used in this chapter are held at the Reuben Library, The British Film Institute, London.
7. Not even able to mention Strunk's name, Granville-Barker (1937) complains of how any academic could 'quite wantonly' sanction this film, especially the cutting of 'the rhyme out of the rhymed couplets'. See 'Alas, Poor Will', *The Listener* XVII (3 March): 387–9 (388). These early sound films are discussed as the 'first' Shakespeare adaptations in Deborah Cartmell (2015) *Adaptations in the Sound Era: 1927–37* (New York and London: Bloomsbury), pp. 23–53.
8. *Taming of the Shrew*, Pressbook.
9. *As You Like It* (1937) Pressbook (British Film Institute Collection) (np).
10. *As You Like It*, Pressbook.
11. *As You Like It*, Pressbook.
12. Luke McKernan and Olwen Terris (1994) *Walking Shadows: Shakespeare in the National Film and Television Archive* (London: BFI), p. 190.
13. A brief discussion of this film is in Megan Murray-Pepper (2013) 'The "Tables of Memory": Shakespeare, Cinema and the Writing Desk' in Judith Buchanan (ed.) *The Writer on Film: Screening Literary Authorship* (Basingstoke: Palgrave), pp. 92–105 (pp. 94–5).
14. Stephen M. Buhler (2001) *Shakespeare in Cinema: Ocular Proof* (New York: SUNY Press), p. 39.
15. Laurence Olivier (1984) *Henry V: Screenplay* (London: Lorrimer), p. v.
16. 'Shakespeare in Love on Film' (2004) *Shakespeare in Love*, Universal Studios, DVD.
17. *Screenland* (1948), October, p. 239, http://www.archive.org/stream/screen land5235unse/screenland5235unse#page/n239/mode/2up/search/hamlet, date accessed 14 August 2015.
18. Sue Summers (1999) *Daily Telegraph* 'Arts', 16 January, p. 49.
19. Q.D. Leavis (1932; rpt. 2000) *Fiction and the Reading Public* (London: Pimlico), p. 94.
20. Richard Burt (2000) '*Shakespeare in Love* and the End of the Shakespearean: Academic and Mass Culture Constructions of Literary Authorship', in Mark Thornton Burnett and Ramona Wray (eds) *Shakespeare, Film, Fin de Siècle* (Basingstoke: Palgrave), pp. 180–231 (p. 225).

21. Samuel Crowl (2008), *Shakespeare and Film: A Norton Guide* (New York: Norton), p. xiii.
22. Charles Gant (2015) 'The Numbers Shakespeare', *Sight and Sound* (December), 25:12, p. 15.
23. Michael Anderegg (2003) 'James Dean Meets the Pirate's Daughter: Passion and Parody in *William Shakespeare's Romeo + Juliet* and *Shakespeare in Love*' in Richard Burt and Lynda E. Boose (eds) *Shakespeare, the Movie, II: Popularizing the Plays on Film, TV, Video, and DVD* (London and New York: Routledge), pp. 56–71 (p. 70).
24. Marc Norman and Tom Stoppard (1998) *Shakespeare in Love: A Screenplay* (New York: Miramax), p. 4.
25. Douglas M. Lanier (2012) 'Marketing' in Arthur F. Kinney (ed.) *The Oxford Handbook of Shakespeare* (Oxford: Oxford University Press), pp. 498–514 (p. 498).
26. Andrew Higson (2013) 'Brit-lit Biopics, 1990–2010' in Judith Buchanan (ed.) *The Writer on Film: Screening Literary Authorship* (Basingstoke: Palgrave), pp. 106–20.
27. Higson, 'Brit-lit Biopics, 1990–2010', p. 110.
28. Rick Altman (1999) *Film/Genre* (London: BFI/Palgrave), pp. 38–44.
29. I discuss this film and the demonization of the British accent through the casting of Charles Laughton in the 1930s in *Adaptations of the Sound Era: 1927–37*, pp. 97–121.
30. *Shakespeare in Love*, Universal Studios DVD, 2004, commentary.
31. Norman and Stoppard, *Shakespeare in Love: A Screenplay*, p. 73.
32. Norman and Stoppard, *Shakespeare in Love: A Screenplay*, p. 70.

Select Bibliography

Altman, Rick (1999) *Film/Genre* (London: BFI/Palgrave).
Anderegg, Michael (2003) 'James Dean Meets the Pirate's Daughter: Passion and Parody in *William Shakespeare's Romeo + Juliet* and *Shakespeare in Love*' in Richard Burt and Lynda E. Boose (eds) *Shakespeare, the Movie, II: Popularizing the Plays on Film, TV, Video, and DVD* (New York: Routledge), pp. 56–71.
As You Like It (1937) Pressbook (British Film Institute Collection).
Buhler, Stephen M (2001) *Shakespeare in Cinema: Ocular Proof* (New York: SUNY Press).
Burt, Richard (2000) '*Shakespeare in Love* and the End of the Shakespearean: Academic and Mass Culture Constructions of Literary Authorship' in Mark Thornton Burnett and Ramona Wray (eds) *Shakespeare, Film, Fin de Siècle* (Basingstoke: Palgrave), pp. 180–231.
Cartmell, Deborah (2015) *Adaptations in the Sound Era: 1927–37* (New York and London: Bloomsbury).
Crowl, Samuel (2008) *Shakespeare and Film: A Norton Guide* (New York: Norton).
Fischlin, Daniel, Tom Magill and Jessica Riley (2014) 'Transgression and Transformation: *Mickey B* and the Dramaturgy of Adaptation' in Daniel Fischlin (ed.) *OuterSpeares: Shakespeare, Intermedia and the Limits of Adaptation* (Toronto, Buffalo and London: University of Toronto Press), pp. 153–97.
Granville-Barker, Harley (1937) 'Alas, Poor Will', *The Listener* XVII (3 March): 387–9.

Higson, Andrew (2013) 'Brit-lit biopics, 1990–2010' in Judith Buchanan (ed.) *The Writer on Film: Screening Literary Authorship* (Basingstoke: Palgrave), pp. 106–20.

Lanier, Douglas M. (2012) 'Marketing' in Arthur F. Kinney (ed.) *The Oxford Handbook to Shakespeare* (Oxford: Oxford University Press), pp. 498–514.

Leavis, Q.D. (1932; rept. 2000) *Fiction and the Reading Public* (London: Pimlico).

McKernan, Luke and Olwen Terris (1994) *Walking Shadows: Shakespeare in the National Film and Television Archive* (London: BFI).

Murray-Pepper, Megan (2013) 'The "Tables of Memory": Shakespeare, Cinema and the Writing Desk' in Judith Buchanan (ed.) *The Writer on Film: Screening Literary Authorship* (Basingstoke: Palgrave), pp. 92–105.

Norman, Marc and Tom Stoppard (1998) *Shakespeare in Love: A Screenplay* (New York: Miramax).

Norman, Marc (2004) *'Shakespeare in Love* on Film', *Shakespeare in Love* (Universal Studios DVD).

Olivier, Laurence (1984) *Henry V Screenplay* (London: Lorrimer).

Taming of the Shrew (1929) Pressbook (British Film Institute Collection).

Willson Jr., Robert F. (2000) *Shakespeare in Hollywood 1929–1956* (Cranbury, NJ, London, Mississauga, ON: Associated University Presses).

5
Shakespearean Actors, Memes, Social Media and the Circulation of Shakespearean 'Value'

Anna Blackwell

A young boy slopes late into his English classroom after skipping school to watch a blockbuster starring his favourite action hero, Jack Slater. His teacher introduces a clip from Laurence Olivier's 1948 *Hamlet* to the dismay of her charges, telling them that they might recognize its British actor from the Polaroid commercials or, with slight resignation, 'as Zeus in *Clash of the Titans*'. The boy is Danny Madigan (Austen O'Brien), the protagonist of *Last Action Hero*; his favourite star is played by Arnold Schwarzenegger and, pleasingly, his English teacher by Joan Plowright. Satirizing the associations of different cultural modes such as Shakespearean drama, classical music and the action genre, the 1993 film subverts the audience's expectations in order to parody them. Olivier becomes the man from the Polaroid commercials and his expressionistic *Hamlet* a Slater star vehicle. Contemplating Hamlet's most famous line, Schwarzenegger decides, 'To be or not to be … *Not to be*'. Meanwhile, Olivier's noirish colour palette is lit by sparks from the play's newly interpolated action scenes. Although a comic adaptation, *Last Action Hero*'s blockbuster *Hamlet* offers a valuable introduction to the subject of this chapter: the role of actors in the shaping of our understanding of Shakespearean 'value' (in both an economic and a cultural sense). As *Last Action Hero* reveals, key to this is the potential permeability of cultural hierarchies. Danny's action-*Hamlet* thereby satisfies his impatience with Olivier's Dane, who shies away from murdering Claudius at his prayers – 'Don't talk, just do it!' – and provides us with a pop cultural adaptation of the play, shaped more by the action genre than by the narrative significance of Hamlet's hesitation. Furthermore, although an imagined *Hamlet,* the reference to Olivier's Polaroid advert, Plowright's English teacher and a later cameo of Ian McKellen dressed as Death from Ingmar Bergman's *The Seventh Seal* (1975), demonstrate the real movement of Shakespearean actors and cachet across modes and for varying cultural and economic reasons.

Indeed, though a common practicality of both film and theatre, Olivier's career has evinced the shock and horror that can arise in the transposition of Shakespearean 'value' to a commercial context. Dominic Shellard details the indignation of one individual for whom Olivier's 'ignominious' decision to endorse Gallaher Ltd.'s new brand of 'Olivier' cigarettes was 'inconceivable' and 'besmirch[ed]' his good reputation, a reputation conferred by no less a person than the Queen in his recent knighthood.[1] Similarly, despite the significance of Olivier's decision to advertise Polaroid for one million dollars to actors' capacity to cross genres, modes and media, it was an act that posed great risk to his popularity. As he acknowledged in his autobiography – stating that he took great pains to ensure the advert was not released in Great Britain – the actor was cognizant that while the American and European audiences would recognize his commercial shrewdness, Britain would be offended by a perceived slight to his reputation as a classical performer.[2] It is this affirmation of the actor's role in negotiating cultural hierarchies and the significance of their actions in determining 'Shakespearean' value that I wish to trace in two contemporary Shakespeareans: Tom Hiddleston and Benedict Cumberbatch.

It is worth first further elucidating the subject of my chapter, however. The phenomenon of the 'Shakespearean' actor is a popular one in Western culture. As a descriptor, established discursively in culture and attached to particular (typically British, male) performers, it gestures towards a certain acting style, theatrical background and personal manner, such as a perceived intellectualism or grandiloquence. Indeed, the figure of the 'Shakespearean' is one that is potentially most familiar to us via parody in the melodramatic caricature of the 'luvvie'. But while collections such as *Great Shakespeareans* (edited by Russell Jackson, 2013) or Jonathan Holmes' *Merely Players? Actors' Accounts of Performing Shakespeare* (2004) have focused on such individuals, they have failed to question the implicit value judgements that underline the description of an actor as a Shakespearean. It is, nonetheless, a useful term, and the phenomenon of Shakespearean actors accords with John Gaffney's and Diana Holmes' observation that stars can 'restate, often in new and modern forms, old identities and values, as well as calling a society towards newer and perhaps confused, emergent values'.[3] As I will continue to demonstrate, such actors serve as a conduit through which the transferable commodity value of 'Shakespeare' may be relayed, adapted and reasserted.

Douglas Lanier argues that 'like all brand icons' Shakespeare is a 'signifier' open to 'appropriation, rearticulation, extension, even negation and parody' and, depending upon the needs of the user, ready for rebranding 'should the need arise'.[4] Barbara Hodgdon states similarly that her critical methodology disavows the myth of the definitive text and author in order to regard performances 'as cultural productions or even commodities'.[5] In doing so, Hodgdon acknowledges that the creation of meaning is also firmly dictated by economic situations and the particulars of production. Lanier's and Hodgdon's recognition of the importance of contextual preconditions for a dynamic and adaptable concept of authorship is instructive here: rather than possessing a single, predefined relationship to the playwright, the Shakespearean should be viewed in remembrance of the nature of acting as an occupation. This is one which is driven and shaped by economic conditions and which is not distinguished by a couple of stand-out performances, but by a career of different roles within an industry.

By working outside of a traditionally or expected 'Shakespearean' context in this chapter and by exploring terrains such as social media and Hollywood, the cultural meanings and legacy attached to the Shakespearean actor are brought into a new, stimulating environment. Certainly, situating the 'Shakespearean' actor in contrast with the supposed values of 'high' culture reveals the expectations attached to both apparently exclusive modes and more mainstream ones. A focus on these individuals, moreover, acknowledges the necessity of making money, with the actor as originator of meaning *and* participant in economic exchanges potentially further complicating our understanding of Shakespeare's cultural legacy. This is a point especially significant given the conservative values typically associated with Shakespearean actors, a tradition in which the Shakespearean is frequently coded as a representative of 'high' cultural values. This continues to be true despite a long tradition of working class Shakespeareans, such as Welsh actors Anthony Hopkins and Richard Burton or the Lancashire-born Ian McKellen, actors who have later gained associations of cultural exclusivity but who testify to the potential of a non-elite iteration of British Shakespeareanism. Nonetheless, the current wave of internationally successful British actors are linked by their upper middle class origins in a recent phenomenon that has seen private schools such as Eton regarded as an 'alternative RADA' for their success in training aspiring performers.[6]

Such individuals have participated in a (reciprocal) exchange between 'high' culture and Hollywood which has long utilized the British

Shakespearean and will, presumably, continue to do so. In their most common popular cultural function blockbusters cast Shakespearean actors as antagonists capable of wit, pathos and depth. With the typically grandiloquent quality of these villains' characterization, the Shakespearean actor is actively courted by such franchises because of their ability to articulate an authoritative, viable threat to the protagonist. The popularity of this is evident in the wealth of other male (potentially non-theatrical) actors who have similarly accessed the cachet of being a British performer – qualities such as a seriousness of dramatic intent, eloquence, class and cultural sophistication. Hollywood has thus been a productive employer for figures such as Eddie Redmayne, Ben Kingsley, Chiwetel Ejiofor, Ralph Fiennes, Jeremy Irons and Brian Cox. The Shakespeareans' textual penumbra particularly reinforces this relationship through the contiguity between their villainous roles and their previous theatrical portrayals; for example, the obvious connections between Ian McKellen's Magneto in *X-Men* (dir. Various, 2000) and his performance in *Richard III* (dir. Richard Loncraine, 1995). The overriding impression of this process, however, is the identification of the Shakespearean (and thus Shakespeareanism) with luxuriance and moral relativism. The difference between the villains' formalized mode of expression and the heroes' popular cultural world positions the gap between the Shakespearean and the mainstream as equivalent to that between the villains' corruption and the heroes' virtue. The association of the villain with the intrusion of 'high' culture within the world of popular culture thereby equates their dictatorial intent with the perceived elitism and exclusionary values of their cultural affiliations.

Tom Hiddleston's performance as Loki in the Marvel Cinematic Universe (MCU) confirms precisely this association of 'high' culture with villainy and, in the productive intersections it forges between Hollywood and the 'Shakespearean', exemplifies both Hiddleston's career and an increasing professional model for British actors. A rising international star, Hiddleston received a double first from Cambridge in Classics and graduated from RADA in 2005 before joining Cheek by Jowl for *The Changeling* in 2006 and *Cymbeline* in 2007, playing Alsemero and Posthumus/ Cloten respectively. This was followed in 2008 by *Ivanov* and *Othello* at the Wyndham Theatre, where he starred opposite Kenneth Branagh, a relationship that would lead to *Wallander* (TV, 2008–12) and, most notably, *Thor* (dir. Kenneth Branagh, 2011) in which he would first play Loki. By this point Hiddleston had begun establishing himself as a theatrical performer of note, earning the Ian Charleson Award (Third Prize) and the Laurence Olivier Award for Best Newcomer in 2007 for his role as Cassio.

The actor continued to cement this association with literariness in his early television career, with dramatic roles in period pieces such as *The Gathering Storm* (TV, 2002), *Miss Austen Regrets* (TV, 2008) and *Cranford – Return to Cranford* (TV, 2009). In all three roles Hiddleston is positioned similarly as a gentlemanly ideal (upper middle class, intelligent and romantic) – an archetype Hiddleston continued as the naïve but noble Captain Nicholls in *War Horse* (dir. Steven Spielberg, 2011), the suave former Second World War pilot Freddie Page in *The Deep Blue Sea* (dir. Terence Davies, 2012) and the aristocratic Sir Thomas Sharpe in *Crimson Peak* (dir. Guillermo del Toro, 2015).

That this tendency has been in part founded on the qualities of Hiddleston's star persona is underlined in superlative reportage from the press. Hiddleston is described by Giles Hattersley as 'costume drama fodder', by Ben Beaumont-Thomas as possessing a 'brand ... [of] guileless old-school grace' and by James Mottram as 'quintessentially English'.[7] Indeed, when paired alongside the biographical details of his life (which include the fact that he boarded at Eton at the same time as Prince William) Hiddleston's somewhat old-fashioned aesthetic contributes to the romantic allure which the world of upper class privilege still holds for many individuals. Bruce Babington argues that British actors 'give things to home audiences that Hollywood luminaries cannot – reflections of the known and close at hand'.[8] Although undeniably the nature of Hiddleston's upbringing (Eton then Cambridge) separates him from many in contemporary society, his portrayal by the press and his early acting roles establish the values he embodies as an idealized, aspirational image, within which his Shakespeareanism constitutes an essential characteristic of cultural sophistication. Hiddleston represents a class-bound vision of white, male Englishness predicated upon qualities of eloquence, restraint and social privilege. And as Ian Shuttleworth observes, since the 'heyday of Ronald Colman and Sir Cedric Hardwick in the 1930s', an English accent in an American film has been used as an 'easy shorthand to denote a certain kind of "class", whether romantic, intellectual or villainous'.[9]

Hiddleston's most famous role – Loki – exemplifies this practice. Having originally auditioned for the titular role in *Thor* and having bulked up suitably for the occasion, Hiddleston was urged to re-audition for the role of Loki, the hero's scheming malcontent brother. He won the part as, according to Branagh, Hiddleston couldn't 'turn off' his intelligence.[10] Indeed, Loki's power in both mythology and the Marvel comics is predicated on deception and misdirection. By contrast, Thor's need for eloquence comes second to his impressive physicality; his character conforms to more traditional markers of masculinity which are, at times, coded as pertaining to a lower class than the pseudo-intellectualism of superhero villains. Thor, though an Asgardian Prince, is characterized by his adherence to a stereotype of Viking primitivism and coarseness. See, for instance, the humour derived from transposing his abrasive social etiquette from the Norse mead halls to a New Mexico coffee shop. Or witness a visual corollary of the distinction between Loki's intellect and Thor's force in the contrasting brute force wielded through Thor's hammer, Mjölnir, and the capoeira-inspired martial art Loki employs, which utilizes speed and deceptive feints.

That Hiddleston's perceived intelligence reinforces the Shakespearea-nism of his star persona is thus further argument for the productive interplay between his earlier theatrical work and his popular cultural characters. Branagh was chosen to direct the production precisely because Marvel felt his experience of adapting Shakespeare could make the more formal style of dialogue attributed to the Asgardians relatable and even humorous. And the subsequent film carries numer-ous Shakespearean echoes, the majority of which are conscious artistic decisions made by Branagh.[11] The contiguity between *Thor's* theatrical intertexts and Loki's appearances elsewhere in the MCU, moreover, further underline both the thematic significance of the character's Shakespeareanism and Hiddleston's continued contribu-tion to this effect.

Loki's second appearance, in *Avengers Assemble* (dir. Joss Whedon, 2012), takes place at a Stuttgart concert hall. As the only non-American location in the film, the selection of Stuttgart suggests an association between Loki and Europe, or the Old World. This is a connection fur-ther enhanced by the *mise en scène* conveying the tenor of the classical music event through the architectural grandeur of the building, the upper middle class connotations of the guests' and Loki's formal even-ing attire (complete with cane) and the accompaniment of Schubert's String Quartet in A Minor. In an ironic reference to this setting Tony Stark later notes that Loki is a 'full tilt diva' and it is Stark, moreover, whose sardonic voice often offers a postmodern, self-reflexive critique of the genre, who establishes a crucial distinction between the camp excess of the Earth superheroes and the Asgardians' overly formalized speech and dramatic costuming:

THOR: You have no idea what you are dealing with.
TONY STARK: Uh, Shakespeare in the park? Doth mother know you weareth her drapes?

Stark's cod-Shakespearean phrasing and bantering reply of 'Uh, Shakespeare in the park?' identifies the tempestuous relationship between Thor and his brother as the stuff of Shakespearean dramatic convention. A potential in-joke reference to Branagh's involvement in the franchise, Stark's feigned anachronisms – 'doth', 'weareth' – continue the association between the Asgardians and outmoded cultural values. The description of Thor's outfit as his mother's 'drapes' denigrates these values as old fashioned and obfuscated, particularly in contrast with the sharply pop culture-infused vernacular of Stark. Similarly to Captain Nicholls and Freddie Page, Loki's 'high' cultural quality is at odds with mainstream modernity, a cultural and linguistic difference used to reiterate his alterity, even from Thor. Furthermore, overt reference in the dialogue to Nazism in the Stuttgart scene posits Loki's 'high' cultural values as not only irrelevant but dangerously dictatorial.[12]

In spite of this, however, Loki has enjoyed a productive afterlife on the internet, where his character has undergone something of a rehabilitation. Digital artefacts such as memes and social media texts reveal both the contradictions within, and potential flexibility of, Hiddleston's performer identity.[13] They acknowledge Loki's framing as a villain, but also the inherent tragedy of his narrative as well as his appealing humorousness (and Hiddleston's own personable manner); Marvel's configuration of the Shakespearean as antiquated and obscure, but Loki's prevalence as a popular cultural figure; and, as I will continue to elucidate, Hiddleston's active engagement with internet culture, but the conservatism of his Shakespearean associations. Indeed, Hiddleston's online persona is characterized by a high degree of self-awareness and an 'innate understanding of what makes internet memes tick'.[14] An illustrative example of this is the 'accidentally groping' meme. On 8 November 2013 YouTube personality Smooth posted an interview with Hiddleston in which he impersonated Natalie Portman's pose on the international poster for *Thor: The Dark World*.[15] The following day this coquettish pose was photoshopped onto the poster itself (see Figure 5.1) by Tumblr user The King Himself, gaining 35,000 notes in the first four days of being online.[16]

This spawned an internet phenomenon with Hiddleston's pose pasted onto images from various media franchises, with manipulations mirroring the work of fan projects such as the Hawkeye Initiative.[17] Similarly, after the enormous success of a fan-made parody of the 2013 Daft Punk song 'Get Lucky', Hiddleston sang his own version of 'Get Loki' for YouTube, demonstrating both his understanding of those values attached to his (and Loki's) online presence, and his willingness to sustain them.[18]

Figure 5.1   The first example of the 'accidentally groping' meme

An essential part of Hiddleston's star persona is founded upon the contrast between his conversance with popular culture and perpetuating the kind of anachronistic English gentility of his Shakespearean identity. Particularly when viewed from an American or international framework, Hiddleston's performance of these aspects of his star persona demonstrates his awareness of the expectations of 'Englishness', in accordance with Katherine W. Jones's conceptualization of national identity as partially self-constructed.[19] A retweet of the account VeryBritishProblems, for instance, epitomizes the delicate balance Hiddleston strikes between earnestness and self-mockery (see Figure 5.2).

Hiddleston's promotion of the account demonstrates his identification with, and inclusion in, those shared values – an image of Britishness as restrained, eccentric, genteel and gently comic. Engagements with fan culture articulate a receptiveness towards Shakespeare's works and the *popular* association made in America between Englishness and perceived 'high' cultural knowledge, moreover. One conversation with fans on

↻ Tom Hiddleston retweeted

VeryBritishProblems @SoVeryBri... 3d
Being unable to properly concentrate
on the conversation while there's still
one roast potato left

Figure 5.2 Twitter screen capture from Tom Hiddleston's account
Source: Tom Hiddleston (@TWHiddleston), RT, 16 February 2014.

the topic of Hiddleston's favourite Shakespeare line prompts a detailed response on the beauty of *King Lear* and the complexity of *Othello* before settling on *Cymbeline*'s 'Hang there like fruit, my soul,/Till the tree die!'.[20] Prevaricating after this selection between *Henry V* and *Coriolanus*, Hiddleston admits, 'that wasn't a very good answer, was it?', to which his American interviewer and co-star, Zachary Levi, responds: 'it was a great answer. I've just never felt more uncultured in my life'.

This appeal of English romanticism to Anglophilic international audiences who have similarly celebrated upper middle stars such as Hugh Grant or Colin Firth is, in the case of Hiddleston, in alignment with his Shakespeareanism. Hiddleston's performance as Henry V (dir. Thea Sharrock, 2012) for the final installment of the BBC's *The Hollow Crown*, for instance, emphasizes the King's nobility; this despite his earlier portrayal of Hal in *Henry IV* (dir. Richard Eyre, 2012) referencing Loki's tricksiness and the actor stating his suspicion that contemporary politicians only ever 'reveal themselves after a time' – making speeches and promises only to break them. Hiddleston has, however, also posited his belief in Henry's 'piety' and 'chivalric code' and this reading is matched by Thea Sharrock's direction, which repeatedly frames central narrative events in a manner that contributes to Henry's characterization as a just, principled King.[21] The violent speech at Harfleur is included in the film, but Hiddleston's eyes are visibly moist as he delivers it, his tone aggressive but his face conveying obvious distress. Meanwhile, unlike Kenneth Branagh's 1989 interpolation of Henry's tacit involvement in the act, Bardolph's death occurs without Henry's knowledge and causes instant sorrow. Finally, when Henry prays to God before battle, the camera focuses in upon his clasped hands, revealing the mismatched gloves as evidence of the promise made to Williams in Act Four, Scene One. At all points Hiddleston's Henry recognizes his responsibility for his men's lives and the cost of violence that necessitates that his soldiers' deaths are meaningful.

Director Josie Rourke's 2013 *Coriolanus* at the Donmar Warehouse is similarly straightforward in its representation of its military hero. The Roman general, though coldly imperious, is still a dedicated father and husband and is not too strenuously criticized by the production. Hiddleston's own description of the character also betrays a desire to assist the audience in identifying with him, praising his simplicity and his conviction: 'you get what you see'.[22] His sympathetic and conservative interpretations of Henry and later Coriolanus thus not only confirm more traditional associations of Shakespeare with emotional sincerity and inspirational sentiment, but align Hiddleston's star capital with the same values.

Hiddleston's career therefore indicates a clear (and productive) conversation between popular culture and Shakespeareanism – this in spite of a caution from his agent that Hiddleston could easily be pigeonholed as a period actor.[23] Indeed, Hiddleston's two most recent Shakespearean performances as Hal and Henry V in *The Hollow Crown* prove the irony of the warning. Initially Hiddleston had been secured only to play the former. With production starting as early as 2010 it can be safely assumed that Hiddleston's casting as only Hal recognized his relative obscurity at this point. Certainly, when previous adaptations starred Kenneth Branagh and Laurence Olivier, it does not beggar belief that a little-known actor (though suitable for the role of Hal) was deemed an insufficient draw. After the success of *Thor*, however, Hiddleston suddenly became both economically and culturally viable as Henry; little could the series' casting agents and producers have anticipated the size of the audience Hiddleston would ultimately bring with him to the role. Meanwhile, as I have argued elsewhere, *Coriolanus* is clearly indebted to the kind of Hollywood blockbuster with which Hiddleston made his name: the qualities he brings to the production 'as both a theatrical and film star opens up the already richly symbolic nature of Coriolanus's body, reframing it in discussions surrounding modern celebrity and cultural performances of masculinity'.[24] As a play founded on a discussion of a male soldier's body – both active, violent and violated – Rourke's *Coriolanus* thus invokes the kind of muscular masculinity which Hiddleston was deemed too cerebral and too inherently upper class to occupy during *Thor*.

Within only a four-year period, Hiddleston's career thereby demonstrates how the Shakespearean actor as a site of adaptive encounter embodies the cross-cultural, intertextual and frequently circular exchange of cultural capital. This interrelatedness is characterized by Judith Buchanan and Marvin Carlson through a language of spectrality.

Buchanan employs Stephen Berkoff's description of 'boxing with ghosts' in order to discuss the potential visibility of former inhabitants of a role and an actor's own past performances in their present iteration. Meanwhile, Carlson's haunted stage is a 'repository of cultural memories', in which the spectres of past performance, the theatre space and actors experience a constant process of recycling and renegotiation.[25] Hiddleston's performance in *Coriolanus* thus locates him as the hub of an adaptive journey which has taken him from being rejected as Thor for possessing too much intelligence as an actor, to Loki's Shakespearean characterization, Hal's impish Loki-ness, Henry's Thor-like heroism and back to Shakespeare, an action blockbuster *Coriolanus* with its body-conscious aesthetic and the muscular, wounded body of its hero as the site of meaning. And so we return to *Thor* .... For Hiddleston, as an example of a Shakespearean actor, this circularity exists not only in terms of characterization, however. Such interrelatedness reflects the series of cultural and economic exchanges which structure the Shakespearean actor's professional life and which consequently shape Shakespeare's evolving cultural 'value'.

A recent Jaguar advertising campaign explores the contradictory appeal of malcontents such as Loki, as well as their early modern antecedents. The advert thus asks, 'Have you ever noticed how in Hollywood movies all the villains are played by Brits?'. Each of its stars (Mark Strong, Ben Kingsley and Hiddleston) contributes a hypothetical answer and, in doing so, confirms the qualities of this popular stereotype. Sat in an open helicopter cockpit Hiddleston proposes, 'We're more focused. More precise .... And we're obsessed by power! ... Stiff upper lip is key'. Surrounded by a microcosm of English gentility, Hiddleston is dressed in a three-piece tweed suit, seated next to a small lampshade and sipping a cup of tea, even as he is buffeted by the wind. A later version of the advert even more explicitly summarizes the traditional qualities of the British 'baddie', acknowledging Hiddleston's upper-class Shakespeareanism in statements such as: 'They say Brits play the best villains ... But what makes a great villain? Firstly, you need to sound distinct. Speak with an eloquence that lets everyone know who's in charge'. An audio recording of John Gielgud performing John of Gaunt's speech from *Richard II* ('This happy breed of men') seemingly provides an example of this desired gravitas.[26] The advert continues to then reinforce a cultural association between formal sophistication and Shakespeare as 'high' culture by reiterating the speech, this time performed with relish by Hiddleston while driving accompanied by the explicitly patriotic strains of Elgar's Nimrod and the roar of the Jaguar engine. Indeed, Brand Vice President for Jaguar, Jeff Curry, explains that Hiddleston's recitation of the 'classic words of England's most famous playwright' advertises the coupé in an 'unforgettable manner', demonstrating the importance of an idealized Englishness to Jaguar's brand identity and Shakespeare as a quintessence of this.[27] That Hiddleston's is the only advert in the campaign to reference the playwright, despite the transparency of the connection between Hollywood villains and a British theatricalism, further indicates the configuration of his star capital as originating from an explicitly Shakespearean source. Shakespeare, as an epitome of 'high' culture, is thereby still regarded as a safe site in which to invest capital. Eoin Price's reading of a press release made by the Globe Theatre, London, in May 2015 interrogates this underlying assumption and its significance for the commodification of the early modern. In promotion for the Sam Wanamaker Playhouse's autumn/ winter season the Globe announced on Twitter: 'After 2 yrs experimenting, for first time we're staging Shakespeare's late plays'. Price notes that such 'rhetoric' explicitly imagines the SWP's previous non-Shakespearean performances as nothing but 'experiment[s]' which, though 'wonderful in their own right', can only ever be viewed as 'half-successes' and ultimately as precursors to the main event: Shakespeare.[28]

Benedict Cumberbatch's involvement in Lyndsey Turner's 2015 production of *Hamlet* at the Barbican, however, evinces an increasing overlap between the value traditionally expected of the 'Shakespearean' and the newer sites of cultural capital created through popular, internet and fan culture. As I will continue to explore, Cumberbatch's reputation as a significant dramatic talent had been confirmed in acclaimed theatrical work, including Shakespeare, but the role which brought him popular fame and thus made him a potentially attractive lead for a Shakespeare production was as the star of the BBC series *Sherlock* (TV, 2010). Indeed, it is worth noting that *Hamlet* is Cumberbatch's first Shakespearean role since beginning his career at the Open Air Theatre, Regent's Park in 2001–02 and since his acting debut, aged 12, as Titania in a school production of *A Midsummer Night's Dream*. Despite Shakespeare's presence at this early stage, the roles with which Cumberbatch established his theatrical ability were non-Shakespearean, including an Olivier-nominated turn in *Hedda Gabler*, a multi-award-winning revival of *After the Dance* in 2010 and a joint lead role in Danny Boyle's *Frankenstein* with Jonny Lee Miller for the National Theatre in 2011 (for which he received Olivier, Evening Standard and Critics' Circle Theatre awards). Nonetheless, the unique qualities of Cumberbatch's *Hamlet* and its reception indicate the usefulness of considering both the play and the actor in relation to 'Shakespearean' cultural capital, not least because of his established association with some of the qualities commonly attributed to other Shakespeareans by popular culture.

From a similarly privileged background to Hiddleston (he attended Harrow and is a distant relative of Queen Elizabeth II, Lady Jane Grey and Richard III), Cumberbatch consolidated theatrical work with acclaimed television credits and Hollywood roles. Like Hiddleston, the bulk of Cumberbatch's filmography consists of adaptations, both period and modern – a pattern no doubt cultivated by a tendency to cast Cumberbatch in roles marked by a non-Hollywood model of masculinity that is intellectual rather than physical. Certainly, both men share a similar build and patrician quality, developing substantial international followings for their perceived sophistication, but also for their willingness to engage with their fans through internet creative practices. Leading roles in modern adaptations such as *Sherlock*, *Tinker Tailor Soldier Spy* (dir. Tomas Alfredson, 2011), *Parade's End* (TV, 2012), *Atonement* (dir. Joe Wright, 2007), *The Imitation Game* (dir. Morten Tyldum, 2014) and *War Horse* thus sit alongside historically situated works, including *12 Years A Slave* (dir. Steve McQueen, 2013) and *Amazing Grace* (dir. Michael Apted, 2006). Participating in a tradition of 'quality' film and television, such roles thereby perpetuate Cumberbatch's persona as upper middle class, sophisticated and intellectual. These are traits that are widely disseminated in the actor's digital representations and are further reinforced in his casting as typically 'Shakespearean' villains in international film franchises, such as Smaug in *The Hobbit* (dir. Peter Jackson, 2012–14) and Khan in *Star Trek: Into Darkness* (dir. J. J. Abrams, 2013). Like Loki, these intellectual, charismatic characters articulate an association between Britishness and an urbanity and intelligence that is conducive to both discerning taste and moral detachment. Cumberbatch's performance as Sherlock the 'high-functioning sociopath' has most successfully capitalized on this tendency, as a character whose intellectual sophistication causes him to declare characteristically that 'sentiment is a chemical defect found on the losing side'. Indeed, that Cumberbatch's return to theatre at a point of unprecedented fame has occurred with a record-breaking production of *Hamlet* demonstrates the conflation of general British cultured theatricality with Shakespeareanism. It is Shakespeare – and *Hamlet* in particular – that is viewed simultaneously as both a test of ability *and* a confirmation of stardom. As Price's reading of the Globe's so-called experimentation reveals, successful theatre capital is *Shakespearean* capital.

Demonstrating this popular conflation of Shakespeareanism, 'high' culture and Britishness, Cumberbatch's perceived cultural capital has been utilized similarly to Hiddleston by companies such as Dunlop and, again, Jaguar. Hired to be the face of Dunlop China, Cumberbatch is posed in adverts for the tyres dressed in a suit and with his hair slicked back. This image is accompanied by the campaign slogan and a small illustration of the British Isles with '1888' next to it.[29] Like Jaguar, this reference to Dunlop's specific national and historical origins promotes the brand through identifying its heritage and thus its perceived 'classic' British quality. Indeed, one interview in which Cumberbatch acts as brand ambassador for Jaguar also includes an advert for Belstaff – another British luxury brand – and is published in British Airways' inflight magazine, *High Life* (the title here opaquely indicating the company's branding aspirations). On these occasions the aspect of Cumberbatch's star persona that is invoked are those that – again – mirror qualities associated with Shakespeareanism: a seriousness of purpose and a cultivated and sophisticated sense of taste.

Elsewhere, Cumberbatch's cultural 'value' again follows similar patterns to Hiddleston's with his Englishness also coded as an essentially romantic quality. Popularly regarded as the 'internet's boyfriend', Cumberbatch was the most reblogged actor on Tumblr from 2014–15. And while memes that aligned Loki and Hiddleston proclaimed the uneasy but essentially humorous incongruity of fans romanticizing a genocidal patricide, an image of Cumberbatch laughing is accompanied by the statement: 'Entire fandom calls themselves Cumberbitches ... Tells them to change it to Cumberbabes because its [sic] less sexist'.[30] This is not a unique article, furthermore, but a contribution to a popular meme, 'Good Guy Benedict', and shares a perpetuation of Cumberbatch's star persona as simultaneously progressive and gentlemanly, idiosyncratic (see 'Cumberbombing') and sweetly eccentric (see 'pengwins'). Besides taking place on internet sites that function through private companies and advertising revenue streams, this aspect of Cumberbatch's persona has also been involved in the more traditional economic exchanges that typify his brand work. One page of Mel Elliott's *Colour Me Good: Benedict Cumberbatch* adult colouring book, for instance, explicitly sources the actor's nationality and proficiency ('ooh get me I'm so English and great at acting') as the 'cutest thing on the internet', a statement proclaimed by the previous incumbents of the role – the many cats of the internet – who sit admiringly next to an outline of Cumberbatch's face.[31] Itself a unique document of the economic and cultural capital the 'Shakespearean' possesses and its intersections with digital commerce and fan culture, texts such as *Colour Me Good* demonstrate the potential versatility of 'Shakespearean' capital online. As an embodied site of adaptation the Shakespearean thus demonstrates the evolution of the cultural industry, including the new sites of economic exchange opened by social media and the diversification of theatrical experience. Indeed, the actor is an increasingly mobile and visible participant in Shakespeare's continuing history and a reflection of changes to the profession. Even for Kenneth Branagh's generation the possibility of bestriding the classical and the popular – as Olivier had attempted to – seemed 'impossible' and 'fairly exotic'.[32] Instead, the accepted convention was to attain larger and larger roles within a repertory theatre system in which the actor's fame was second to the complex working of the company. Only then, and with sufficient star appeal, could they finally traverse into popular culture. Even so, an actor could still risk diminishing a hard-won theatrical reputation. As Sarah Crompton notes, Peter O'Toole's obituary still reported that the actor was 'destined for greatness on stage until in 1962 David Lean's *Lawrence of Arabia* turned him into a film star'.[33] Actors such as Cumberbatch and Hiddleston, however, have forged their performer identities in conversation with the mainstream as individuals who not only acknowledge the presence of digital culture but actively participate with their fans and their online representation. Cumberbatch's cultural capital, in particular, has been determined by the strength of the Sherlock Holmes fan community, a wide group of devoted individuals who engage creatively *and* critically with Conan Doyle's character in many varied ways (see *Sherlock and Transmedia Fandom* for evidence of the richness of this phenomenon).

It is here, I maintain, that a fundamental distinction between these and earlier generations of Shakespeareans exists. Digital texts like memes are explicitly intertextual in nature: they invoke and sustain comparisons between different modes and media and destabilize previously held cultural hierarchies in order to produce creative productive intersections. Echoing the now commonplace movements between 'high' and 'popular' culture that are a practical reality of the profession, fans work to draw connections, interpret and engage with the entirety of an actor's oeuvre. As Paul Booth writes, fans do 'more than passively view media' – they 'make explicit what we all do implicitly: that is, we actively read and engage with media texts on a daily basis'.[34] It is these individuals, furthermore, who constituted a large section of *Hamlet*'s audience and who helped the production to become the fastest-selling London theatre show in history and the highest-attended National

Theatre Live screening. Indeed, the ticket website Viagogo reported more than 20,000 people queuing online in the minutes after tickets were released and stated that the show registered 214% more searches during this period than global music stars Beyoncé's and Jay Z's On The Run tour.[35]

Although Turner's *Hamlet* thus constituted a traditional performance of Shakespearean cultural capital, the show was influenced by its star and the origins of his fame in a production that both purposefully and inadvertently disrupted convention in terms of performance, reception and critical practice. The media discourse surrounding the production both reported on and perpetuated the uniqueness of the cultural event, taking great pains to interview Cumberbatch's followers about the experience of attending *as* a fan: questioning first their relationship with the actor and his performances and then *if* and how their enjoyment would transpose to a Shakespearean context. Certainly, Cumberbatch's international fan base appeared to articulate differing concerns than those one might expect from a more typical theatre-going audience. For these individuals, their expectations and anxieties revealed them as cultural tourists: their attendance was driven first by Cumberbatch's involvement and the immediacy of the live form (through which they could, conceivably, be closer to the star). That the event provided them with the opportunity to see Shakespeare performed for, potentially, the first time, just underlined an association already present in popular culture between Cumberbatch and a uniquely British cultural sophistication. Indeed, Naomi Roper, convenor of the Cumberbatchweb Twitter stream, reported concern from the account's followers about matters of theatre etiquette, including dress code and practical aspects such as where to charge a phone or where to get mobile signal at the Barbican. Itself a telling indicator of the exclusively 'high' cultural cachet theatre is seen to possess, Roper's engagement with fans ('maintaining a constant Q&A with fans [...] for the last 18 months') demonstrates their practical concerns and their desire to integrate their behaviour as consumers to the unique para-performances of theatre-going. Similarly, Whatsonstage.com published an article detailing tips for *Hamlet*'s first time theatre-goers, including the well-intentioned but somewhat patronizing reminder for silence because, 'unlike Tom Cruise's latest *Mission Impossible* currently booming into cinemas around the world, Bendy [Cumberbatch] doesn't have the luxury of Dolby Surround Sound speakers'.[36]

The Cumberbatch fans who made up such a large proportion of the Barbican's audience and many of whom were 'reading *Hamlet* or watching previous film versions to swot up for the play', thus represented a distinct interpretive voice.[37] In comparison to critics or more frequent theatre-goers, the virgin audience members for *Hamlet* refer to a largely different frame of references and one which (as described above) works to link disparate pop cultural texts, genres and communities through fan practices. Posting on Tumblr, the account the-fellowship-of-erdemhart, for instance, shares a grainy photograph of Tom Hiddleston, apparently taken at the Barbican. It notes that if the 'fangirls aren't completely *done* by the end of watching BC [Cumberbatch]' that they will 'implode' witnessing Loki at the theatre: 'We all remember the last time Loki went out to "appreciate the arts"'.[38] Other related posts include an illustration by tiniestjohn of Cumberbatch's Hamlet in a 'chibi' style – an artistic convention popular amongst fan artists and adopted from Japanese anime – in which the young Prince is drawn in a cartoonishly 'cute' and boyish manner.[39] Drawn by an artist who typically focuses on depictions of John Watson from *Sherlock* (to whom the 'tiniest' in the name refers), Cumberbatch's presence here demonstrates the capital Hamlet possesses but as an extension of the *Sherlock* world. By utilizing the same chibi-style, tiniestjohn's illustration thereby works to cohere the disparate parts of the adaptation's active fan community – its characters and actors, its actors and their past/future endeavours – and bring them into a comparable, cohesive virtual space.

It was not only the production's audience who challenged traditional theatrical practices, however. Journalists from *The Times* and *The Telegraph* broke with protocol by releasing reviews before the end of previews, with *The Daily Mail* publishing grainy camera-phone photographs. Although Ian Rickson, former artistic director of the Royal Court, likened the act to an art critic reviewing a half-dry canvas, other commentators, such as Terri Paddock, acknowledged the ambiguous status of these early performances, which charged the same £125 ticket price as the rest of the run.[40] Meanwhile, 'To be or not to be' was initially located at the beginning of the play, a decision which, though not unique or particularly incongruous, caused consternation amongst theatre critics.

Hamlet is, of course, a play that has been associated historically with well-known individuals, a tendency explained by the play's structure, with its uniquely famous soliloquies necessitating the visibility of its lead. In Turner's production these were delivered with a spotlight on Cumberbatch, illuminating him while the rest of the stage and its potential inhabitants moved as in slow motion. Scott Jordan Harris argues, though, that from the 'response in the house' this staging is intensely self-reflexive, acknowledging the origins of Cumberbatch's fame and cultural capital. Harris continues, with their curiously out-of-time temporality, the soliloquies – though lasting minutes for the audience – are experienced as thoughts of mere seconds to the other characters.[41] They are, in short, 'carefully choreographed theatrical re-creation[s]' of *Sherlock*'s distinctive visualization of the detective's thought processes. That such emphasis was placed in staging on marrying the singular nature of Cumberbatch's fame with the uniquely well-known quality of his character's lines proved problematic to some. Regarded with mixed success, the majority of critics praised Cumberbatch's performance. But, perhaps in reflection of this fact, some individuals including Michael Billington, Ben Brantley and Quentin Letts observed a lack of integration between the performance of Hamlet's most famous soliloquies, emphasized through a singular focus on Cumberbatch in staging and the rest of the production. Brantley, for instance, noted the actor 'riding Shakespeare's rushing words like a surfboard, as if saving his interior energy for the monologues'.[42] In a final iteration of Cumberbatch's significance, the actor has also been uniquely visible in *Hamlet*'s peripheral moments, issuing a public plea for fans not to record or take photographs and delivering an appeal for charity for Syrian refugees at the end of many performances (including the NT Live screenings).

The visibility of Cumberbatch thus underlines the significance of the contemporary Shakespearean actor in shaping Shakespeare's cultural capital. The significance of Hamlet's final pronouncement of silence is lost in a production and its reception that emphasizes Cumberbatch's stardom from its opening to its close. By bringing his personal politics into the periphery of performance, the ambiguous, transformative site of the curtain call witnesses the shift not from Hamlet to the (expected) weary yet appreciative Cumberbatch but to the activist, a moment of individualism made all the more potent for its placement at a point when the lead traditionally receives judgement from the audience, but also cedes attention to the rest of the cast and crew and back to the crowd. At times congruent with *Hamlet*'s dramatization of identity, at other times a visible entry of popular cultural associations or disruption of traditional theatrical practices, the *Sherlock* star arrives in the production pre-loaded with cultural meaning, his star persona the site and occasion for exchanges that take place digitally, culturally and economically the world over. Lyndsey Turner's *Hamlet* reassigns its famous opening line – 'Who's there?' – to the young Prince. The answer, of course: Benedict Cumberbatch.

Notes

This chapter has been adapted in part from my doctoral thesis, 'The Contemporary Shakespearean actor as the Site of Adaptive Encounter' (Unpublished doctoral thesis, De Montfort University, Leicester, 2014).

1. Lieutenant-Colon. C.J. Barton-Innes cited in Dominic Shellard (2008) 'Stability, Renewal and Change: Gielgud and Olivier in 1957' in Dominic Shellard (ed.) *The Golden Generation* (London: British Library), p. 69.
2. Laurence Olivier (1982) *Confessions of an Actor* (New York: Simon and Schuster), p. 298.
3. John Gaffney and Diana Holmes (2007) 'Introduction' in John Gaffney and Diana Holmes (eds) *Stardom in Postwar France* (New York: Berghahn Books), p. 1.
4. Douglas Lanier (2007) 'Shakespeare™: Myth and Biographical Fiction' in Robert Shaughnessy (ed.) *The Cambridge Companion to Shakespeare and Popular Culture* (Cambridge: Cambridge University Press), p. 94.
5. Barbara Hodgdon (1998) *The Shakespeare Trade* (Philadelphia: University of Pennsylvania Press), p. xi.
6. 'Eton's motto, "Floreat Etona" ("Let Eton flourish"), has never seemed more apt, as former pupils such as Hugh Laurie, Dominic West, Damian Lewis, Eddie Redmayne, Tom Hiddleston and Harry Lloyd dominate our stage and screens'. Andrew Wilson (2012) 'Eton's Class Act' *Daily Mail*, 14 July, http://www.dailymail.co.uk/home/moslive/article-2172578/Etons-class-act--renowned-school-turning-new-generation-actors.html, date accessed 15 September 2014.
7. James Mottram (2012) 'Soldier of Fortune: Tom Hiddleston Is Set to Become 2012's Hottest New Star' *The Independent*, 8 January, http://www.inde pendent.co.uk/news/people/profiles/soldier-of-fortune-tom-hiddleston-is-set-to-become-2012s-hottest-new-star-6284844.html, date accessed 21 January 2014; Ben Beaumont-Thomas (2013) 'Tom Hiddleston's Thor PR Antics Are a Lesson in Mischief as Marketing' *The Guardian*, 20 November, http://www.theguardian.com/film/filmblog/2013/nov/20/thor-tom-hiddleston-publicity-social-media, date accessed 21 January 2014; Giles Hattersley (2013) 'Kneel, for I Shall Be Lord of the Multiplex' *The Sunday Times*, 3 November, p. 5.
8. Bruce Babington (2001) 'Introduction: British Stars and Stardom' in Bruce Babington (ed.) *British Stars and Stardom: From Alma Taylor to Sean Connery* (Manchester: Manchester University Press), p. 8.
9. Ian Shuttleworth (1995) *Ken & Em: The Biography of Kenneth Branagh and Emma Thompson* (Reading: Headline), p. 242.
10. Amy Raphael (2011) 'Tom Hiddleston: From Theatre to Thor' *The Guardian*, 24 April, http://www.theguardian.com/culture/2011/apr/24/tom-hiddleston-thor, date accessed 13 February 2014.
11. For more detail on *Thor*'s Shakespearean intertexts and Branagh's own Shakespearean identity see: Anna Blackwell (2014) '"Yes, I Have Gained My Experience" (*As You Like It*, 4.3.23) Kenneth Branagh and adapting the 'Shakespearean' Actor' *Critical Survey*, 25.3: 29–42.
12. Loki's instruction to the public to kneel is met with an elderly German man getting to his feet and retorting, 'Not to men like you'. When answered by Loki's boast, 'There are no men like me', the man states: 'There are *always*

men like you'. This reference to Nazi Germany is consolidated by Steve Rogers' appearance (an American super soldier resurrected from the 1940s) remarking, 'You know, the last time I was in Germany and saw a man standing above everyone else, we ended up disagreeing'.

13. Although it was primarily used to explore genetics and evolution, Richard Dawkins (amongst others) has since distinguished the internet meme as a cultural unit that is deliberately altered by human creativity. In practice it contains the possibility for a variety of different forms, including viral videos, image macros (an image superimposed with text for humorous effect), hashtags or intentional misspellings. Richard Dawkins (1989) *The Selfish Gene*, 2nd edition (Oxford: Oxford University Press), p. 192.

14. Beaumont-Thomas.

15. 'Loki Interview Prank' *YouTube*, 8 November 2013, http://www.youtube.com/watch?v=5K2AI44XI0s#t=380, date accessed 20 February 2014.

16. The King Himself, 'So I Made a Thing' 9 November 2013, http://the-king-himself.tumblr.com/post/66450388581/so-i-made-a-thing, date accessed 20 February 2014.

17. Created in December 2012, the Initiative uses Hawkeye and other male comic characters to illustrate how 'deformed, hyper-sexualized, and impossibly contorted women are commonly illustrated in comics, books, and video games.' Web page, http://thehawkeyeinitiative.com/faq, date accessed 11 November 2015.

18. 'Tom Hiddleston sings Get Loki' *YouTube*, 30 October 2013, http://www.youtube.com/watch?v=oU-MLOh6YME, date accessed 20 February 2014.

19. Katherine W. Jones (2001) *Accent on Privilege: English Identities and Anglophilia in the U.S.* (Philadelphia: Temple University Press), p. 7.

20. 'Conversation with Tom Hiddleston – Nerd HQ' *YouTube*, 21 July 2013, https://www.youtube.com/watch?v=jLX-tdqEjUg, date accessed 2 July 2014.

21. *Times* Talks Madrid, 'Tom Hiddleston' *YouTube*, 6 August 2013, http://www.youtube.com/watch?v=lD-E-ddTp8E, date accessed 1 June 2013.

22. Frances Wasem (2014) 'Tom Hiddleston on *Coriolanus' Harper's Bazaar*, 1 December, http://www.harpersbazaar.co.uk/culture-news/tom-hiddleston-on-coriolanus-shakespeare-national-theatre-live, date accessed 11 November 2015.

23. 'Tom Hiddleston Industrial Scripts Interview' *YouTube*, 16 January 2013, https://www.youtube.com/watch?v=WTnJIW-IuO8, date accessed 1 November 2014.

24. Anna Blackwell (2014) 'Adapting *Coriolanus*: Tom Hiddleston's Body and Action Cinema', *Adaptation*, 7.3: 350.

25. Judith Buchanan (2005) *Shakespeare on Film* (Harlow: Pearson), pp. 207–8; Marvin Carlson (2003) *The Haunted Stage: The Theatre as Memory Machine* (Ann Arbor: University of Michigan Press), p. 2.

26. William Shakespeare (1997) *Richard II* in Stephen Greenblatt et al. (eds) *The Norton Shakespeare* (New York and London: Norton) 2.1.45–50.

27. 'Jaguar continues British villains storyline' 2 April 2014, http://finance.yahoo.com/news/jaguar-continues-british-villains-storyline-120000395.html, date accessed 5 June 2014.

28. Eoin Price (2015) 'Shakespeare Season' *Asidenotes*, 28 May, https://asidenotes.wordpress.com/2015/05/28/shakespeare-season/, date accessed 1 June 2015.

29. Nabanita Singha Roy, 'Voice of Jaguar' 25 June 2014, Web Page, http://www. rushlane.com/dunlop-china-benedict-cumberbatch-12123001.html, date accessed 1 July 2015.

30. N.d., http://memegenerator.net/instance/22976163?urlName=Good-Guy-Benedict&browsingOrder=New&browsingTimeSpan=AllTime, date accessed 9 November 2015.

31. Mel Elliott (2015) *Colour Me Good: Benedict Cumberbatch* (Banstead: I Love Mel), n.p.

32. 'Kenneth Branagh: A Life in Pictures' 19 November 2011, Video [PDF also available], BAFTA, http://guru.bafta.org/kenneth-branagh-life-pictures-video-interview, date accessed 1 May 2013.

33. Sarah Crompton (2015) 'Why Benedict Cumberbatch Is Luckier than Richard Burton' *The Guardian*, 31 July, http://www.theguardian.com/stage /2015/jul/31/benedict-cumberbatch-richard-burton-hamlet, date accessed 29 September 2015.

34. Paul Booth (2010) *Digital Fandom: New Media Studies* (New York: Peter Lang Publishing) p. 12, p. 18.

35. Rachel Stewart (2014) 'Cumberbatch's Hamlet Most In-demand Show of All Time' *The Telegraph*, 11 August, http://www.telegraph.co.uk/culture/theatre/ theatre-news/11025625/Cumberbatchs-Hamlet-most-in-demand-show-of-all-time.html, date accessed 26 November 2015.

36. Ben Hewis (2015) '5 Tips for First-time Theatre-Goers Going to Watch Cumberbatch in Hamlet' 4 August, Web Page, http://www.whatsonstage. com/london-theatre/news/benedict-cumberbatch-hamlet-barbican-tips-etiquette_38448.html, date accessed 10 December 2015.

37. Hannah Furness (2015) 'Cumberbatch Fans Swot Up on Shakespeare and Etiquette Ahead of Hamlet' *The Telegraph*, 3 August, http://www. telegraph.co.uk/news/celebritynews/11781259/Cumberbatch-fans-swot-up-on-Shakespeare-and-etiquette-ahead-of-Hamlet.html, date accessed 10 December 2015.

38. The-Fellowship-of-Erdemhart, 10 October 2015, Web Page, http://the-fellowship-of-erdemhart.com/post/130908733626/tom-hiddleston-making-sure-that-if-the-fangirls, accessed 10 December 2015.

39. Tiniest John (2015) 'Barbican-Hamlet' 26 August, Web Page, http://tiniest john.tumblr.com/post/127632031088/barbican-hamlet, accessed 10 December 2015.

40. Mark Brown (2015) 'Benedict Cumberbatch's Hamlet' *The Guardian*, 19 August, http://www.theguardian.com/culture/2015/aug/19/benedict-cum-berbatchs-hamlet-media-accused-of-contempt-and-hysteria, date accessed 27 November 2015.

41. Scott Jordan Harris (2015) 'Benedict Cumberbatch's *Hamlet* Could Usher in a New Era of Blockbuster Shakespeare' *Slate*, 31 August, http://www. slate.com/blogs/browbeat/2015/08/31/benedict_cumberbatch_s_hamlet_could_usher_in_an_era_of_blockbuster_shakespeare.html, date accessed 1 October 2015.

42. Ben Brantley (2015) 'Review' *The New York Times*, 25 August, http:// www.nytimes.com/2015/08/26/theater/review-benedict-cumberbatch-in-hamlet-cocooned-in-an-aura-on-a-london-stage.html?_r=2, date accessed 27 November 2015.

Select Bibliography

Babington, Bruce (ed.) (2001) *British Stars and Stardom: From Alma Taylor to Sean Connery* (Manchester: Manchester University Press).

Blackmore, Susan (1992) *The Meme Machine* (Oxford: Oxford University Press).

Jones, Katherine W. (2001) *Accent on Privilege: English Identities and Anglophilia in the U.S.* (Philadelphia: Temple University Press).

Lanier, Douglas (2002) *Shakespeare and Modern Popular Culture* (Oxford: Oxford University Press).

Olivier, Laurence (1982) *Confessions of an Actor* (New York: Simon and Schuster).

Shellard, Dominic (1999) *British Theatre Since the War* (New Haven, CT and London: Yale University Press).

Stein, Louisa Ellen and Kristina Busse (ed.) (2012) *Sherlock and Transmedia Fandom: Essays on the BBC Series* (Jefferson: MacFarland).

6
Ales, Beers, Shakespeares

Graham Holderness and Bryan Loughrey

I

> *Boy* Would I were in an alehouse in London. I would
> give all my fame for a pot of ale and safety. (*Henry V,*
> 3.2.10–11)[1]

Here the Boy in *Henry V*, on the night before Agincourt, expresses his homesick longing to be out of danger, in a familiar alehouse, drinking a pot of ale. Far from the 'vasty fields of France' (1.Prologue.10), the national drink comes to represent shelter and safety; an alehouse in England, a pot of ale that is home. The Boy is of course killed the next day, so he never makes it home, and his pot of ale remains eternally untasted.

English ale was indeed so embedded in social life as to figure in the imagination as a necessity of an abundant, or even a subsistence life. Literally it was a 'staple' of the common diet. *Magna Carta* (1215) promised free-born Englishmen not only relief from arbitrary arrest but also a 'standard measure' for many of life's essentials, including 'ale'[2] – leading eventually to the adoption, 'in perpetuity', of the ubiquitous 'Imperial Pint' throughout Britain and much of the Commonwealth.[3] Shakespeare's various references to 'ale' frequently bear similar associations with patriotism, local loyalties, and a demotic entitlement to popular pleasure. At least one of them, Sir Toby Belch's remonstrance against Malvolio's puritanical abstinence in *Twelfth Night*, is firmly established in common parlance as a well-known phrase or saying:

> Dost think because thou art virtuous
> there shall be no more cakes and ale?
> (*Twelfth Night*, 2.3.110–111)

Clearly, in Sir Toby's view, 'cakes and ale' belong to the Englishman's birth right, and the notion of their being withheld on the grounds of religious exclusivity and ethical intolerance is anathema. Sir Toby is a knight of the realm, but more often in Shakespeare ale is associated rather with lower-class figures, like the Boy in *Henry V*. Autolycus in *The Winter's Tale* affirms that 'a quart of ale is a dish for a king' (*The Winter's Tale*, 4.2.8); but he himself is an itinerant tinker, petty thief, and confidence trickster. Puck in *A Midsummer Night's Dream* knocks the cup from an old 'gossip's' lips, so the ale runs down her chin. In the Induction to *The Taming of the Shrew*, the drunken tinker Christopher Sly calls for 'a pot of small ale' (*Taming of the Shrew*, Induction 2.1). Two clowns in *The Two Gentleman of Verona* construct a list of ideal feminine qualities, which includes the ability to 'brew good ale' (*Two Gentlemen of Verona*, 3.1.296).

Shakespeare also refers, on fewer occasions, to 'beer', and the allusions are interestingly different. In *Henry VI, Part II* a mock-heroic duel is fought between the armourer Thomas Horner and Peter Thump. Horner is fortified with 'double beer' which intoxicates him to such a degree that he is easily killed by his opponent. In the same play one of the unreasonable utopian demands of the notorious rebel Jack Cade is to outlaw 'small beer', and to require the 'three-hooped pot' to be expanded to ten hoops; so the working population would be permanently in the same inebriated condition as the unfortunate Horner. In one of his most scathing and cynical satires, Hamlet reflects on the decomposition of the human body, which returns to earth, and might therefore be fashioned into a clay plug for a beer-barrel. Nothing, it seems, could be more depressing. Equally depressed is Prince Hal in *Henry IV, Part I*: 'Doth it not show vilely in me to desire small beer?' (2.2.5).

Since the terms 'ale' and 'beer' have become virtually interchangeable, the discrepancy in Shakespeare's attitude towards the two terms deserves some explanation. In fact, Shakespeare's distinction between the two drinks, his attribution to them of contrasting values and his clear preference for ale over beer, reflects the deep fault-line of a competition between two types of brewing which marked the industry in England for centuries and is still alive today, at least in terminology (even though nothing available today would be akin to what Shakespeare knew as 'ale').[4]

Ale in Shakespeare's time was brewed in England simply from water, malted barley, and yeast, with the possibility of additional flavourings such as rosemary and thyme. It was fundamental to the diet of many in the medieval period, providing significant nutritional benefits to a largely agrarian workforce, boosting vitamin intake, especially in the B spectrum; and crucially (in an age in which cholera and typhus were still widely prevalent) the brewing process ensured that ale was far safer to consume than drinking water of often dubious quality. Brewing of ale was therefore an important domestic responsibility, a task undertaken largely by women – the descriptor 'ale-wife' being then a term that was certainly not pejorative. Although ale was brewed primarily for home consumption, the sale of both the drink and its ingredients also presented lucrative business opportunities. Historical records indicate that Shakespeare in 1598 possessed more malt, the basic ingredient of ale, than was needed for his household, strongly suggesting some of it was for sale. In 1604 Shakespeare sued a neighbour for non-payment in respect of malt supplies, so clearly some of it *was* sold. As Lena Cowen Orlin points out, since 'malt-making would have been a business conducted and supervised by women', this would have been all within Anne Shakespeare's domestic control: Shakespeare's wife was an 'ale-wife'.[5] Excavations at Shakespeare's house, New Place, have turned up stone pads which archaeologists think may indicate the presence of an on-site brew-house.[6]

In Shakespeare's time there were essentially three grades of ale. The premium quality ale, often referred to as double ale, was derived from the first batch of ingredients, or mash, which was particularly strong in alcohol content. This obviously enhanced its inebriating qualities, no doubt an important attribute in the many social rituals in which ale was intimately involved, one of the more notorious being the 'church ales': essentially parties where alcohol was sold to raise money for church repairs and the relief of the poor, but which gained such a reputation for drunken licentiousness that Queen Elizabeth attempted to suppress the practice. Probably the nearest modern analogues to the taste of premium ales in Shakespeare's time are the super-strong lagers Special Brew[7] and Tennent's Extra – both 9% alcohol by volume (ABV) – more than double the strength of the traditional modern English beer. The recycled second mash of ale was subsequently brewed into single ale available at approximately half the ABV for half the price; and when further diluted became weak or 'small beer', a near universal alternative to drinking water that accompanied all meals, including breakfast, for men, women, and children.

The key difference between ale and beer is that beer has the additional ingredient of hops. Ales were unhopped; beers were hopped. Ale had been brewed without hops in England for centuries. Hops were introduced from continental Europe from the mid-fifteenth century, and were soon grown locally, particularly in Kent. Their inclusion within the brewing process had two distinct outcomes. One was a distinctive 'hoppy' taste that became the characteristic flavour of English bitter beers. The other was that the preservative powers of the hop flowers meant beers could be stored for far longer.

By the early-modern period, ale and beer were separate and competing enterprises, with beer gradually taking a larger market share. They were produced separately by rival enterprises. London in 1574, when Shakespeare was ten, had 58 ale breweries and 32 beer breweries. In 1564 Norwich had five 'comon alebrewers' and nine 'comon berebrewers'. In 1606, St Albans agreed to restrict the number of brewers in the town to four for beer and two for ale. In 1571 the Parish of St Olave's, where Shakespeare was later to lodge, had 14 Dutch brewers, all producing beer on the continental, hopped, model.[8]

The gradual ascendancy of beer, valued for its taste and longevity, should not disguise the fact that ale continued to be preferred by many as the more natural, healthier, and more English refreshment. In 1615 Gervase Markham published *The English Huswife*, a handbook containing 'all the virtuous knowledges and actions both of the mind and body, which ought to be in any complete woman' (the kind of conduct manual or inventory that Shakespeare parodied in *The Two Gentlemen of Verona*):

> The general use is by no means to put any hops into ale, making that the difference between it and beer ... but the wiser huswives do find an error in that opinion, and say that the utter want of hops is the reason why ale lasteth so little a time.[9]

Markham's text shows that ale was commonly being converted into beer by the addition of hops; but also that there was a strong residual prejudice against this practice. For some two centuries restrictive practices had been applied to keep ale free from hops. In 1471 the 'common ale brewers' of Norwich were forbidden from brewing with hops. In 1483 the ale brewers of London were complaining to the Mayor about 'sotill and crafty means of foreyns' who were 'bruing of ale within the said Citee', by 'puttyng of hopes and other things in the ale, contrary to the good and holesome manner of bruying of ale of old tyme used'.[10]

In 1542 Andrew Boorde published a medical self-help book *A Dyetary of Helth* which promoted ale over beer. 'I do drinke ... no manner of beer made with hopes'. 'Ale for an Englyshmann is a natural drinke', while beer was a 'a natural drynke for a Dutche man'. Beer production has been:

> Of late days ... much used in Englande to the detryment of many Englysshe men; specialy it kylleth them the whiche be troubled with colyck and the stone, and the strangulion; for the drynke is a cold drynke; yet it doth make a man fat and doth inflate the bely, as it doth appear by the Dutche mens faces & belyes.[11]

As late as 1651, John Taylor, in his *Ale Ale-vated into the Ale-titude*, asserted that 'Beere is a Dutch Boorish Liquor, a thing not knowne in England till of late dayes, an Alien to our Nation till such time as Hops and Heresies came amongst us: it is a sawcey intruder into this Land'.[12] Earlier poet Thomas Randall wrote of ale and beer as Catholic and Protestant respectively:

> Beer is a stranger, a Dutche vpstart come
> Whose credit with us sometimes is but small;
> But in the records of the empire of Rome
> The olde Catholicke drink is a pot of good ale.[13]

In 1630 John Grove wrote in his *Wine, Ale, Beer and Tobacco Contending for Superiority* that wine was the drink for the court, beer for the city, but 'Ale, bonny Ale, like a lord of the soil, in the Country shall domineer'.[14]

Ale was therefore the traditional English drink, familiar from centuries of universal local practice; beer was a relatively new-fangled and foreign import, emanating from Germany and the Low Countries, that could be regarded as an unnecessary innovation. The allusions in Shakespeare's plays to both drinks strongly suggest that in his mind ale was traditional, popular, and the stuff of harmless pleasure; while beer was excessively strong and dangerous, associated with violence, innovation, and the chaos of unbridled appetite.

II

Shakespeare's own connections with the production, distribution, and regulation of ale are intimate and well documented. John Shakespeare, William's father, son of a local tenant farmer, initially moved to Stratford to sell the produce of the family's farm, including wheat, wool, leather, and that staple of the brewing industry, malt. He was clearly a skilled craftsman and entrepreneur, who quickly diversified his business interests, becoming a successful maker of high-quality gloves and other handmade leather goods. Business success brought higher social standing. He was eventually appointed in 1571 to the illustrious position of the Town's Chief Alderman, having previously held the offices of Borough Constable (1558), Affeeror (responsible for determining penalties for crimes where these were not specified by statute, 1559), Borough Chamberlain (1561), and Alderman (1565). But his first public office was that of the Town's official Ale Taster (1556).[15]

The Ale Taster, often known as ale-conner, was expected to assay the quality of beers within his jurisdiction, judge upon purity and quality, and where fault was found enforce remedy, through the courts if necessary. In some cases he also had the powers to set the price of ales and beers within the locality. Although there is little direct evidence for this possibly apocryphal extension of the ale taster's duties, in later centuries it was widely believed the ale-conner would also check for the sugar content in beverages by pouring a quantity of beer onto a wooden seat, and while wearing leather breeches sit upon it for half an hour to test for 'stickiness'. As a maker of leather goods John Shakespeare would have been well qualified for this particular aspect of the job! Nevertheless, despite, to modern sensibilities at least, the comic potential of the role, it was one that was then taken extremely seriously and the holder was required to swear a formal oath, pledging to uphold the public interest.[16]

It seems likely, then, that William Shakespeare, by way of his upbringing and exposure to the general social milieu, had a thorough knowledge of the brewery trade and personal experience of ale houses, taverns, and inns.[17] At any rate, the numerous quotations from within his plays give the impression of a ready familiarity. We know that John Shakespeare possessed malt and grain, since he traded in them illegally. Some of these stores must have been used to make ale for the family, proving that Shakespeare drank it, probably from a very early age. He may have graduated to finer drinks, such as sack, when he became a successful London playwright; but he must have been born and bred on ale.

III

So Shakespeare drank ale, grew up in an ale-redolent environment, and wrote about ale in his plays. It is hardly surprising that when, after his death, people began to recollect and record incidents in his life, the presence of ale and ale-houses should be a constant factor.

Although most ales were home brewed and consumed there or, in the case of agrarian labourers, in the field, convivial souls with time to spare could gather in an ale house, where those that could afford it drank from their own 'pot', while others shared not only seating at the long trestle tables but also access to 'communal pots' (from which the Boy in *Henry V* may have been hoping to drink). Taverns were rather more upmarket destinations, offering not only ale, but meals to order, and in some cases fortified wines: 'sack'. Most up-market of all were inns, often elaborate buildings constructed around a courtyard, that gradually sprang up along English highways to provide lodgings and higher quality refreshment to travellers and their entourage. An inn of this type, with subsequent architectural renovations, is preserved from Shakespeare's time in the form of the George (formerly the George and Dragon) in Borough High Street, Southwark. The modern 'traditional' English pub shares its genealogy from all three. Taken together there were a vast number of retail outlets: a survey in 1577 recorded 19,000 alehouses, taverns, and inns in England and Wales catering for a population of circa 4 million: i.e. there was at least one pub for every 250 residents. For comparison, there were in 2014 throughout the entire UK just 48,000 pubs serving a population of circa 64.5 million: i.e. just one pub for every 1,300 or so residents.[18]

An impressive number of early biographical legends cluster around Shakespeare and taverns, as demonstrated by Samuel Schoenbaum. In London, he may have shared the company of his fictional characters, Falstaff and Hal, at the sign of the Boar in East Cheap. Perhaps there really was a Globe Tavern in Blackfriars frequented by the players of the Globe Theatre – though conflation over time between public house and public theatre would be understandable. There certainly was, until destroyed in the Great Fire, nearby to St Paul's a Mermaid Tavern – and contemporary documents demonstrate that Shakespeare knew its owner, though they neither confirm nor deny it was the scene of the celebrated encounters between the Bard and Ben Jonson. There are passing references to the Red Lion in the Edgware Road, the atmospherically named Devil Tavern, and the Three Pigeons in Brentford, while in the nineteenth century the Bankside's Falcon advertised itself as the 'daily resort of SHAKESPEARE, and his Dramatic Companions'. Shakespeare has also been associated with pubs in Stratford, including the Greyhound, and inns on the route between London and Stratford, particularly the Olde Shipe Inne of Grendon Underwood.[19]

The association of Shakespeare himself with alcohol (not necessarily beer) can be clearly seen in the three more elaborate tavern narratives popularised by the late-seventeenth-century diarist John Aubrey.[20] If the Shakespeare biography is restricted to documented facts, it tends towards the respectable and dull: hard work, an obsession with financial security and flinty dealings over property, debts, and enclosures. The 'tavern tales', like the legends of Shakespeare's youthful misdemeanours as deer-hunter and runaway apprentice, provide a rather different perspective. Individually some at least show that the use of Shakespeare's reputation to drum up business for venues of entertainment has a long pedigree – affording rudimentary though no doubt locally effective marketing strategies. Collectively, however, they suggest an alternative narrative for a life of Shakespeare: the smooth-talking ladies' man; the bar room wit; the lover of life. A humanised fellow with whom it would be a pleasure to share a pint in your 'local'.

IV

In marketing, images trump words. The familiar 'received' image of the Bard, which adorns countless advertisements worldwide, has become iconic, an instantly recognisable signifier of high culture (Shakespeare metaphorically endorses those products he vicariously and posthumously endorses).[21]

Pubs were 'early adopters' of Shakespeare iconography. Richard I introduced legislation that required every ale house, tavern, and inn in England to display a sign that could be recognised by the official Ale Taster. Given a largely illiterate population, such signs inevitably depended on recognisable icons. The Red Lion (the heraldic insignia of Richard I) and the King's Head (Henry VIII's now predominates) were and remain the most popular. But Shakespeare's remarkable visage and universal popularity ensured his features began to adorn pub signs from the seventeenth century onward. As of 2011, there were still at least some 35 pubs bearing his name and portrait, although there used to be many more.[22] So the association, in the popular culture of pub names and signs, between Shakespeare and alcohol was established at an early stage: partly on the basis of his status as a great historical character, but also on account of the presence within his work of portrayals of tavern culture and of copious drinking, which in turn fuelled the growth of those legends of Shakespeare as drinker and frequenter of pubs.

Eventually Shakespeare, pubs, and beer came together into a decisive rapprochement in his home town of Stratford-upon-Avon. The Industrial Revolution led to a concentration of workers in Britain's cities, and thus to economies of scale in the brewing industry based upon population growth, innovation in brewing technologies that improved the stability of the product, and improved transportation links between urban conurbations. Large-scale brewing conglomerates became established as a response, particularly in London and the long-time brewing centre of Burton-on-Trent. Meanwhile, in rural Stratford, Edward Flower opened his Stratford brewery in 1831.[23] In its early stages this enterprise remained defiantly local, using produce from local farms and selling into local, sometimes tied, outlets; but also managing to brew one world-renowned product, a bottled Pale Ale exported across the Far East. The brewery eventually became the largest employer in Stratford, and one of the largest in Warwickshire. Stratford, however, had been linked to Birmingham by canal in 1816 and by train in 1859. The Flower Brewery, by now Flower & Sons, took advantage of this expanding market and introduced state-of-the-art 'tower brewery technology' in 1870. By this time Charles Edward Flower (who gradually took full control of the family-owned business, his brother William Henry becoming Director of the Natural History Museum) had already begun to demonstrate a lifelong commitment to Stratford's Shakespeare connections by purchasing on behalf of the brewery the 'Shakespeare' inns in nearby Welford-on-Avon and Harvington.

Charles Edward Flower created a unique legacy based upon an extraordinary blend of capitalist enterprise, inspired Bardolatry, and exemplary public service, recognised through his appointment as Mayor of Stratford. After the 1864 Shakespeare Centenary celebrations in Stratford, several local committees were established to promote the idea of establishing a Memorial Theatre. These committees immediately fell into internecine strife concerning 'matters, not unconnected with self-interest on the part of the advocates' of this idea.[24] Charles Flower eventually resolved the local conflict by offering a grant of land on the bank of the Avon and a donation of £1,000 to establish a Memorial Theatre that was to include a public Art Gallery and Library.[25] In many ways he shepherded in the establishment of Stratford as both a site of veneration to the National Poet and an elite tourist destination.

The opening of the first Memorial Theatre in 1879 (the Library had to wait till 1880) was not, however, without controversy, despite recruiting the famous, if ageing, Helen Faucit as the leading lady for an opening-night performance of *Much Ado About Nothing*. By all accounts, Stratford entered into the spirit of the occasion: the town was bedecked with garlands and a party spirit prevailed. But the national press, particularly the *Telegraph*, were more curmudgeonly in their view, taking umbrage that a sleepy backwater such as Stratford should have the temerity to deem itself an appropriate site for a National Monument to the Bard. Cartoons were published depicting an audience of local yokels, and lead articles complained of a parochial atmosphere.[26]

This in no way deterred Charles Flower, who had already begun assiduously to incorporate Shakespearean features into the brewery's marketing strategy. He was assisted by the passing of the 1875 Trade Mark Registration Act, which allowed formal registration of trademarks with the Patent Office. The first such registered trademark was for Bass beer, with its distinctive bright red triangular design. To deter counterfeit, the design was burnt onto each Bass barrel, establishing the modern marketing understanding of the term 'branding'.[27] In 1876 Flower & Sons applied for two trademarks (5,244 and 5,255) based upon portraits of Shakespeare derived from the Holy Trinity bust.[28] Shakespeare's image began insistently to appear on Flower's signs, posters, mugs, and beermats, and, in figurine form, even to adorn its ashtrays. The theatre, Stratford's soon regular theatrical and musical festivals, and the town's nascent tourism industry created a wider market for the company's distinctively traditional beers, which could now be sent on reliably by train for resale in Birmingham, Oxford, and London. The marketing image was reassuringly pastoral, its figurehead the eminent Burgher of Stratford in the rural county of Warwick (see Figure 6.1). A safe pint to enjoy in genteel good company.

Figure 6.1　Flowers beer mat
Source: Photo by Graham Holderness.

In 1926 the original theatre burnt down. Fortunately, there were no injuries despite the fact that the local populace formed a heroic human chain to rescue the majority of the treasures it contained from the flames. This contrasts with the fate of Shakespeare's own Globe theatre, which burnt to the ground in 1613 during a performance of *Henry VIII*. There too there was no loss of life, despite one man's breeches catching fire. Tragedy was averted when a 'provident wit' doused the flames with 'bottle ale'.[29]

Sir Archibald Flower, nephew to Charles Edward and his successor as the company's Chairman (and like him Mayor of Stratford) led the fundraising exercise to establish a new theatre. By this time, the national mood, and the mood of the national newspapers, had swung in favour of Stratford rather than London being recognised as the spiritual home of the National Poet. Fundraising was endorsed by both the Prime Minister, Stanley Baldwin, and the Leader of the Opposition, Ramsay MacDonald, with Thomas Hardy in a supporting role; when the General Strike disrupted fundraising activities in the UK these were diverted, entirely successfully, to the USA and Canada. The new theatre was established under Royal Charter with George V as its first Patron. Sir Archibald Flower became Chairman of its Board of Trustees, and the Flower family have remained intimately concerned with the organisation of the Royal Shakespeare Company ever since.

The opening of the new theatre in 1932 was a dazzling extravaganza, one presided over by the Prince of Wales (the future Edward VII) and Sir Archibald Flower, the Brewer-Mayor of Stratford. A crowd of 40,000 packed the banks of the Avon, and no doubt Flower & Sons' beer flowed from the town's pubs. Visiting dignitaries included the Prime Minister, the Ambassadors of the USA and France, many Commonwealth diplomats, and George Bernard Shaw. The Prince of Wales arrived by private plane, landing on the surrounding fields, and then opened events by pressing from his gallery in the Bancroft Gardens an electronic button, to be followed immediately by the unfurling of the flags of 74 nations in honour of William Shakespeare:

> It was an unforgettable scene. In the back-ground the stately front of the theatre, then line upon line of distinguished visitors, then the Prince upon the canopied platform; in the foreground the splendid array of the flags of the world above a huge concourse of people; to the left more crowds, to the right the imperturbable waters of the Avon, and beyond, the unspoiled meadowlands.

After a speech of welcome from Sir Archibald Flower, the Prince stepped forward to the microphone and spoke to the hearts of men and women in every part of the world.[30]

The event was the apotheosis of a consistent 100-year-old marketing strategy, allying a once-local brewery to a National Poet. But the national taste was about to change.

V

At the time of the coronation of Queen Elizabeth II in 1953, 'bottom fermented' chilled lagers accounted for only 3% of total beer sales in Britain, despite its universal popularity in every other major world market for beer.[31] The reasons for British beer 'exceptionalism' were often hotly debated in bar rooms of the period. Some pointed to high rates of tax on higher strength European lagers; others denounced dismal British summer weather; connoisseurs pointed towards the complex flavours of 'top fermented' traditional British bitter beers served at cellar temperature. One thing, however, was clear – that in the post-Second World War baby-boom years there was an increasing youth market for beer. And although advertisements such as Flower's might tempt a young man to share a pint with his father, it was not a 'cool drink' to share with his mates. And what was true for young men was equally true for young women, even if they sometimes adulterated their lager with lime. Lager was the beer of the future, or more accurately lagers were the beers of the future, and indeed they now account for over 70% of the beer sales in Britain. Some breweries, such as Heineken, Carlsberg, Budweiser, and Stella, could increase market share by appeal to their heritage and inherent quality. But it was the Canadian Carling Black Label brand – which in truth had virtually no heritage and very little quality – that both broke the mould in marketing terms, and embraced Shakespeare into a new alcohol-based alliance.[32]

For one thing, the company relied upon a new mass medium, television. Its transformative campaign began with an inverted homage to the 'Dam Busters' Second World War raid upon the dams powering the Ruhr industrial heartlands of Germany – normally celebrated as a triumph of British heroism and technological innovation. A low-ranking German soldier emerges sleepily from his guard hut, and lights a cigarette, only to hear, in the distance, the low drone of approaching Lancaster bombers. The soldier drops his rifle, shrugs off his greatcoat and, at first although hesitantly, adopts the stance of the professional goalkeeper. He staggers ineptly under the impact of catching the first of the flying 'football-bombs'; but as more follow, he becomes increasingly acrobatic and adept in protecting his dam/goal line, dealing with the final bomb with bravura insouciance. Like 'good sports', the public-school-accented RAF pilots acknowledge defeat (and heroism) gracefully, paying the lone, lowly protagonist beneath them the greatest laconic compliment at their disposal: 'I bet he drinks Carling Black Label'.[33] This became the catchphrase of a long-running series of high production value, and high budget televisual commercials that caught the subversive zeitgeist of the time.

Released in 1989, the Carling Black Label parody of Shakespeare's *Hamlet* remains one of the most innovative and creative examples of Shakespeare in advertising.[34] Taking its cue from popular Shakespeare parodies of the time by Peter Sellers, Morecambe and Wise, and Lenny Henry, the advert exploited the contrast between a middle and upper class theatrical culture and the common experience of the targeted lager drinker. We see a formally dressed theatre audience, though one of its members can be seen incongruously holding a pint of Carling Black Label in his hand. Hamlet addresses the skull: 'Alas poor Yorick'. The actor accidentally drops the skull, catching it like a football on his toe. A sequence follows, familiar from sports programmes, demonstrating the ball control of professional footballers, with the skull bouncing from foot, head, and shoulders, to excited 'Oohs' and 'Aahs' from the theatre audience. Horatio enters with 'My noble Lord Hamlet' – but noting the revised theatrical context immediately reverts to proletarian vernacular – 'over 'ere, son. On me 'ead'. Finally Hamlet kicks the skull into the lap of the evening-suited drinker of Black Label seated in one of the boxes. The advertisement concludes with the skull, now as ventriloquist's dummy, announcing 'I bet he drinks Carling Black Label'. Derek Longhurst records that another version of the advert had the same line delivered by a bust of Shakespeare, draped in a football scarf:

Clearly the targeted market is essentially male lower or middle class and the identity of the product is created by disrupting and supplanting 'alien' cultural practices with a comic spectacle of the performance of expert skills in a familiar cultural activity, an association of the popular leisure pursuits of football and beer-drinking.[35]

VI

By the 1990s there were in Britain only five brewers with national reach: Scottish Courage; Bass; Whitbread; Carlsberg-Tetley; and Guinness, the Irish exception to the rule.[36] Flower & Sons had long before been swallowed up by Whitbread, and its beers are no longer available – even in Stratford. In one sense that process of consolidation, despite changes of nomenclature, has accelerated. In November 2015 the largest brewer in the world, the US–Belgian–Brazilian multinational Anheuser-Busch, announced it is to merge with the UK-based international conglomerate SABMiller plc, the second largest brewer in the world: the new entity will control some 30% of the world's beer production.[37] The age of brewing globalisation has truly arrived.

Globalisation, however, invariably provokes its discontents. In the case of British brewing these discontents were first articulated by the Campaign for Real Ale (CAMRA), which since 1971 has championed the distinctive, complex flavours of cask- and bottle-conditioned beers. Clearly, the organisation has been a phenomenally successful pressure group, with local branches throughout the UK. It has also managed to resuscitate the term ale – although CAMRA applies it to a far wider range of drinks than in Shakespeare's time, encompassing all cask- or bottle-conditioned beers, even though virtually all of these in fact are hopped beers. Largely as a result of this groundswell of support for quality and diversity, there has been a resurgence of locally and regionally based brewing SMEs, including microbreweries. The 'Shakespeare' brand has been resurrected within this new brewing space, particularly in Warwickshire.

When you cross the borders of Warwickshire by car, the first thing you see is the County's road sign. In its centre is the county name. To the right-hand is the heraldic insignia of the county, the Bear and Ragged Staff, which has been associated with Warwickshire since at least the fourteenth century. The third component of the design is the strap line reminding us of Warwickshire's most famous denizen: 'Shakespeare's County'. Although not included within road signs, Warwickshire in 1931 consolidated its official Shakespearean identity by adopting as its heraldic motto 'Non Sanz Droit' (Not Without Right), proudly declaring that the county (rather than say London) has the right to represent Shakespeare, by appropriating the motto contained within the Coat of Arms granted to John Shakespeare in 1596 which legally entitled his children to bear the same. The countryside you drive through thereafter remains even today remarkably rural, virtually untouched by its proximity to the conurbation and industrial complex of the nearby city of Birmingham.

According to Jerry Lewitt, a representative of the Warwickshire Beer Company, Warwickshire road signs directly inspired the marketing of its product, 'Shakespeare's County', a bottled-beer of 5% ABV 'with a slightly spicy and a delicate floral, smooth bitterness'.[38] The label on the back of the bottle notes 'The leafy lanes and rolling countryside of Warwickshire provided inspiration to Shakespeare. Enjoy the refreshing taste of beer from the heart of the County'. The front label foregrounds an image of the Bard derived from the Droeshout engraving of the First Folio (see Figure 6.2). Perhaps surprisingly the company prefers the Droeshout engraving to the Janssen Bust, the more 'local' image of Shakespeare erected in Holy Trinity Church, Stratford (although perhaps it is paying homage to the so-called Flower portrait of Shakespeare purchased by the Flower family and subsequently donated to the Royal Shakespeare Company). Above his forehead, 'WARWICKSHIRE' is picked out by colour and capitalisation to emphasise locality. Below, the strap line emphasises heritage: 'a timeless classic'.

This is the nearest marketing campaign we have found to that pioneered by Flower & Sons, one based upon pastoral, familiarity, and a safe association with the local and national poet. It is clearly a strategy that works: 'Shakespeare's County' remains the company's most popular product, gaining the majority of its sales through outlets in Stratford, and in particular The Shakespeare Birthplace Trust's official shop. There is, however, no lack of marketing innovation within the company: it also makes one other Shakespeare-themed beer for a single outlet, the Student Union Bar of Warwick University. Its 'Dirty Duck' beer has a rather more tongue in cheek identity, derived from the nickname of the pub immediately opposite Stratford's Royal Shakespeare Theatre that serves as a pre- and post-performance 'watering hole'.

The 'William Shakespeare Strong Ale' range of beers (they are all hopped) also has a Warwickshire connection, though in this case there is a considerably more complex chain of association, production, and supply. The 'common brew' that underpins the entire range is originally brewed in Nottinghamshire by the family-owned Pheasantry Brewery, which can trace its pedigree back to the seventeenth century – and due to legal requirements that company's name must appear on the labelling on the bottles. According, however, to one of its co-owners, Mark Easterbrook,[39] the Pheasantry Brewery does not oversee either the final flavour, strength, or marketing of the range. Instead it forwards the common base brew to Harry & Parker, a microbrewery based in Southport, Lancashire. But having been brewed in Nottinghamshire and adapted in Lancashire, the largest proportion of the company's sales result from re-export into the Warwickshire heartland of Stratford's 'Shakespeare' market. Unusually, Harry & Parker is a microbrewery that

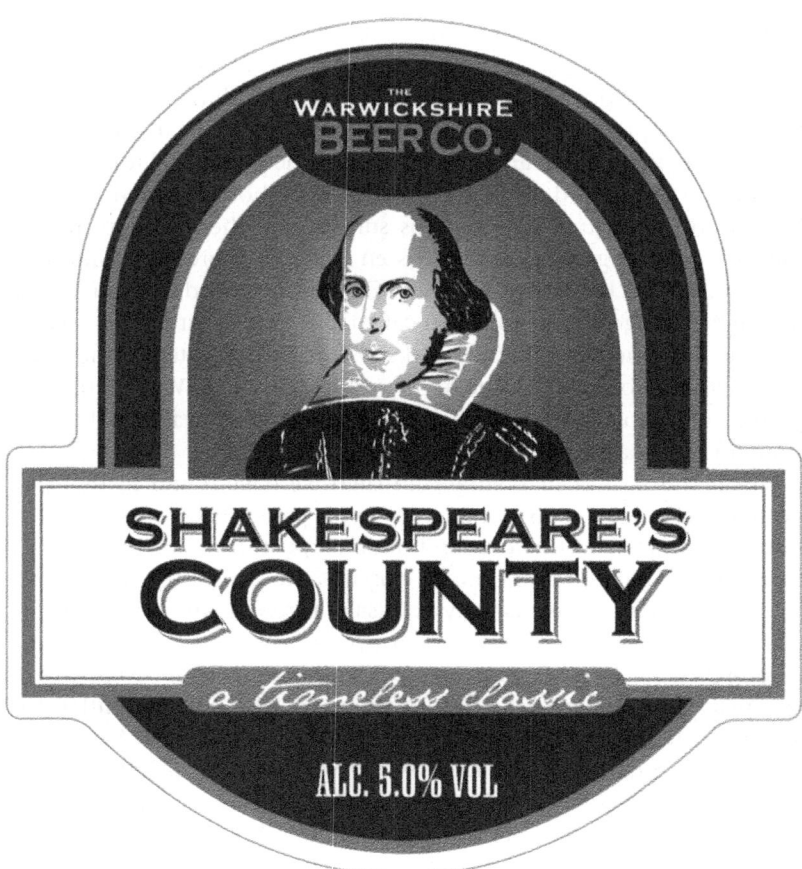

Figure 6.2   'Shakespeare's County' label
Source: Warwickshire Beer Company.

is also a 'brand consultancy', offering marketing advice to a wide range of regional SMEs in various business fields.[40] The company's representative James Snowling explained that Harry & Parker's strategy in relation to their own product is to sell 'bespoke and rebadged ales' that are closely identified with the names of individual Shakespeare plays.[41] Thus the ABV of the 'Romeo & Juliet Strong' ale is boosted to 5%, reflecting the strength of passion between the lovers. The palest beer of the range is the 'As You Like It', suggesting the play's lightness of tone. The dark, almost porter-like colour of the 'Macbeth Dark' beer, ABV 4.2%, again reflects the tenor of Shakespeare's play (and perhaps even alludes to the Porter in the play). Their 'Hamlet' is another dark beer, although this time flavoured with a berry, perhaps suggestive of the poison – which would have been derived from the berries of either hemlock or yew – by which Claudius murdered Hamlet's father (but having tasted the beer we are happy to affirm it is certainly not a poisonous brew!). The 'Tempest Amber' suggests the colour of the ale and the ambergris washed onto the shores of remote islands. One of the best sellers in the range is the company's 'Shakes-beerd', a full strength alcoholic ginger beer featuring on its label a stylised image of the Bard (although it is far more elaborate than those provided for the company's more mainstream beers, which derive from Picasso's famous sketch) with red hair and ginger beard (see Figure 6.3).

Harry & Parker hope that by emphasising the plays rather than traditional images of the Bard such diversity will promote 'convivial bar room conversation': for example, 'Did Shakespeare really have a ginger beard?'. Equally importantly, the company believes that by associating their products with Shakespeare these will gain a 'halo' of 'prestige' and 'authenticity'.

Harry & Parker rely on in-house marketing expertise to sell their Shakespeare beers. Church End Brewery relies on a very different strategy. For one thing, the brewery owns two pubs, and the majority of its sales are through these outlets, supplemented by orders for guest beers

Figure 6.3 'Shakes-beerd' label
Source: Harry & Parker.

from other local Warwickshire pubs and the tourist-driven Stratford trade. According to the Manager of the brewery, Karl Graves,[42] the company is acutely aware of market drivers ('You can brew lovely beer but you have to sell it') and its sometimes eccentric marketing strategy is driven by the colourful character of the brewery's owner, Stewart Elliott, who has ensured that since the company's foundation in 1994 it has maintained a more or less constant rolling programme of specialist 'occasional beer' campaigns, sometimes campaigning on local issues such as the closure of HP Sauce's Aston factory. The company has forged a close and longstanding relationship with Rees Bradley Hepburn Ltd (RBH), an award-winning advertising agency that is regularly featured in the trade press. Here, for example, is *The Drum*'s announcement for RBH's 2010 Shakesbeer campaign:

Church End brewery transforms Shakespearen (sic) sonnets into liquid gold

Church End Brewery and communications agency Rees Bradley Hepburn are celebrating the 446th birthday of William Shakespeare in appropriately British fashion, by launching a series of new beers.

The alcoholic promotion will see a series of specially concocted Elizabethan ales produced to excite the palette, each with an appropriately Shakespearean sounding name in recognition of the English master's greatest works.

A series of phased launches will commence with the bard's April 23 birthday whereupon patrons of real ale pubs stocking Church End beers will be able to refresh with a jar of 'Shakesbeer', a blend of four hops and four malts with just a hint of chocolate. A series of tasty tipples will follow in a succession of staggered launches including 'Much A Brew About Nothing'.[43]

'Shakesbeer' is perhaps a slightly hackneyed term that has been used for beer festivals worldwide and by at least one other brewer: Greene King sell a bespoke 'Shakesbeer' (unusually a draft rather than bottled beer) from Stratford's oldest pub, the Garrick Inn. There is certainly, however, nothing hackneyed about the overall approach of RBH's campaign, which is based, according to the company's Creative Director, Mike Kalin,[44] on an attempt to 'conjure the Bard without his words – which have become overfamiliar'. This is done by 'subverting traditional images' of the Bard, creating 'parodic … visually distinctive, but instantly recognisable, caricatures' through 'distortion and transposition' (see Figure 6.4). These have proved popular on labels, posters, beer mats, videos, and social media. He believes there is now a 'cult following' for Church End beers and its 'Brewery memorabilia', with a thriving market for the latter on the online auction site Ebay.

Figure 6.4 'Shakesbeer' Shakespeare 'Portraits'
Source: Rees Bradley Hepburn Ltd.

The marketing of Tunnel Brewery's 'Quill' range of beers also embraces the Bard, with a combination of striking visuals and dense textuality. The owner of the Brewery, Bob Yates, has a background in the fine arts, and conceived and designed the marketing materials himself, in conversation describing his efforts as a 'labour of love', although wryly noting that, given the relatively low volume of production, not one that was 'necessarily cost effective'.[45] In fact, following the intervention of the Birthplace Trust, he created two versions of both the beers and the marketing materials: Quill 1 and Quill 2, which we cannot resist calling Q1 and Q2.

Q1 was a deliberately strong 7% ABV bottled beer, reflecting the likely strength of a premium beer in Elizabethan times, with a strap line above an illustration of 'Shakespeare' in his library that read 'Plays wot I wrote' (see Figure 6.5).

The playful, parodic titles on the spines of the volumes on the library shelves read:

> TWELFTH NIGHT CAP
> OTHALEO
> VERY MERRY WIVES OF WINDSOR
> TIGHT AS ANDRONICUS
> THE WINTER'S ALE
> PERICALES

$QUILL$ 7% Trappist Style Ale

3rd Birthday / 200th Brew

Whilst settling down on a gloomy candlelit eve to write another play, Will Shakespeare bumped his desk and spilt his ink. What was he to do! In his hand he had a goblet of dark ale. He tentatively dipped his nib and discovered to his amazement that his quill flowed effortlessly across the pages. In no time at all he penned one of his finest plays. This Trappist Style Dubbel Ale should also flow smoothly and sweetly across your tongue. The play he wrote that night was of course....... Alls ALES! Well That Ends Well!

 Dark   Fruity   Delicious

Ingredients: Water, Barley, Hops and Yeast. Allergen advice: Contains gluten.

Best before date or see cap:

TUNNEL BREWERY

Vol 330ml e
7 % ABV

Tunnel Brewery Limited
Birmingham Road, Ansley Village
North Warwickshire CV10 9PQ
Tel: 024 7639 4888
E: info@tunnelbrewery.co.uk
www.tunnelbrewery.co.uk

 2.3 UK Units

DRINKAWARE.CO.UK

Figure 6.5 'Quill 1' label
Source: Tunnel Brewery Ltd.

KING BEER
MUCH ADO ABOUT BREWING
RICHARD'S III
A MIDSUMMER NIGHT'S CREAM STOUT
THE MERCHANT'S ARMS IN VENICE
THE TEN PISSED

Sitting in front of his works is a deliberately 'smug, supercilious'-looking 'Shakespeare' whose features are loosely derived from both the Droeshout engraving and the Janssen bust, though he has grown a beer belly and sports an ear ring. His left hand grips a goblet labelled Tunnel Quill, dimly illuminated by a candle. In his left he holds a quill pen and is in the act of writing 'ALL'S (scratched out) Ales! Well that ends ...'. Beside the parchment is an ink bottle that has been knocked over, its ink spilling over the desk. The back story to this accident is explained in the printed commentary to the side of the library shelves:

Whilst settling down on a gloomy candlelit eve to write another play, Will Shakespeare bumped his desk and spilt his ink. What was he to do! In his hand he had a goblet of dark ale. He tentatively dipped his nib and discovered to his amazement that his quill flowed effortlessly. In no time at all he penned one of his finest plays. This fine Old English ale should also flow smoothly and sweetly across your tongue. The play he wrote that's of course ..., 'All's (scratched out) Ales! Well That Ends Well!'

When the beer was offered to the Birthplace Trust to sell in its retail outlet, Tunnel Brewery was asked to make two significant changes that effectively established Q2. The first of these was to reduce the ABV of the liquor to 5.2%, something that was relatively easily achieved by substituting for the original another popular beer in the Tunnel range, its 'Henry Tudor', which is also rebadged for the Warwickshire Wildlife Trust. The quest for 'authenticity' in the form of unusually strong beer was rejected in favour of an understandable preference for 'responsible drinking'. According to the website of the 'BeerAdvocate Community' this did not detract from the taste, which revealed 'complex flavors of malts and a light amount of associated sweetness and notes of fruity yeast. No bitterness is perceptible. It feels medium-bodied and a little smooth on the palate with a low amount of carbonation. I enjoyed this beer because it was quite complex despite the low alcohol content, which makes this very easy to drink'.[46]

The second change asked for was to substitute for the original facetious 'Plays wot I wrote' strap line (derived of course from the comedians Morecambe and Wise) the more functional 'The Shakespeare Birthplace Trust' (see Figure 6.6). The Brewery's web site notes that all profits derived from the sale of the Quill range are donated to the Trust. Tunnel Brewery also sells suitably inscribed commemorative Quill tankards and goblets, often at local farmers' markets, including Stratford's. The Trust currently has plans to open a Shakespeare-themed pub in Henley Street, close to the Birthplace itself. This development could hardly be more appropriate, given that the Birthplace, sometime after Shakespeare's death, operated as a pub before it became a museum.

VII

When the relations between Shakespeare and alcohol, including ale and beer, were first explored in the 1980s, the emphasis was invariably on the tendency of capitalist enterprise to appropriate Shakespeare for profit, and in the process to render his image, reputation, and achievement into flattened, attenuated, superficial commodities. *The Shakespeare Myth*, the first publication to discuss these relations critically and theoretically, operated within a Frankfurt School paradigm that viewed all business, including tourism and brewing, as culturally inferior to 'critical knowledge'.[47] All attempts at using Shakespeare to reinforce 'heritage' and 'authenticity' were mercilessly mocked, and the Flower's beermat was ritually displayed as a classic instance of commodity fetishism.

Much has changed since then (not least our own critical and theoretical parameters), but more significantly the depth and subtlety of Shakespeare appropriation within the brewing industry. As the examples given above indicate, the production and marketing of Shakespeare-related beer demonstrate an extraordinary capacity to incorporate critical ideas, deconstructive instabilities, and knowing postmodern pastiche into their appropriations and representations of Shakespeare. Capitalism can now produce Shakespearean materials that display a textual richness and diversity that do justice to the dramatic works from which the material originally derives. Shakespeare, ale and beer are now reunited, as synchronised as they were when Mary Arden was busy brewing, John Shakespeare was out tasting, and little William longing, like the Boy in *Henry V*, for his own 'pot of ale'.

QUILL No.2 Old English Ale
5.2% ABV VOL 330ml e

Whilst settling down on a gloomy candlelit eve to write another play, Will Shakespeare bumped his desk and spilt his ink. What was he to do! In his hand he had a goblet of dark ale. He tentatively dipped his nib and discovered to his amazement that his quill flowed effortlessly across the pages. In no time at all he penned one of his finest plays. This fine Old English Ale should also flow smoothly and sweetly across your tongue. The play he wrote that night was of course....... All's ALES! Well That Ends Well!

 Dark Ruby    Really Fruity    Absolutely delicious

Ingredients: Water, Barley, Hops and Yeast. Allergen advice: Contains gluten.

Best before date or see cap:

TUNNEL
BREWERY
www.tunnelbrewery.co.uk

drinkaware.co.uk

1.7 UK Units

Produced exclusively for The Shakespeare Birthplace Trust by Tunnel Brewery. All proceeds from the sale of this item support the work of The Shakespeare Birthplace Trust.
Registered Charity Number 209302

Figure 6.6 'Quill 2' label
Source: Tunnel Brewery Ltd.

Notes

1. All Shakespeare quotations from Stanley Wells and Gary Taylor (eds) (1988) *William Shakespeare: The Complete Works* (Oxford: Clarendon Press).
2. See the British Library's *English Translation of Magna Carta* (1215), clauses 34 and 39.
3. British *Weights and Measures Act,* 1824. Contrary to near-universal pub banter, it has never been illegal to order half a pint! Indeed even one third of a pint glasses are legal.
4. Despite its name, The Campaign for Real Ale (CAMRA) exists to promote 'cask conditioned' beers rather than traditionally brewed ales. See www.camra.org.uk.
5. Lena Cowen Orlin (2014) 'Anne by Indirection', *Shakespeare Quarterly*, 65.4: 447.
6. See *BBC News*, 22 January 2015, http://www.bbc.co.uk/news/uk-england-coventry-warwickshire-30938157, date accessed 28 November 2015.
7. Carlsberg Special Brew, with its distinctive gold can, has an indirect Shakespearean link. Carlsberg created the lager in the immediate aftermath of the Second World War specifically to celebrate Winston Churchill's contribution to the Allied victory. Samples were shipped to London for Churchill's personal approval. A state visit to Denmark followed shortly thereafter. It included an official banquet in Kronborg Castle, Helsingor (Shakespeare's 'Elsinore'), where we imagine Special Brew was served.
8. See Martyn Cornell (2015) *Strange Tales of Ale* (Stroud: Amberly Publishing), p. 130.
9. Gervase Markham (1623) *Countrey Contentments, or the English Huswife* (London: R. Jackson), p. 225.
10. See Cornell, *Strange Tales of Ale*, p. 132.
11. Quoted in Cornell, *Strange Tales of Ale*, p. 133.
12. Quoted in John Ayto (1990) *The Diner's Dictionary: Word Origins of Food and Drink* (Oxford: Oxford University Press), p. 27.
13. Thomas Randall (1613) 'High and Mightie Commendation of the Vertue of a Pot of Goode Ale', quoted in Anonymous (2012) *In Praise of Ale* (Los Angeles: Library of Alexandria), n.p.
14. Quoted in Cedric C. Brown (2004) 'Drink as a Social Marker in Seventeenth Century England' in Adam Smyth (ed.) *A Pleasing Synne: Drink and Conviviality in Seventeenth Century England* (Cambridge: D.S. Brewer), p. 7.
15. See David Fallon (2015) 'His Father John Shakespeare' in Paul Edmondson and Stanley Wells (eds) *The Shakespeare Circle: An Alternative Biography* (Cambridge: Cambridge University Press), pp. 26–39.
16. See Garrett Oliver (ed.) (2011) *The Oxford Companion to Beer* (Oxford: Oxford University Press), p. 28.
17. See Pete Brown (2014) *Shakespeare's Local* (London: Macmillan) for a lively discussion of the possibility that Shakespeare drank at, and possibly also performed in, London's sole surviving galleried inn, The George, located in Southwark a short distance from the site of The Globe Theatre.
18. Harry Wallop (2014) 'The Perfect Pub: Is There One Left in England?' *The Daily Telegraph*, 15 October.
19. Samuel Schoenbaum (1991) *Shakespeare's Lives* (Oxford: Clarendon Press), pp. 48–49.

20. See Samuel Schoenbaum (1975) *Shakespeare: A Documentary Life* (Oxford: Oxford University Press), p. 224; 'Mr Seward's Preface' (1811) *The Dramatic Works of Ben Jonson and Beaumont and Fletcher* (London: John Stockdale), p. xxiv; and Roland Mushat Frye (1967) *Shakespeare's Life and Times: A Pictorial Record* (Princeton, NJ: Princeton University Press), p. 72.

21. See Graham Holderness and Bryan Loughrey (1991) 'Shakespearean Features' in Jean E. Marsden (ed.) *The Appropriation of Shakespeare* (Hemel Hempstead: Harvester Wheatsheaf).

22. See the pub-mapping website www.pubstops.co.uk. From personal observation we believe this figure might be a serious underestimate, perhaps not reflecting variants such as the Shakespeare's Head.

23. See Jonathan Reinars (1998) 'The Social History of a Midland Business: Flower & Sons Breweries, Stratford-upon-Avon, 1870–1914' (unpublished PhD thesis, University of Warwick) available online http://go.warwick.ac.uk/wrap/4308, date accessed 15 November 2015.

24. See A. K. Chesterton (1934) *Brave Enterprise: A History of the Shakespeare Memorial Theatre* (London: J. Miles & Co. Ltd), p. 7.

25. *Brave Enterprise*, p. 9.

26. See Christy Desmet (2012) 'Helen Faucit and the Shakespeare Memorial Theatre, Stratford-upon-Avon, 1879', *Critical Survey*, 24.2: 4.

27. See Pete Brown (2010) *Man Walks into a Pub: A Social History of Beer* (London: Pan Books), p. 107.

28. Its current legal status can be found at https://trademarks.justia.com/752/97/flowers-original-trade-mark-special-flower-sons-75297774.html, date accessed 26 November 2015.

29. See J. R. Mulryne and Margaret Shewring (eds) (1997) *Shakespeare's Globe Rebuilt* (Cambridge: Cambridge University Press), p. 186.

30. *Brave Enterprise*, p. 50.

31. *Man Walks into a Pub*, pp. 237–268.

32. *Man Walks into a Pub*, pp. 217–236.

33. The Carling Dam Busters ad can be viewed at https://www.youtube.com/watch?v=yCmhR2JK1VE, date accessed 30 November 2015.

34. The Carling *Hamlet* ad can be viewed at https://www.youtube.com/watch?v=ZsbUZTP--bg, date accessed 30 November 2015.

35. Derek Longhurst (1988) '"You Base Football-Player!": Shakespeare in Contemporary Popular Culture' in Graham Holderness (ed.) *The Shakespeare Myth* (Manchester: Manchester University Press), p. 67.

36. *Man Walks into a Pub*, p. 323.

37. See 'Beer giants AB InBev and SABMiller agree takeover terms' (2015), *BBC News*, 13 October, http://www.bbc.com/news/business-34513520, date accessed 28 November 2015.

38. Notes derived from a telephone conversation between Jerry Lewitt and Bryan Loughrey on 4 November 2015.

39. Notes derived from a telephone conversation between Mark Easterbrook and Bryan Loughrey on 4 November 2015.

40. See http://www.harryandparker.co.uk.

41. Notes derived from telephone conversations between James Snowling and Bryan Loughrey on 4 November 2015 and 11 November 2015.

42. Notes derived from a telephone conversation between Karl Graves and Bryan Loughrey on 9 November 2015.
43. See *The Drum* (2010), http://www.thedrum.com/news/2010/04/15/church-end-brewery-transforms-shakespearen-sonnets-liquid-gold, 15 April, date accessed 25 November 2015.
44. Notes derived from telephone conversations between Mike Kalin and Bryan Loughrey on 23 and 25 November 2015.
45. Notes derived from a telephone conversation between Bob Yates and Bryan Loughrey on 24 November 2015.
46. Tasting notes from BeerAdvocate Community, available at http://www.beeradvocate.com/community/.
47. 'Preface' (1988) in Graham Holderness (ed.) *The Shakespeare Myth* (Manchester: Manchester University Press, 1988).

Select Bibliography

Ayto, John (1990) *The Diner's Dictionary: Word Origins of Food and Drink* (Oxford: Oxford University Press).
Brown, Cedric C. (2004), 'Drink as a Social Marker in Seventeenth Century England' in Adam Smyth (ed.) *A Pleasing Synne: Drink and Conviviality in Seventeenth Century England* (Cambridge: D.S. Brewer), pp. 3–20.
Brown, Pete (2010) *Man Walks into a Pub: A Social History of Beer* (London: Pan Books).
Brown, Pete (2014) *Shakespeare's Local* (London: Macmillan).
Chesterton, A. K. (1934) *Brave Enterprise: A History of the Shakespeare Memorial Theatre* (London: J. Miles & Co. Ltd).
Cornell, Martyn (2015) *Strange Tales of Ale* (Stroud: Amberly Publishing).
Desmet, Christy (2012) 'Helen Faucit and the Shakespeare Memorial Theatre, Stratford-upon-Avon, 1879', *Critical Survey*, 24.2: 4–21.
Fallon, David (2015) 'His Father John Shakespeare' in Paul Edmondson and Stanley Wells (eds) *The Shakespeare Circle: An Alternative Biography* (Cambridge: Cambridge University Press), pp. 26–39.
Frye, Roland Mushat (1967) *Shakespeare's Life and Times: A Pictorial Record* (Princeton, NJ: Princeton University Press).
Holderness, Graham (ed.) (1988) *The Shakespeare Myth* (Manchester: Manchester University Press).
Holderness, Graham and Bryan Loughrey (1991) 'Shakespearean Features' in Jean E. Marsden (ed.) *The Appropriation of Shakespeare* (Hemel Hempstead: Harvester Wheatsheaf), pp. 141–59.
Longhurst, Derek (1988) '"You Base Football-Player!": Shakespeare in Contemporary Popular Culture' in Graham Holderness (ed.) *The Shakespeare Myth* (Manchester: Manchester University Press), pp. 59–73.
Markham, Gervase (1623) *Countrey Contentments, or the English Huswife* (London: R. Jackson).
Mulryne, J. R. and Margaret Shewring (eds) (1997) *Shakespeare's Globe Rebuilt* (Cambridge: Cambridge University Press).
Oliver, Garrett (ed.) (2011) *The Oxford Companion to Beer* (Oxford: Oxford University Press).

Orlin, Lena Cowen (2014) 'Anne by Indirection', *Shakespeare Quarterly*, 65.4: 421–454.

Randall, Thomas (1613) 'High and Mightie Commendation of the Vertue of a Pot of Goode Ale', quoted in Anonymous (2012) *In Praise of Ale* (Los Angeles: Library of Alexandria).

Reinars Jonathan (1998) 'The Social History of a Midland Business: Flower & Sons Breweries, Stratford-upon-Avon, 1870–1914', unpublished PhD thesis, available online http://go.warwick.ac.uk/wrap/4308.

Schoenbaum, Samuel (1975) *Shakespeare: A Documentary Life* (Oxford: Oxford University Press).

Schoenbaum, Samuel (1991) *Shakespeare's Lives* (Oxford: Clarendon Press).

Wallop, Harry (2014) 'The Perfect Pub: Is There One Left in England?' *The Daily Telegraph*, 15 October.

Wells, Stanley and Gary Taylor (eds) (1988) *William Shakespeare: The Complete Works* (Oxford: Clarendon Press).

7
A King Rediscovered: The Economic Impact of Richard III and *Richard III* on the City of Leicester

Dominic Shellard

For those seeking to rehabilitate the reputation of Richard III from centuries of opprobrium (primarily for allegedly both deposing his nephew Edward V in 1483 and then having him and his brother, Richard, murdered in the Tower of London), Shakespeare's play offers a significant and, at times, irritating challenge.

One of the leading figures in the remarkable project to discover where the king's remains actually resided, the leading Ricardian Philippa Langley, is quite explicit about this at the start of her book, *The Search for Richard III*.[1] Indeed, she argues that the playwright's creation has played such a crucial (and possibly malign) role in the historical depiction of the short-reigned fifteenth-century monarch that it:

> has long been recognized that only a discovery as important as Shakespeare's drama is compelling would provide a counterpoint to the Tudor villain the playwright portrayed.[2]

Langley and her fellow members of the indefatigable Looking for Richard project, which was founded by her in February 2009 with the aim to 'search for the grave of Richard III, and, if found, honour him with a reburial and tomb' (as well as 'to attempt to bring to life the real man behind the myth'), were always quite clear that this important 'discovery' would be the unearthing of the remains of the King.[3] Inspired by the research of John Ashdown-Hill that would lead to the publication of his book *The Last Days of Richard III* (2013), she surmised that these would lie in the long-buried remnants of the church of the Greyfriars, the friary of the Franciscans, in the heart of the city of Leicester.

126

The complexity of the historiography of Richard III is such that it is perhaps inevitable that aspects of the historiography of the actual search for his remains are already contested. The Looking for Richard Project received key support from Leicester City Council in September 2010, before Langley approached Richard Buckley, Co-Director, University of Leicester Archaeological Services (ULAS), in early 2011 to undertake the search for Richard III.[4] Buckley writes in the University of Leicester's own account of the discovery, *The Bones of a King* (published in 2015), that, with the appropriate caution of the expert archaeologist, he initially agreed to this commission 'because it offered a chance to reveal new knowledge about this important friary [Greyfriars]'.[5] Langley, perhaps with the understandable passion of the devotee, was quite clear on the other hand that the prime focus for her was the discovery of Richard.

A flavour of her intense passion can be gleaned from her account of a visit to Leicester in 2004, when, having conducted her own research (which in turn had been inspired by Michael Jones's *Bosworth 1485: Psychology of a Battle*), she was drawn to a car park close to the reputed site of the Church of the Greyfriars:

It was a large open space for seventy or more vehicles, surrounded by Georgian buildings with a large red-brick Victorian wall running north to south straight ahead of me. I found myself drawn to this wall and, as I walked towards it, I was aware of a strange sensation. My heart was pounding and my mouth was dry – it was a feeling of raw excitement tinged with fear. As I got near the wall, I had to stop, I felt so odd. I had goose bumps, so much so that even in the sunshine I felt cold to my bones. And I knew in my innermost being that Richard's body lay here. Moreover I was certain that I was standing right on top of his grave.[6]

This was five years before the Looking for Richard Project was founded and eight years before the remains were exhumed. This romanticism, serendipity, even mysticality have all added a significant allure to the Richard III story.

The co-existence of academic rigour and committed devotion was always likely to create pinch points and it is the contention of this chapter that both the brilliance and far-reaching influence of Shakespeare's momentous play, together with the differing perspectives on the mag-nificent search for the remains (most visible at the public reinterment of Richard III on 26 March 2015, as I shall discuss later) have added to the aura of controversy that has surrounded the King. This controversy has, in turn, further enhanced the undoubted economic impact of the extraordinary discovery in 2012 of the skeleton of the King of England who reigned from 1483 to 1485 in a turbulent and mesmerising period. Why then is Shakespeare's *Richard III* so problematic for Ricardians? Philippa Langley herself offers a plausible explanation when she states that 'Shakespeare created a play so sinister and darkly seductive that it still remains the portrait most are drawn to'.[7] A brilliant depiction of cynical opportunism, the banality of evil and the initial triumph of the underdog against supreme odds (a happenstance much beloved by the British), the stage Richard has been etched into public consciousness through compelling and inventive interpretations by Laurence Olivier, Ian McKellen and Antony Sher, for example. None of Shakespeare's Histories have been performed as often as the one about him, and the king literally dominates the play, appearing in 15 of its 25 scenes – with only Hamlet appearing in more – and most unusually opening the action himself with a portentous soliloquy whose very cadence, seeming simplicity and cunning wordplay ('son/sun') beguiles the audience in the same way that so many of those whom he is soon to encounter are beguiled:

> Now is the winter of our discontent
> Made glorious by this son of York,
> And all the clouds that loured upon our house
> In the deep bosom of the ocean buried.[8]

The son he refers to is his elder brother, Edward IV, whose defeat of the Lancastrian, Henry VI, had secured the kingship but whose accession to the throne had lit up the prospects of his youngest brother, too.

Richard also utters lines throughout the play that have become mainstays of popular culture ('A horse, a horse, my kingdom for a horse!'[9] is such an example) and in a magnificent first act, scarcely rivalled in its audaciousness by any other that Shakespeare wrote, we witness the extraordinary rise of somebody whom the Elizabethan audience would have felt scarcely had it within them to prosper so malignly. Richard makes quite clear in his opening soliloquy that he has disabilities:

> I, that am curtailed of this fair proportion,
> Cheated of feature by dissembling Nature,
> Deformed, unfinished, sent before my time
> Into this breathing world, scarce half made up,
> And that so lamely and unfashionable
> That dogs bark at me as I halt by them –

Why, I, in this weak piping time of peace,
Have no delight to pass away the time,
Unless to see my shadow in the sun
And descant upon my own deformity.[10]

– but he is in no way cowed by these. Indeed, they inspire him to action
and revenge against a contemporaneous world that would have viewed
his famous stage hunchback as a sign of moral depravity:

And therefore, since I cannot prove a lover
To entertain these fair well-spoken days,
I am determined to prove a villain
And hate the idle pleasures of these days.[11]

This counterpointing of an appealing bravura with an immediate confirmation to the audience of his villainous intent quickly paves the way
for a series of outrageous proleptic actions that he will seek to engineer.
In what is soon to become his pithy signature style of address, Richard
informs the audience that George, Duke of Clarence, the middle brother
between him and Edward IV, will die at his instigation:

Simple, plain Clarence, I do love thee so
That I will shortly send thy soul to heaven,
If heaven will take the present at our hands.[12]

And this is quickly followed by his desire to see the sickly Edward IV
pass away, but only at a time that suits his stratagems: 'He cannot live,
I hope, and must not die/Till George be packed with post-horse up to
heaven'.[13]

Before he makes one of his most audacious and scarcely credible
statements of intent, his desire to secure for himself as his wife the
woman whose husband, Prince Edward, he himself has (according to
Shakespeare) murdered:

What though I killed her husband and her father?
The readiest way to make the wench amends
Is to become her husband and her father.[14]

Much of this is, of course, without historical foundation. The famous
wooing of Lady Anne is completely invented, the *Henry VI* trilogy ques-
tionably makes Richard responsible for the murder of Prince Edward, by

following the sources of Edward Hall's *Union* and Raphael Holinshed's *Chronicles*[15] (which, in turn, were both derived from the distinctly unsympathetic *History of King Richard III* by Sir Thomas More),[16] and the whole of the first act actually covers a period of 12 years of action. This is obviously immensely frustrating to those who wish to see a more benign depiction of Richard's life. Even more so when, in spite of being called a 'lump of foul deformity',[17] 'unfit for any place but hell'[18] and only fit for a 'dungeon'[19] by Anne at the outset of their encounter in front of the corpse of her father-in-law (which bleeds afresh in the presence of his murderer), such is Richard's sophistry, charisma and cunning and her gullibility, weakness and fragile political state, that she eventually accepts his protestations of remorse ('and much it joys me too/To see you are become so penitent'[20]), as well as his protestations of love and agrees to wear his ring.

The audience scarcely has time to gasp – though most audiences do when the ring is placed on Anne's finger – before Richard revels in his cynicism:

> Was ever woman in this humour wooed?
> Was ever woman in this humour won?
> I'll have her, but I will not keep her long.
> What? I that killed her husband and his father,
> To take her in her heart's extremest hate,
> With curses in her mouth, tears in her eyes,
> The bleeding witness of my hatred by,
> Having God, her conscience and these bars against me,
> And I, no friends to back my suit withal
> But the plain devil and dissembling looks?
> And yet to win her? All the world to nothing![21]

With bombast as brilliant and as depraved as this, it is quite accurate of Langley to describe the persona of the Shakespearean Richard III as 'darkly seductive'.[22]

But he is repellent, too, and has to be, if as an Elizabethan playwright Shakespeare was to end the work on a note that would not offend the Tudor authorities. Richard's amorality is rammed home in the way that at the end of the breathless first act Clarence is starkly and pitiably murdered in front of the audience, believing almost to the end that his brother was working to save him from imprisonment rather than conspiring to bring about his brutal dispatch. But for Richard's evil to thrive, the credulity, myopia and political vulnerability of hierarchical figures such as Anne, Hastings and the Mayor need to weaken their judgment, and it is no coincidence that one of the first signs of his decline comes when the citizens of London, in spite of Richard having instructed Buckingham to infer 'the bastardy of Edward's children',[23] remain, according to Buckingham, resolutely unpersuaded by his claim to the crown:

> they spake not a word,
> But like dumb statues or breathing stones
> Stared each on other and looked deadly pale.[24]

As so often in Shakespeare's plays there is a subversive hint that the acuity of the masses is occasionally preferable to the moral indolence and self-serving nature of the ruling classes.

The character of Hastings is the epitome of this, and his inadvertent culpability for Richard's triumph has the most dire consequences for him personally and for the kingdom at large. No sooner has he pronounced on Richard's moral rectitude in Act 3 Scene 4:

> I think there's never a man in Christendom
> Can lesser hide his love or hate than he,
> For by his face straight shall you know his heart[25]

– than he is being urged a mere forty or so lines later by Ratcliffe (with almost comic impetuosity) to make haste for his death:

> Come, come dispatch. The Duke would be at dinner.
> Make short shrift. He longs to see your head.[26]

The short, pithy sentences of the morally indifferent adherents of Richard are linguistically juxtaposed against the ornate but completely ineffectual lament of the anagnorisis of Hastings:

> O, bloody Richard! Miserable England,
> I prophesy the fearfull'st time to thee
> That ever wretched age hath looked upon.[27]

Indeed, the more Richard outwits his foes, the starker his rhetoric becomes. This reaches its apotheosis when he states – with a clear foreshadowing of Macbeth's 'I am in blood/Stepp'd in so far that, should I wade no more,/Returning were as tedious as go o'er'[28] – that he is 'so far in blood that sin will pluck on sin', but such is his compelling deviousness up to the seizure of the crown that he is able to both ape the rhetoric of his opponents and pretend that he shares their moral compass. This is most spectacularly evident in Act 3 Scene 5, when Lovell and Ratcliffe bring him Hastings' head (which often occasions grotesque stage business). The nadir of his hypocrisy occurs when he outrageously dissembles his true feelings of triumph:

> So dear I loved the man that I must weep.
> I took him for the plainest harmless creature
> That breathed upon the earth a Christian.[29]

But, as with Macbeth, the actual seizure of the crown brings the usurper neither triumph nor ease, but ever-gathering problems. This clearly reinforces the Elizabethan message that the deposition of a monarch will inevitably cause a breach of nature, but it also highlights, as new historicists such as Kiernan Ryan rightly point out, the desire of Shakespeare to point out the complicity of a society that allows such over-reachers to prosper.

As soon as Richard literally ascends the throne in Act 4 Scene 2, the newly crowned king betrays his inevitable insecurity when he shares with Buckingham his anxiety that young Prince Edward, whose claim to the throne he has elbowed away, still lives:

> *King Richard*: Thus high, by thy advice
> And thy assistance is King Richard seated.
> But shall we wear these glories for a day?
> Or shall they last, and we rejoice in them?
> *Buckingham*: Still live they, and forever let them last.
> *King Richard*: Ah Buckingham, now do I play the touch
> To try if thou be current gold indeed:
> Young Edward lives; think now what I would speak.[30]

Uncharacteristically – or possibly with deliberate intent, having had enough of the murders – Buckingham is slow to pick up the hint, so Richard reverts to his bald, stark form of expression to reveal his real intentions:

> Cousin, thou was not wont to be so dull.
> Shall I be plain? I wish the bastards dead,
> And I would have it suddenly performed.[31]

Buckingham's hesitancy condemns him in Richard's eyes and he immediately starts the process of distancing, which will result in him ending the play in a state of near tragic isolation:

> The deep-revolving, witty Buckingham
> No more shall be the neighbour to my counsels.
> Hath he so long held out with me, untired,
> And stops he now for breath? Well, be it so.[32]

This will eventually lead to Richard refusing to honour his promise to grant Buckingham the reward of the Earldom of Hereford ('I am not in the giving vein today'[33]), which in turn prompts Buckingham's inevitable desertion for reasons of self-preservation:

> And is it thus? Repays he my deep service
> With such contempt? Made I him king for this?
> O, let me think on Hastings and be gone
> To Brecknock while my fearful head is on.[34]

By the time Richmond, the future Henry VII, has invaded England to challenge Richard for the crown, the King is diminished and painfully alone, followed under compulsion rather than through love or loyalty: 'He hath no friends but what are friends for fear', Blunt presciently advises Richmond.[35] He suffers terrifying dreams before the eve of the Battle of Bosworth and even his courage on the battlefield, as described by Catesby, simply emphasises an existential isolation:

> The King enacts more wonders than a man,
> Daring an opposite to every danger.
> His horse is slain, and all on foot he fights,
> Seeking for Richmond in the throat of death.[36]

At the end of the play Richard utters the desperate cry of terrifying isolation that has become a hallmark of the work – 'A horse, a horse, my kingdom for a horse!'[37] – and it is no coincidence that Richmond's triumphant shout – 'The day is ours; the bloody dog is dead' is in its alliterative baldness a linguistic echo of Richard at the height of his powers.[38]

Shakespeare's play makes no mention of any of the good works that the historical King Richard undertook during his reign. These include his interest in the law and justice, his establishing of the College of Arms and his foundation of colleges in both Oxford and Cambridge.

The conclusion of the play, too, makes it quite clear that his reign was a terrible aberration and his death necessary to correct a breach of nature and permit an end to the devastating Wars of the Roses. Richmond is adamant that his own regicide has brought a corrective unity:

> The true succeeders of each royal house,
> By God's fair ordinance conjoin together;
> And let their heirs, God, if Thy will be so,
> Enrich the time to come with smooth-faced peace,
> With smiling plenty and fair prosperous days.[39]

And the very final couplet uttered by the new Henry VII suggests God's approval for the deposition of the King:

> Now civil wounds are stopp'd; peace lives again.
> That she may long live here, God say amen.[40]

But as if this was not offensive enough for some Ricardians, even worse is the clear assertion in the play that Richard was personally responsible for the murder of the Princes in the Tower, perhaps the most controversial element of the historical Richard's entire reign. Whether Richard was actually implicated has been bitterly contested for over 500 years, and even Ricardians are split on the issue. Indeed, in their jointly authored book, Philippa Langley and Michael Jones offer a fascinating appendix where the former exonerates him of the charge and the latter considers his involvement to be likely.[41] They preface their debate by acknowledging that the:

> fate of the two sons of Edward IV, the Princes in the Tower, is one of the great mysteries of Richard III's reign and a controversy so powerful and compelling that it has often overshadowed all other aspects of Richard's life and kingship.[42]

Shakespeare's play brooks no equivocation, however, and this above all is why many Ricardians claim the work to be a simple piece of Tudor propaganda.

From the moment the stage Richard encounters the loquacious Prince Edward, he makes his intentions clear in a sinister aside: 'So wise so young, they say, do never live long'.[43] As we have seen, his explicit request to Buckingham to dispatch them could not be clearer and in full view of the audience Tyrrell commissions the murder of the two Princes by Dighton and Forrest following the king's request and then chillingly confirms its execution to the audience:

> The tyrannous and bloody act is done,
> The most arch deed of piteous massacre
> That ever yet this land was guilty of.[44]

In spite of this emotive and hyperbolic claim, it would be a mistake to see the stage Richard as a one-dimensional depiction of pure evil, however. If that were the case, some of the finest actors since the Second World War would not have been repeatedly drawn to the role. Two of the most famous stage depictions of Richard were performed at the New Theatre in 1944 and at the Old Vic in 1949 by Laurence Olivier. Part of the reason that these interpretations have gone down in theatre history as some of the most compelling ever produced is that he had the great good fortune to be reviewed by two of the finest theatre critics who ever wrote, Harold Hobson of the *Sunday Times* and Kenneth Tynan, soon to be of the *Observer*.

Tynan's and Hobson's styles were very different. Tynan favoured the coruscating and often cutting phrase, the brilliant impetuosity of youth and the locating of a production within the context of the time in which it was performed. Hobson, on the other hand, favoured encapsulating the atmosphere of a performance, the idiosyncrasy of middle age and the magnificence of a single, often overlooked, stage moment.

Tynan's 1944 review, therefore, is resplendent with scintillating phrases, such as 'Olivier's Richard eats into the memory like acid into metal, but the total impression is one of lightness and deftness'[45] and 'Craggy and beetlebrowed, Olivier's face is not especially mobile: he acts chiefly with his voice'.[46] But it is Tynan's description of the way Olivier portrays Richard's nihilistic, impotent and furious death that leaves the truly lasting impression:

> when the end approaches, his hoarse, strangled roar for a horse sums up all the impotent fury of a Machiavellian who must yield up his life and the fruits of his precise conspiring because of an accident of battle. To be vanquished by the ill luck of being unseated is a final ignominy to this enormous swindler. His broken sword clutched by the blade in both hands, he whirls, dreadfully constricted, and thrashes about with animal ferocity, writhing for absolute hate; he dies, arms and legs thrusting and kicking in savage, incommunicable agony, stabbing at air.[47]

Interestingly, although Hobson had been struck down by polio as a young boy, his review, magnificently entitled 'The Theatre Justified', highlighted the monstrous elements of Olivier's depiction:

From the moment when Sir Laurence's malign hunchback first hobbles across the stage, after entering through a door whose lock he avariciously fingers as if to see that decency and generosity have been shut out, this performance amuses, delights and astonishes. Mark how, in that opening soliloquy, by a waving of the arms, and a swaying of his crooked body, a mad nodding of his monstrously-nosed head, and a rapid quickening of his speech, he creates a choking, snaring forest: and mark, too, the effect, at once pitiful and revolting, when he drops on his knee to court the Lady Anne, and falls to one side in his deformity. These things prepare one for the greater achievements to come.

Hobson's greatest reviews tended to focus on particular stage moments that left a deep impression on him and Olivier provided him with two:

The first is after he has accepted the invitation of Buckingham and half a dozen seedy citizens to be king. He has been reading a prayer book in a window, and Buckingham thinks that he is a man whom he can manage. But when the last citizen has departed, Richard flings the book of devotion aside, leaps from the window, gains the centre of the stage, and extends his hand for Buckingham to kiss in a gesture of royalty horrible, evil, twisted and grotesque, but sickeningly powerful. The relationship between the two men changes on the instant without a word being spoken. With one astounded look Buckingham realizes that what he thought was a lizard was a rattlesnake.

The second encapsulates Olivier's famous athleticism and his willingness to push his body to the limits to create an extraordinary stage tableau. It is also the moment that made such a deep impression on Tynan, too:

[Olivier] leaves the fighting to Kean, but after Richmond, foot planted on his beast, has spiked him on his sword, he is tremendous. Convulsively freeing himself from his enemy, but still lying on his back, he performs what, with its shooting out of the legs like the darting tongue of the viper, can only be described as a horizontal dance. It is an amazing end to a memorable evening.[48]

For many people, even those who could not possibly have seen the stage version but may have witnessed Olivier's later film version, this remains the defining image of Richard III.

But is Shakespeare's depiction of Richard III, solidified and codified in popular culture by performances such as Olivier's, actually fair? Not so according to Ricardians, who offer the not unreasonable contention that Shakespeare's work is supremely political and that much of our perception of the king has been shaped by Tudor propaganda that inevitably contends that Richard's deposition was a necessary act in the light of the alleged depravities of his reign. They cite in particular the two accounts of Richard written by the priest, John Rous, who was a direct contemporary. The first account, written before Henry VII's accession, portrays a very different view of Richard from the historical norm:

> The most mighty Richard, all avarice set aside, ruled his subjects in his realm full commendably, punishing offenders of his laws, especially extortioners and oppressors of his commons, and cherishing those that were virtuous, by which discreet guiding he got great thanks from God and love of all his subjects, rich and poor, and great praise of the people of all other lands about him.⁴⁹

The second reverts to a type that we have long been familiar with, demonising Richard instead. This would be followed by the hostility of Polydore Vergil, Henry VII's court historian, and in particular, Sir Thomas More's *History of King Richard III*, written between 1513 and 1518. More's work is a key source for Shakespeare (as well as Hall's *Union* and Holinshed's *Chronicles*) and, as James R. Simeon points out, supplies some of the most vivid moments in the play, including 'King Edward's deathbed attempt to reconcile hostile factions (2.1); Buckingham's sleazy sophistry (3.1); Hastings' betrayal (3.4); the commoners' skepticism (3.6); Buckingham's failure to manufacture public support (3.7); Richard's staged reluctance to rule (3.7); his break with Buckingham (4.2); and his commissioning of Tyrrell to murder the princes (4.2)'.⁵⁰

More is also responsible for the articulation of the extreme physical deformities of the king, which are equated with moral depravity and which have passed into folklore. Richard is thus:

> little of stature, ill fetured of limes, croke backed, his left shoulder much higher than his right, hard fauoured of visage, and suche as is in states called warlye, in other menne otherwise. He was malicious, wrathfull, enuious, and from afore his birth, euer frowarde. It is for

trouth reported, that the Duches his mother had so muche a doe in her travaile, that shee coulde not bee deliuered of hym vncutte: and that hee came into the worlde with the feete forwarde, as menne bee borne outwarde, and (as the fame runneth) also not vntothed.[51]

We get the picture. And certainly by the time that Shakespeare came to write the play in the 1590s, More's colourful victor's account had become accepted fact and Richard was a familiar bogeyman. Shakespeare's play then cemented in people's mind the notion that Richard was a despot for the next 400 years or so.

So Shakespeare's play represented a well-known backdrop against which the dig to discover the remains of the king took place. Beginning on Saturday 25 August 2012, Richard Buckley, the lead archaeologist, drew on several sources to determine where his team should dig the first trench. Polydore Vergil – notwithstanding the fact that he might have been a less than objective observer – had stated that 'tasting what he had more often served to others, [the king] ended his life miserably, and finally he was buried among the Friars Minor of Leicester, in the choir'.[52] The friary had been decommissioned in 1538 as part of the dissolution of the monasteries and, although the grave had long gone, Christopher Wren's father had visited Robert Herrick, the owner of the site in the early seventeenth century and noted that in a part of the garden where the friary had been located he was shown 'a handsome Stone Pillar, three Foot high, with this inscription, "Here lies the Body of Richard III. some Time King of England"'.[53] Buckley therefore commissioned Leon Hunt to assemble as much extant information about the precise location of the buried Friary as he could, which together with the intuition and lobbying of Philippa Langley, determined the positioning of the first trench to be cut on a north/south axis of the social services car park.

What happened next is scarcely believable. The team almost immediately discovered human remains, which were quickly covered up to protect them from an imminent thunderstorm.[54] Having established that these were located 'on the division between the choir and the presbytery'[55] of the church of the Friary, osteoarchaeologist Jo Appleby started to excavate the remains on Wednesday 5 September. The skeleton lacked feet – perhaps sliced away during earlier construction work – and the body appeared to have been buried in haste, as there was neither shroud nor coffin.[56] What was manifestly apparent, however, was that the skeleton had a curvature of the spine, in other words 'severe scoliosis – abnormal side-to-side bending of the spine'.[57]

Over the next few months, the University of Leicester undertook extensive testing and research to confirm the identity of the skeleton as the king's and this is set out with clarity in the book, *The Bones of the King* (2015). It was established that the scoliosis would have left little visible sign as the 'S-shaped curve was well balanced, leaving the upper and lower spine still aligned, and his leg bones were well formed so he would not have walked with a limp'.[58] Whilst the right shoulder would have been a little higher than the left, it was contended that he could still have fought a battle and undertaken vigorous activity, a very different condition indeed from the monstrous hunchback of Shakespeare's play.[59]

But the most significant question was whether these actually were the remains of the last King of England to have died in battle. Two descendants of Richard III, Michael Ibsen and Wendy Duldig, were traced and their DNA matched, and so on 4 February 2013 the University of Leicester was able to announce to the world's media – media conditioned by Shakespeare's play and enthralled by the almost banal nature of the final resting place – that the remains had indeed been discovered. 'Bones under parking lot belonged to Richard III' (*New York Times*),[60] 'Skeleton Under Car Park England's Richard III' (*South China Morning Post*)[61] are just two of the headlines that testified to the global interest in this discovery.

The drama did not end there, of course. A year after the exhumation, 15 people who claimed to be living relatives of the king and calling themselves 'the Plantagenet Alliance' launched a legal challenge against the Ministry of Justice, which had granted the archaeological excavation licence to the University of Leicester, to try to get him to be buried not in Leicester Cathedral but in York Minister. The licence stipulated that the king's remains should be 'deposited in [Leicester's] Jewry Wall museum or else be reinterred at [the city's] St Martin's Cathedral or a burial ground in which interments may legally take place', but the petitioners argued that since Richard had been brought up in Middleham in Yorkshire and had allegedly claimed that he wished to be buried after his death in York, the Minster was the more appropriate resting place.[62] This conveniently ignored, of course, the fact that he had actually been born in Fotheringay, Northamptonshire, and that archaeological convention states that exhumed bodies are generally buried as close to their place of exhumation as is practicable.

It was not lost on many that there was an economic dimension to this row – 'Any [burial] site is likely to attract a significant tourist business', the *Guardian* wryly observed – and the issues pertaining to the economic impact of the discovery would now come increasingly to the fore.[63] The Plantagenet Alliance's claim for judicial review was dismissed in the High Court in May 2014, when the judges stated that it was time to give the king 'a dignified burial'.[64] Chris Grayling, the then Justice Secretary, was scathing about the challenge and interestingly framed his response in monetary terms:

> I am ... frustrated and angry that the Plantagenet Alliance – a group with tenuous claims to being relatives of Richard III – have taken up so much time and public money. This case, brought by a shell company set up by the Alliance to avoid paying legal costs, is an example of exactly why the Government is bringing forward a package of reforms to the judicial review process.[65]

The way was now clear for the king to be reinterred at a Service of Reinterment in Leicester Cathedral on 26 March 2015, an event I was most fortunate to attend myself in my capacity as Vice-Chancellor of De Montfort University. There had been much speculation as to whether a senior member of the Royal Family would attend and perhaps it was a sign of the ongoing nervousness about the persona of Richard III that a relatively junior member, the Countess of Wessex, was the presiding Royal. The Queen, nevertheless, sent a message that was unequivocal in its recognition of the importance of the day:

> The reinterment of King Richard III is an event of great national and international significance. Today we recognize a King who lived through turbulent times and whose Christian faith sustained him in life and death. The discovery of his remains in Leicester has been described as one of the most significant archaeological finds in this country's history.[66]

– and the service itself, broadcast live by Channel 4, was an impressive juxtaposition of the medieval rite of burial with a reading by Benedict Cumberbatch (and a third cousin, 16 times removed of King Richard III) of a specially composed poem by the Poet Laureate, Carol Ann Duffy. His reading of the first three lines:

> My bones, scripted in light, upon cold soil,
> a human braille. My skull, scarred by a crown,
> emptied of history.[67]

– seemed particularly portentous.

Although the Looking for Richard team and the University of Leicester team processed into the cathedral together, relations appeared to the outside world to be strained when John Ashdown-Hill was caught on camera theatrically rolling his eyes during the service. The *Daily Express* headline was suitably provocative: 'Did "rude" Richard III historian roll his eyes at reburial because HE got no mention?'.[68] Ashdown-Hill later explained in an interview with Krishnan Guru-Murthy of Channel 4 that he had been dismayed by what he claimed were factual errors in the service and his sense that the contribution of the Looking for Richard team had been deliberately diminished (not something that was apparent to me during the service and subsequent television coverage, I should add).[69]

His bitterness reached its apotheosis when he published his book, *The Mythology of Richard III* in 2015. Stating that the Looking for Richard team was 'the body ultimately responsible for the discovery of the remains',[70] he argued that 'many aspects of the written agreement were not honoured by ULAS'[71] and tendentiously claimed that Buckley was not often on site, because he was 'reconstructing his own kitchen'.[72] Whilst the general public had had some inkling of these tensions between the exhumation and the reinterment when there was a dispute as to whether Richard's bones should remain in the university's laboratory or be placed in a Catholic place of repose, the revelation of Ashdown-Hill's dyspepsia was a surprise. Further charges that he levelled included the accusation that members of the Looking For Richard team were excluded from press conferences,[73] the temporary exhibition about the discovery of the body at St Martin's excluded mention of Looking For Richard, the eventual Visitor Centre did not 'accurately reflect' their role,[74] the cathedral was too negative about Richard[75] and, most extraordinarily, that the University of Leicester 'aimed at attempting to boost public perception of its role in the discovery of Richard III's remains at my expense'.[76]

Whatever the validity of these slightly hysterical claims (and it should be pointed out that both Ashdown-Hill and Langley were awarded MBEs for being 'instrumental in the discovery of Richard III's remains', according to the BBC),[77] they contributed yet another layer to the atmosphere of controversy that surrounded Richard III. As if the fiercely debated events of his life, the domineering impression created by Shakespeare's play and extraordinary discovery under a car park were not enough, we now had an ongoing controversy about the nature of his exhumation. And all of this added to the undoubted economic impact to Leicester of the discovery of the remains in August 2012, a point Ashdown-Hill rather archly makes when he observes:

> there can be very little doubt that, since the discovery of his remains in August 2012, Leicester City Council has perceived Richard III as a potentially huge source of income, leading the mayor of Leicester to announce that only over his dead body would the king's bones be removed from the city.[78]

Whether one agrees with his claim that there is an 'ongoing process of mythologizing the story of the discovery',[79] it is indisputable that Richard III 'has become a new source of income for Leicester in various ways'[80] and it is useful to conclude this chapter by examining how the economic impact of Richard III's discovery has manifested itself.

Nobody could dispute that the increased number of visitors and their attendant economic activity in relation to transport, restaurants, shopping and hotel stays has created significant additional income for the city. This can be evidenced in a number of ways. Shortly after the announcement was made that Richard had been discovered, a small temporary exhibition centre was established in the Guildhall in February 2013 to tell the story of the discovery, set Richard's life in context and display a replica of the skeleton. People flocked to see it, with over 150,000 visitors entering the rather cramped venue by the end of the year. The day that I visited in March 2013 there were scores of people clustered around the exhibits from all over the world and there was an air of palpable excitement, curiosity and even reverence. With Shakespeare's depiction of the king looming over the storyboards, it was an immediate sign of the renewed interest in Richard, the indelible link with the playwright and the potential for significant tourist business for Leicester.

Following news of the High Court ruling in May 2014, Leicester Cathedral swiftly spent £2.5m to restore its gardens, conscious that the eyes of the world would be upon it when his remains were finally laid to rest.[81] With commendable prescience, Sir Peter Soulsby, the elected City Mayor of Leicester, secured in November 2012 the freehold of the former Alderman Newton school (last used as Leicester Grammar School in 2008), which was directly adjacent to the by now world-famous car park, to establish a permanent Visitors Centre at a cost of £4 million. This was opened on 24 July 2014 and during the first month alone 10,000 people visited the centre.[82] And the Diocese of Leicester launched a fundraising campaign to reorder the Cathedral and build the tomb at an eventual cost of £2.54 m (£2 m of which was eventually raised through donations).[83]

Hotels, restaurants and bars have all reported additional revenue from increased numbers of visitors, and local traders have all got in on the act, with Richard III spectacles, chocolates and posters all making variously fleeting appearances. The street furniture of the city centre has been significantly improved, the area around the Cathedral restyled in a most appealing way and throughout the city centre high-quality information boards have been installed by the City Council to tell the story not just of Richard's association with Leicester (both before and after Bosworth) but of the local history of the area.

All of this activity has created a significant economic impact, but how big has that actually been? In the spring of 2015, the City Council commissioned Focus Consultants to undertake an economic impact study of the discovery of Richard III from the period of his exhumation in September 2012 to the week before his reinterment at the end of March 2015 (accepting that that event would generate its own significant impact). Focus established that visitor numbers to the city had increased by 5% (more than 600,000 people), the additional visitor spend in Leicester in that period was £54.5 m and that an additional 1000 jobs had been created.[84] They also discovered that £4.5 m of extra impact had been generated by the week of reinterment activities alone, 8,000 volunteering hours equated to a benefit of £144,000 and visitor numbers to the Bosworth Battlefield visitor centre had increased by 40%. The cost of the reinterment had been £484,000 (£272,000 for the City Council and £212,000 for the County Council), which was an excellent return on investment by any calculation.[85] This articulated what so many of us who live in Leicester have witnessed over the past three years, namely an increasing international profile for the city, which has palpably resulted in an influx of visitors and a previously unseen dynamism. This is most evident in the quiet daily queues to visit Richard's dignified and reposeful tomb.

Michael Jones argues that 'Shakespeare, more than any other, has shaped our reaction to this deeply controversial monarch'.[86] His contested portrait of the king now juxtaposed against the reality of his discovery clearly contributes to the undeniable economic impact that his interment is bringing to the city of Leicester. The fact that his play provides such a whetstone to Ricardians merely adds to our fascination and further stimulates people's desire to get closer to the king. That this is directly causing economic benefit is made manifest when you pull into Leicester train station and see a huge billboard advertising the new King Richard III Visitor Centre. Beneath the motif of a crown underpinned by the words 'Dignity, Death and Discovery' is the pitch made to entice people in: 'Discover the **controversial** [my emphasis] story of the last English king to die in battle and the first to be DNA tested. www.kriii.com'.

Thanks to Shakespeare, controversy clearly sells.

Postscript

As the Vice-Chancellor of De Montfort University (DMU) in Leicester, a friend of the University of Leicester, whose archaeological skill and scientific expertise in the discovery is clear for everyone to see, and an admirer of the devotion of Philippa Langley and the persistence of the Looking for Richard project, I cannot claim to be a wholly disinterested observer. This is perhaps most manifest in the fact that in the basement of the Hawthorn building of the Faculty of Health and Life Sciences at DMU lie the two remaining arches of the medieval Church of the Annunciation, where Richard's body is likely to have lain for two days immediately after his death in battle, before being transferred to Greyfriars and presumably a somewhat hasty burial.[87]

Shortly after the University of Leicester had made their announcement to the world in February 2013, DMU began to notice an increasing number of visitors to the campus who wished to see the arches. Staff and students were curious, too. That they were not accessible to the public in any meaningful way was clearly very frustrating to them, so a decision was taken to create a small Heritage Centre which could tell the history of the university, the history of the surrounding area of the Newarke and the context of the arches which formed part of the original crypt of the church.

John Ashdown-Hill argues that universities have 'been transformed into commercial, money-seeking, competitive bodies',[88] and whilst it is true that we need to be financially sustainable and recruit the highest calibre students given that the vast majority of our income now comes from student tuition fees, the Heritage Centre was not created to secure a new income stream, but to recognise our responsibilities as custodians of these architectural remains and to allow them to be safely and enjoyably viewed.

The Heritage Centre was designed by students from Graphic Design, Interior Design and Architecture and, following careful cleaning of the arches, was opened to some acclaim on 12 March 2015. It is now sought out by many visitors drawn to Leicester to absorb as much as they can of the life and death of Richard III and its impact is therefore as much social, cultural and educational as it is economic. Rather like, in fact, the impact of the magnificent and much larger discovery by *both* the University of Leicester and the Looking for Richard team.

Notes

1. The term generally given to people who believe that Richard III's posthumous reputation has been unfairly traduced.
2. Philippa Langley and Michael Jones (2013) *The Search for Richard III* (London: John Murray), p. xi.
3. Langley and Jones, p. 14.
4. The Greyfriars Research Team with Maev Kennedy and Lin Foxhall (2015) *The Bones of a King: Richard III Rediscovered* (Chichester: Wiley), p. 6.
5. Kennedy and Foxhall, p. 6.
6. Langley and Jones, pp. 5–6.
7. Langley and Jones, p. xi.
8. William Shakespeare (2009) *Richard III*, ed. James R. Simeon (London: Bloomsbury), 1.1.1–4, pp.133–4.
9. Shakespeare, *Richard III*, 5.4.1.
10. Shakespeare, *Richard III*, 1.1.18–27.
11. Shakespeare, *Richard III*, 1.1.28–31.
12. Shakespeare, *Richard III*, 1.1.118–120.
13. Shakespeare, *Richard III*, 1.1.145–6.
14. Shakespeare, *Richard III*, 1.1.154–6.
15. Shakespeare, *Richard III*, footnote 154, p.147.
16. Shakespeare, *Richard III*, p. 3.
17. Shakespeare, *Richard III*, 1.2.57.
18. Shakespeare, *Richard III*, 1.2.111.
19. Shakespeare, *Richard III*, 1.2.113.
20. Shakespeare, *Richard III*, 1.2.222–3.
21. Shakespeare, *Richard III*, 1.2.230–40.
22. Langley and Jones, p. ix.
23. Shakespeare, *Richard III*, 3.5.75.
24. Shakespeare, *Richard III*, 3.7.24–6.
25. Shakespeare, *Richard III*, 3.4.51–3.
26. Shakespeare, *Richard III*, 3.4.93–4.
27. Shakespeare, *Richard III*, 3.4.102–4.
28. William Shakespeare (1986) *Macbeth*, ed. Kenneth Muir (London: Methuen), 3.4.135–7.
29. Shakespeare, *Richard III*, 3.5.24–6.
30. Shakespeare, *Richard III*, 4.2.3–10.
31. Shakespeare, *Richard III*, 4.2.17–19.
32. Shakespeare, *Richard III*, 4.2.42–5.
33. Shakespeare, *Richard III*, 4.2.114.
34. Shakespeare, *Richard III*, 4.2.117–20.
35. Shakespeare, *Richard III*, 5.3.20.
36. Shakespeare, *Richard III*, 5.4.2–5.

37. Shakespeare, *Richard III*, 5.4.7.
38. Shakespeare, *Richard III*, 5.5.2.
39. Shakespeare, *Richard III*, 5.5.30–34.
40. Shakespeare, *Richard III*, 5.5.40–1.
41. Langley and Jones, pp. 257–73.
42. Langley and Jones, p. 257.
43. Shakespeare, *Richard III*, 3.1.79.
44. Shakespeare, *Richard III*, 4.3.1–3.
45. Kenneth Tynan (1950) 'Laurence Olivier's *Richard III*' from *He That Plays The King* in Dominic Shellard (ed.) (2007) *Kenneth Tynan Theatre Writings* (London: Nick Hern Books), p. 3.
46. Tynan, p. 4.
47. Tynan, p. 6.
48. Harold Hobson (1949) 'The Theatre Justified' *Sunday Times*, 30 January.
49. Langley and Jones, p. 40.
50. Shakespeare, *Richard III*, p. 54.
51. Shakespeare, *Richard III*, pp.57–8.
52. Kennedy and Foxhall, p. 10.
53. Kennedy and Foxhall, p. 7.
54. Kennedy and Foxhall, p. 175.
55. Kennedy and Foxhall, p. 19.
56. Kennedy and Foxhall, p. 21.
57. Kennedy and Foxhall, p. 71.
58. Kennedy and Foxhall, pp. 72–3.
59. Kennedy and Foxhall, p. 73.
60. 4 February 2013.
61. 5 February 2013.
62. 'Richard III's distant relatives threaten legal challenge over burial', *Guardian*, 26 March 2013.
63. *Guardian*, 26 March 2013.
64. 'Richard of York's relatives gave battle in vain' *Daily Mail*, 24 May 2014.
65. *Daily Mail*, 24 May 2014.
66. Service Booklet for the Service of Reinterment.
67. Service Booklet.
68. *Daily Express*, 25 March 2015.
69. *Daily Express*, 25 March 2015.
70. John Ashdown-Hill (2015) *The Mythology of Richard III* (Stroud: Amberley), p. 143.
71. Ashdown-Hill, p. 144.
72. Ashdown-Hill, p. 144.
73. Ashdown-Hill, p. 152.
74. Ashdown-Hill, p. 153.
75. Ashdown-Hill, p. 154.
76. Ashdown-Hill, p. 155.
77. http://www.bbc.co.uk/news/uk-england-leicestershire-33121465, date accessed 6 November 2015.
78. Ashdown-Hill, p. 10.
79. Ashdown-Hill, p. 157.
80. Ashdown-Hill, p. 163.

81. *Leicester Mercury*, 2 November 2013.
82. http://www.kriii.com/celebrating-our-10000th-visitor/, date accessed 20 October 2015.
83. www.goleicestershire.com/news/RichardIIIEffectBringsAlmost60Million.aspx, date accessed 6 November 2015.
84. 'The Discovery of King Richard III in Leicester: The Economic Impact of Richard III on the Tourism and Visitor Economy in the period from Discovery to the Re-interment (September 2012 to March 20th 2015), www.focus-consultants.co.uk, p. 2, date accessed 6 November 2015.
85. www.goleicestershire.com/news/RichardIIIEffectBringsAlmost60Million.aspx, date accessed 6 November 2015.
86. Langley and Jones, p. 34.
87. Certainly the Chairman of the Richard III Society, Phil Stone, believes this to be the case in a letter to myself dated 5 October 2015: 'It is, indeed, a historical fact that the king's body was displayed in the Church of the Annunciation to show the populace that he was dead and there was no point in raising a rebellion in his name against Henry Tudor'.
88. Ashdown-Hill, p. 169.

Select Bibliography

Ashdown-Hill, John (2015) *The Mythology of Richard III* (Stroud: Amberley).

Kennedy, Maev and Lin Foxhall (2015) *The Bones of a King: Richard III Rediscovered* (Chichester: Wiley).

Langley, Philippa and Michael Jones (2013) *The Search for Richard III* (London: John Murray).

Shakespeare, William (2009) *Richard III*, ed. James R. Simeon (London: Bloomsbury).

8
Shakespeare Is 'GREAT'

Conrad Bird, Jason Eliadis and Harvey Scriven

'Be not afraid of greatness' (*Twelfth Night*, 2.5.126).[1]

While William Shakespeare has had over 400 years to nurture and grow his globally iconic and emblematic brand, the UK Government's highly innovative *GREAT Britain Campaign* ('GREAT') has had just four. Yet, by showcasing the very best the UK has to offer the world in terms of trade, investment, tourism, education and culture, the impact that GREAT has had already on its target markets has been highly significant, in terms of both economic gain and soft power influence. At the heart of GREAT's global message is its focus on promoting UK leadership and expertise in creativity as a way of differentiating the nation against key competitors such as Germany, France and Italy. To achieve this, the GREAT campaign has worked in close partnership with many of the UK's most iconic corporate and personal brands including Jaguar Land Rover, James Bond, British Airways, Burberry, David Beckham and the Royal Family. Given Shakespeare's contemporary relevance globally as a cultural and soft power asset for the UK, it was inevitable that he would also become part of the GREAT campaign and, with the ongoing global celebrations of his key anniversaries, the bard from Stratford-upon-Avon is taking centre stage. His cultural significance globally – indeed his ability to take stories from overseas, add creative value to them and then 'export' them again to the world – continues to have a resonance for modern-day UK business.

Strategic context to GREAT

In today's globalised economy, where consumers have an increasing choice of locations to visit, invest in, trade with or study in, it is essential that a country presents itself as positively as possible to its existing and future target markets, for both economic gain and soft power influence. This process is both highly challenging and long-term, and can often depend as much on intangible factors, such as perception and emotion, as it does on reality and fact. Altering individual opinions, particularly those in another country, can be extremely complex – personal history, individual bias or a lack of knowledge may mean that deeply entrenched opinions are held about a particular location or culture that can be difficult to change. Yet evidence from international research shows increasingly that the more one country trusts another country, the more those countries will trade and invest with each other. For example, the British Council found that 'increased levels of trust in people in the UK are associated with a significantly increased level of interest in opportunities for business and trade with the UK',[2] while an important academic study by Paul Dekker et al. found that a 1% increase in 'mutual trust' between countries correlated to an increase in foreign direct investment stock of almost 3%.[3] In building trust for the long term, it is familiarity – and typically *cultural* familiarity – that is essential, so 'national ownership' of cultural icons already shared by the world, such as Shakespeare, is particularly valuable. However, for governments seeking to influence others proactively, relying in isolation on a long-term 'trust' approach to secure economic growth is too passive, but by *combining* this approach with shorter-term, intensive and carefully targeted strategies that raise positive profile, significantly increased levels of trade, investment, tourism and influence can be generated. Indeed, it is clear that countries worldwide are gradually beginning to recognise the benefits of taking an *integrated* and proactive approach to marketing themselves to the world – a premise that drove the original thinking behind the establishment of the 'GREAT Britain' campaign.

The GREAT Britain Campaign

'The GREAT Britain campaign ... is probably the best example that I have come across of an integrated campaign for a Government and a country across the world.'

Sir Martin Sorrell, Chief Executive Officer,
WPP Group (May 2015)

GREAT is the UK Government's most ambitious international marketing campaign ever – the results have been spectacular, with audited economic benefits of over £2 billion already achieved for the UK economy from increased tourism, education, trade and investment. First announced by Prime Minister David Cameron in New York in September 2011, GREAT was officially launched in February 2012 to take advantage of the Queen's Diamond Jubilee celebrations and the 2012 London Olympics and Paralympics, when the eyes of the world would be firmly fixed on the country. The strategic intention from the outset was clear – the campaign's vision at its launch, and which remains in place today, was 'to inspire the world to think and feel differently about Great Britain now and in the future, demonstrating that we are the best nation to visit, invest in, trade with and study in'. Led and strategically coordinated at the highest level in government through the Prime Minister's Office at Number 10 Downing Street, GREAT has enabled the government for the first time to unify the international promotion efforts of currently 17 key departments and public sector organisations, including the Foreign & Commonwealth Office, UK Trade & Investment, British Council, VisitBritain and VisitEngland.[4] By using the same creative branding across all UK promotional activity overseas, GREAT's partner organisations have successfully implemented an innovative global programme of strategic and tactical marketing initiatives.

Although ground-breaking in itself, ensuring that key government organisations were part of a coordinated and aligned marketing framework was just the first stage in the process of promoting the UK's 'message' more effectively to the world. The next step was to understand what was driving international markets and key decision-makers in detail, and then to determine how the UK could influence them more successfully than ever before. Following comprehensive international customer research and analysis, the campaign developed specific themes or 'pillars' to articulate the UK proposition precisely to overseas audiences – these pillars included overarching themes associated with UK excellence, such as 'Creativity is GREAT', 'Education is GREAT' and 'Culture is GREAT', that allowed the campaign to deliver carefully selected marketing messages to its target sectors and markets. It was evident to GREAT's leadership from the start that UK cultural icons such as Shakespeare could play an important cross-pillar role to support and enhance the campaign's objectives. This measured approach to strategic marketing and communications has proven incredibly successful. For example, the Foreign & Commonwealth Office currently uses the GREAT brand in 96% of its diplomatic posts, while UK Trade & Investment applies the brand in all of its trade and investment activities worldwide. The economic benefits of integrated consistency are substantial, with independent research[5] showing that GREAT consistently has a positive uplift of around 15% on the buying actions of the UK's target decision-makers in the fields of international trade, investment, education and tourism. Combined, this means that GREAT is delivering a strong and proven return for the UK economy, significantly exceeding the cost of the campaign by a factor of more than 20.

With British culture regarded as a world-class asset and a key mechanism in generating familiarity, trust and influence, it was recognised at the launch of GREAT that innovation and creativity would need to be at the heart of the campaign. This approach was reinforced by international market research undertaken by the British Council, GREAT's education lead partner, which found that 'cultural and historic attractions' were perceived as being the most attractive characteristic of the UK by international audiences, with UK 'arts', 'history' and 'people' also rated highly (see Figure 8.1).

Further research was conducted by VisitBritain, GREAT's tourism lead partner, to understand the influence that UK culture and heritage had on the UK's top three markets for *inbound* tourists – specifically visitors from France, Germany and the USA, who represent approximately one-third of all international tourist visits to the UK. The results confirmed that 'culture' and 'heritage' were key factors in determining where tourists choose to visit, underpinning previous research by VisitBritain which showed that approximately half of all tourists go to castles or historic houses when visiting the UK, with 15% attending a ballet, a musical or the theatre. Indeed, heritage-based tourism is worth over £26 billion to the UK and directly supports over 740,000 jobs.[6]

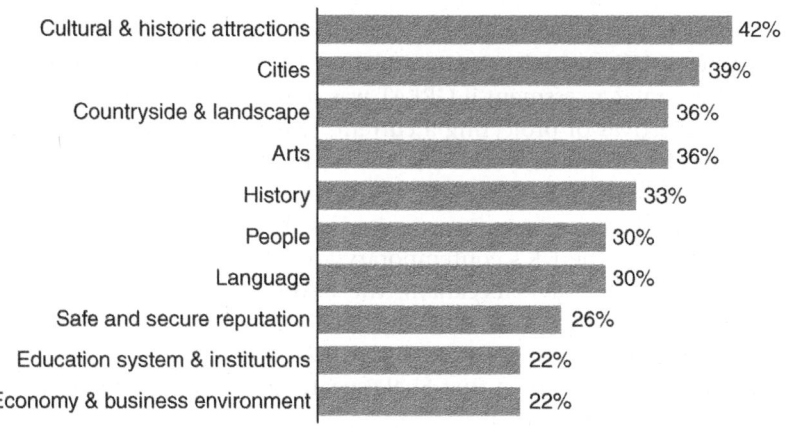

Figure 8.1   What makes the UK attractive to international audiences?
Source: The British Council (2014).

Combining GREAT and Shakespeare

The world's best-known playwright, William Shakespeare, is the focus of a highly successful international industry and an unparalleled exporter of British values, culture and creativity. His work has been translated into over 80 languages worldwide and the Royal Shakespeare Company sells 1.8 million tickets annually for its performances, while the current 'Globe to Globe' *Hamlet* tour being performed by Shakespeare's Globe has already played to over 100,000 people in 141 countries and has the ambitious plan of performing in every country in the world over a two-year period.[7] In the UK, Stratford-upon-Avon attracts over five million visitors each year, generating revenues worth over £335 million for the local economy, with Shakespeare's 'Birthplace' and other local Shakespeare family homes expected to attract 1.2 million visitors in 2016.[8] The underlying generational influence that Shakespeare has in building global familiarity and trust in UK culture will undoubtedly continue, with research from the Royal Shakespeare Company and the British Council finding that Shakespeare's work is studied by half of the world's schoolchildren[9] – indeed, in countries as diverse as the USA, Russia, China, India, Brazil, Mexico, Nigeria and Poland, children study up to three Shakespearean plays in their own language.

As Shakespeare is shared by the world, he potentially presented a far more powerful icon for GREAT to work with than people, products or companies that were just quintessentially British. However, for the leadership of the GREAT campaign it was essential to understand whether, despite his global ubiquity, Shakespeare was associated more with values from the past and might therefore be less relevant to conveying a message of UK creativity and culture for the present and the future. This was a vital assessment if GREAT was to meet its economic and soft power objectives of projecting a current, relevant and forward-looking image of the UK to the world. The answer to this strategic question was striking – international research[10] undertaken by the British Council found that Shakespeare was recognised as the person most frequently associated with the UK's contemporary arts and culture, well ahead of Queen Elizabeth, David Beckham, the Beatles and the UK's strongest contemporary author, J. K. Rowling[11] (the scale of the survey results is illustrated in the 'word cloud' in Figure 8.2).

The research confirmed that Shakespeare provides a strong and current connection between the UK and cultures around the world – he is British and is recognised, respected and valued by all nations. His core value to the international promotional efforts of the GREAT campaign

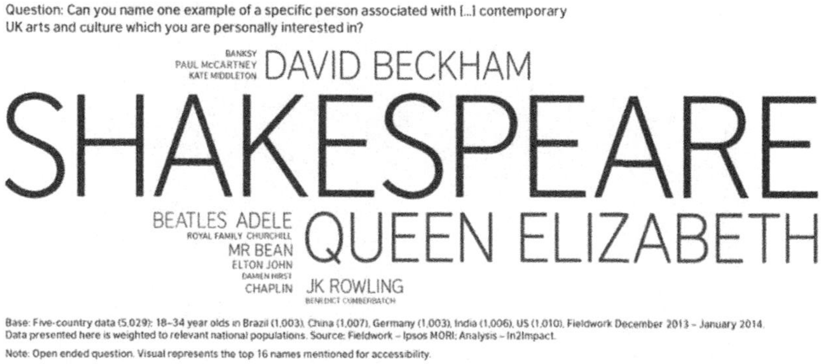

Question: Can you name one example of a specific person associated with [...] contemporary
UK arts and culture which you are personally interested in?

BANKSY
PAUL McCARTNEY DAVID BECKHAM
KATE MIDDLETON

SHAKESPEARE

BEATLES ADELE
ROYAL FAMILY CHURCHILL
MR BEAN QUEEN ELIZABETH
ELTON JOHN
DAMIEN HIRST
CHAPLIN JK ROWLING
BENEDICT CUMBERBATCH

Base: Five-country data (5,029): 18–34 year olds in Brazil (1,003), China (1,007), Germany (1,003), India (1,006), US (1,010). Fieldwork December 2013 – January 2014.
Data presented here is weighted to relevant national populations. Source: Fieldwork – Ipsos MORI; Analysis – In2Impact.
Note: Open ended question. Visual represents the top 16 names mentioned for accessibility.

Figure 8.2   Who is the most associated with contemporary UK arts and culture?
Source: The British Council (2014).

was clearly evident, so his brand became formally integrated into the campaign and began to play an important role in promoting the UK. Shakespeare's 'cultural capital' continues to be as relevant today as it has been over the last four centuries – through GREAT, his soft power value for the UK is being applied to initiatives that deliver direct economic benefits through increased tourism and high-quality international students, while enhancing the UK's reputation with influential stakeholders, businesses and diplomatic networks.

Shakespeare and GREAT tourism

The tourism sector is a highly valuable market for the UK economy, worth over £125 billion and supporting over three million jobs. International tourists are a vital market segment, spending over £21 billion each year in the UK with a forecast annual growth rate of over 6% to 2025.[12] Tasked with increasing the UK's share of international tourism, VisitBritain uses Shakespeare as one of its key cultural assets to attract the interest of tourists through carefully targeted marketing initiatives (see Figure 8.3). These include collaborations with the Royal Shakespeare Company in New York and Canada to target the North American travel trade, and media familiarisation visits to 'Shakespeare's England' for representatives of the international travel industry based in key markets globally. VisitBritain also uses Shakespeare throughout its digital marketing strategies by undertaking innovative email marketing campaigns to directly promote Shakespeare-related UK tourism, placing editorials on global travel media channels such as Yahoo!, and providing dedicated

Figure 8.3   An example of VisitBritain's marketing collateral, 2015
Source: © GREAT Britain campaign.

content for cultural tourists such as guides to Stratford-upon-Avon[13], the 'Best Shakespeare' attractions and 'Shakespeare's Globe'.

VisitEngland, the English domestic tourism promotional agency, is also using Shakespeare as an important component of its marketing strategy. One of its most innovative marketing initiatives to date has been to feature the popular English contemporary characters 'Wallace and Gromit' visiting the Royal Shakespeare Company in Stratford-upon-Avon as part of an overall 'Holidays at Home are GREAT' campaign which generated over £80 million of incremental tourism expenditure for the UK economy. In addition, given the growing requirement for excellence in digital tourism marketing, VisitEngland has developed a dedicated promotional website[14] to encourage tourists to visit Stratford-upon-Avon and its surrounding areas, as well as running an award-winning social media campaign for people to vote for England's most famous internationally recognised person or place – won, unsurprisingly, by Shakespeare!

Shakespeare and GREAT education

In the field of education, Shakespeare has also been used extensively by the GREAT campaign to encourage international students to study in the UK or to learn English. The international education market is fiercely competitive, with countries worldwide seeking to attract high fee-paying internationally mobile students – indeed, the British Council estimates that an overseas university student is worth approximately £25,000 to the UK economy for each academic year studied. The UK is well positioned in the global education market, with education exports of over £17.5 billion each year, the vast majority of which come from the 430,000 international students studying in the UK from countries as diverse as the USA, China, India, Nigeria, Nepal, Malaysia and Saudi Arabia. The British Council, which is responsible for promoting the UK education offer internationally, has undertaken various GREAT marketing activities, including creating 'Shakespeare-inspired' promotional materials to encourage international students to study English literature at a UK university and tailored lesson plans that focus on using idioms originating from Shakespeare's work – these are used extensively by the British Council's network of over 80 English language learning centres in 49 countries. Shakespeare has also taken centre stage in an innovative 'Learn English' app that includes 'Literature is GREAT' videos that highlight his work and legacy – in just 12 months, the app was downloaded by over 300,000 people, a third of whom were in China.

Shakespeare and GREAT diplomacy

Shakespeare's name and brand has not only been used to generate hard and immediate economic returns for the UK from tourism and education. Significantly, the UK's international diplomatic and commercial network – led and coordinated by the Foreign & Commonwealth Office, working closely with the British Council – has placed Shakespeare at the heart of hundreds of initiatives worldwide to enhance the UK's reputation and generate long-term relationships, trust and influence. For example, in Russia – a strategically crucial relationship for the UK – themed initiatives have included performances by the Royal Shakespeare Company in Moscow, a recitation of Shakespeare's plays at the Novaya Opera to celebrate the 450th anniversary of Shakespeare's birth, performances by Shakespeare's Globe at the Mayakovsky Theatre in Moscow as part of the celebrated Chekhov International Festival, and various events to celebrate the UK–Russia year of culture, including lectures in Moscow and St Petersburg which were attended by 1,700 participants and reached a further 100,000 people online.

In the Middle East, UK diplomatic relations were strengthened through a series of Shakespeare-themed cultural and economic activities during the 'Qatar–UK Year of Culture' which included a 'Shakespeare in Translation' panel discussion, a *Romeo and Juliet* production by Shakespeare's Globe, a performance of *Macbeth* by the Doha Players at Hamad bin Khalifa University, and performances of *Othello* by Qatari actors as part of the 'Sam Wanamaker Festival'. Shakespeare has also been used in other parts of the world to advance UK diplomacy and soft power relations. For example, in South America a 'Dining with Shakespeare' event was hosted by the UK Ambassador in Bolivia with guests that included media and local arts personalities, while in the southern African country of Botswana a showcase of UK talent, innovation and culture was held to expose local audiences to Shakespeare's work and provide local educators with new teaching tools. Even in Outer Mongolia, Shakespeare has played an important role, with a 'Shakespeare in Ulaanbaatar' initiative being held by the British Embassy and the Mongolian State Academic Theatre of Drama to host the Shakespeare Globe's *Hamlet* tour, with guests including government ministers, ambassadors, members of Parliament, alumni and several prominent Mongolian and British businesses – and with substantial funds raised for the UK-based charity 'Go Help' that supports local communities across central Asia to access education and healthcare services. UK Ambassadors have even taken a starring role themselves, with the Ambassador to the Czech Republic securing the part of Olivia in a local production of *Twelfth Night*, with her eight performances generating huge publicity across Prague!

Capitalising on Shakespeare's anniversary in 2016

The success of the GREAT campaign since its launch proves the efficacy of its strategy of capitalising on opportunities when the eyes of the world are on the UK – the global profile generated by events such as the 2012 London Olympics and Paralympics, the Queen's Jubilee and more recently the 2015 Rugby World Cup, has enabled GREAT to create additional economic benefits for the UK and enhance its international reputation. In 2016, the global 'moment' belongs to Shakespeare and the attention of the world will once again be on the UK. To maximise this opportunity, the UK government has launched a unique global programme known as 'Shakespeare Lives in 2016' which is being led by the British Council and GREAT, and involves partners such as the BBC, the BFI, the National Theatre, Education UK, the Royal Shakespeare Company, the 'Shakespeare 400' consortium, the Shakespeare Birthplace Trust and Shakespeare's Globe. Shakespeare Lives celebrates Shakespeare's canon and his influence on culture, education and society on the 400th anniversary of his death, and is an opportunity for millions of people in over 140 countries to participate actively in a unique digital collaboration and to experience Shakespeare's works through brand new productions. By actively creating opportunities to share and celebrate Shakespeare's anniversary with the world, the Shakespeare Lives programme is not only helping the UK to generate and reinforce soft power values of familiarity and trust, it is also aiming to secure hard returns of at least £60 million for the UK economy through the attraction of overseas students to study at UK universities, encouraging more tourists to visit, persuading more international companies to invest in the UK and increasing trade opportunities.

The programme involves a unique mass participation digital campaign called 'Play Your Part' based on Shakespeare's work, as well as performances on stage and film, exhibitions, public readings, debates and the provision of educational resources for classrooms and English language learners, both in the UK and internationally. The British Council and BBC Arts are collaborating with key cultural partners to showcase the best of modern British Shakespeare for international audiences, including an online 'Shakespeare Day Live' on 23 April 2016 and a six-month online festival. National Theatre Live Shakespeare films will also be made available globally alongside screenings of historically acclaimed and ground-breaking contemporary Shakespeare productions, including the international premiere of the film of Manchester Royal Exchange Theatre's *Hamlet*. Shakespeare Lives is also supporting a global touring programme of 20 interpretations of Shakespeare's works for the cinema from the BFI National Archive, including 'Silent Shakespeare', Laurence Olivier's *Hamlet*, Franco Zeffirelli's *Romeo and Juliet* and *Richard III* starring Ian

McKellen. In addition, the programme has established a partnership with UK-based charity Voluntary Services Overseas to use the power of Shakespeare's anniversary year to give help to children in some of the world's poorest communities and to raise funds and awareness of the charity's work in education globally – a powerful example of using literature to promote literacy.

In addition to the Shakespeare Lives programme, VisitBritain is also taking advantage of the global focus on Shakespeare by delivering a high-impact international campaign using the UK's wider cultural 'offer' to target prospective tourists. This digitally led initiative, using newly developed Shakespeare-related content, encourages individuals to share their 'amazing moments' experienced in the UK with friends, family and wider social networks. Connected to this, a Shakespeare digital itinerary will bring to life the variety of Shakespeare experiences on offer in the UK, with Shakespeare content featuring strongly within VisitBritain's '*#OMGB*' campaign. In addition, and in order to generate new individual tourist contact information, VisitBritain is running a global competition that offers the opportunity to travel to the UK to explore Shakespeare trails in London, Stratford-upon-Avon and other related destinations.

To specifically target the global education sector, the British Council is undertaking an extensive global programme of Shakespeare-inspired marketing initiatives to promote studying in the UK and the learning of English. These will include innovative digital collateral, such as a series of promotional videos that will be distributed through social media and feature leading UK academics discussing Shakespearean themes of language, literature, society, history, performance and science, along with international students who are studying Shakespeare in the UK. Throughout the year, there will also be a series of Shakespeare lectures and seminars in key target markets with the objective of encouraging international students to choose the UK for their education.

Across the Foreign & Commonwealth Office's global network of 260 cities, Shakespeare will be the centrepiece of an extensive programme of diplomatic and business activities. The programme will use Shakespearean themes (such as 'the rule of law', 'corruption' and 'conflict') to stimulate debate, dialogue and relationship building with hard-to-reach individuals in foreign governments and institutions. To support UK businesses in target markets, commercial opportunities will also be generated – using Shakespeare as a context – for the

UK's key creative sectors of film-making, television production and publishing.

GREAT and Shakespeare: the next chapter

'The GREAT Campaign is an example of consistency, continuity and unsurpassed message clarity.'[15]

The GREAT campaign works and is having an undoubted impact far in excess of its original conception in 2011. The authoritative 'Nation Brand Index' showed that the UK moved up to fourth place globally in 2013 and then maintained this position in both 2014 and 2015 as 'the GREAT Britain nation brand campaign continues to pay dividends'.[16] While Shakespeare's canon has survived, adapted and dominated the literary landscape since first being performed, GREAT in comparison is a relative newcomer, but it has already received over 25 awards and commendations. Perhaps even more meaningfully, it has also attracted the praise of many of the UK's international competitors as being a best practice campaign that immediately captures and conveys the essence of British excellence, particularly in the fields of creativity and culture.

The acceleration of mainstream government recognition for GREAT as a core commercial and soft power asset for the UK has been especially noteworthy. In 2014–15 the National Audit Office undertook an independent and comprehensive review of the effectiveness of the GREAT campaign,[17] which concluded by commending the campaign for its 'strong marketing and communication tools and materials ... [that] provide an important element of consistency ... which helps to embed the brand by creating familiarity among target audiences and markets'. Next, in June 2015, the UK was independently ranked as the world's leading soft power nation because of its 'unmatched combination of strong assets across all categories of soft power ... with particular strengths in "culture", "digital" and "global engagement"'.[18] Shortly afterwards, in September 2015, the GREAT brand was independently valued at £217 million, with the potential to increase to £2.1 billion within five years and be ranked within the UK's top 50 brands.[19] Finally, at the end of 2015 the Chancellor George Osborne confirmed in his five-year Spending Review that the GREAT campaign would continue to receive government funding through to 2020, with a target of securing £1.6 billion a year of additional economic benefits for the UK.

Shakespeare's cultural capital continues to remain strong, and he remains the most important and contemporarily relevant British cultural personality in overseas markets. His role in GREAT – which will be central in 2016 – will continue to be essential to the campaign's success. His universality supports the aims and values of the GREAT campaign, and as one of the UK's core soft power and economic assets, his brand will help to shape and drive the GREAT campaign forward through to the end of the decade. For the UK, Shakespeare is always GREAT, and over the coming five years it will be essential to exploit GREAT's growing global momentum with the additional profile and soft power benefits brought about by the coincidence of Shakespeare's anniversary. In the ongoing international battle for economic growth, if the UK is to fully exploit the wide range of global opportunities available, it must ensure that the GREAT campaign continues to 'make use of time, let not advantage slip'.[20]

Notes

1. William Shakespeare (1997) *Twelfth Night* in Stephen Greenblatt et al. (eds) *The Norton Shakespeare* (London: Norton). All subsequent quotations from Shakespeare will be from this edition.
2. British Council (2012) 'Trust Pays – How International Cultural Relationships Build Trust in the UK and Underpin the Success of the UK Economy' available at https://www.britishcouncil.org/organisation/policy-insight-research/research/trust-pays, date accessed 23 December 2015.
3. Paul Dekker et al. (2006) 'Diverse Europe: Public Opinion on the European Union and Cultural Diversity, Economics and Policy' The Netherlands Institute for Social Research, available at http://www.scp.nl/english/content.jsp?objectid=22013, date accessed 23 December 2015.
4. At least 17 Government departments and public sector organisations are using the GREAT brand including the Department for Business, Innovation and Skills, the Department for the Environment, Food and Rural Affairs, the Department for International Development, and regional bodies such as the devolved administrations in Scotland, Wales and Northern Ireland and major cities such as London, Leeds and Manchester.
5. Ipsos MORI/In2Impact (2015).
6. Kareen El Beyrouty and Andrew Tessler (2013) 'The Economic Impact of the UK Heritage Tourism Economy' (Oxford Economics), available at http://www.oxfordeconomics.com/my-oxford/projects/236505, date accessed 23 December 2015.
7. As of November 2015.
8. Shakespeare's Birthplace Trust Annual Report 2014 (2015), p. 6, available at http://issuu.com/shakespearebt/docs/sbt_2014annualreport_art_singles/1?e=12035869/13648921, date accessed 23 December 2015.
9. Royal Shakespeare Company/British Council (2012) 'Shakespeare: A Worldwide Classroom', see http://theatreanddance.britishcouncil.org/projects/2012/world-shakespeare-festival/, date accessed 23 December 2015.

10. British Council (2014) 'As Others See Us: Culture, Attraction and Soft Power' available at https://www.britishcouncil.org/organisation/policy-insight-research/research/as-others-see-us, date accessed 23 December 2015.
11. The survey was carried out amongst people aged 18 to 34 in China, India, Brazil, Germany and the USA, as well as their UK contemporaries.
12. Deloitte (2013) 'Tourism: Jobs and Growth. The Economic Contribution of the Tourism Economy in the UK' (Oxford Economics), available at http://www.oxfordeconomics.com/my-oxford/projects/246555, date accessed 23 December 2015.
13. www.visitbritain.com/en/Things-to-do/Culture/Britains-best-Shakespeare-attractions.htm, date accessed 23 December 2015.
14. www.shakespeares-england.co.uk, date accessed 23 December 2015.
15. Brand Finance (2015) 'Nation Brands 2015' available at http://brandfinance.com/images/upload/brand_finance_nation_brands_2015.pdf, date accessed 23 December 2015.
16. Brand Finance (2014), 'Nation Brands 2014' available at http://brandfinance.com/knowledge-centre/reports/brand-finance-nation-brands-2014/, date accessed 23 December 2014.
17. National Audit Office (2015) 'Exploiting the UK brand overseas' available at https://www.nao.org.uk/report/exploiting-the-uk-brand-overseas/, date accessed 23 December 2015.
18. Portland Communications (2015) 'The Soft Power 30 – A Global Ranking of Soft Power' available at http://www.portland-communications.com/the-soft-power-30/, date accessed 23 December 2015.
19. Brand Finance (2015).
20. William Shakespeare, *Venus and Adonis* (1593) in *The Norton Shakespeare*, l. 129.

Select Bibliography

Beyrouty, Kareen El and Andrew Tessler (2013) 'The Economic Impact of the UK Heritage Tourism Economy' (Oxford Economics), available at http://www.oxfordeconomics.com/my-oxford/projects/236505.

British Council (2014) 'As Others See Us: Culture, Attraction and Soft Power' available at https://www.britishcouncil.org/organisation/policy-insight-research/research/as-others-see-us.

British Council (2012) 'Trust Pays – How International Cultural Relationships Build Trust in the UK and Underpin the Success of the UK Economy' available at https://www.britishcouncil.org/organisation/policy-insight-research/research/trust-pays.

Dekker, Paul, et al. (2006) 'Diverse Europe: Public Opinion on the European Union and Cultural Diversity, Economics and Policy' The Netherlands Institute for Social Research, available at http://www.scp.nl/english/content.jsp?objectid=22013.

Deloitte (2013) 'Tourism: Jobs and Growth. The Economic Contribution of the Tourism Economy in the UK' (Oxford Economics), available at http://www.oxfordeconomics.com/my-oxford/projects/246555.

National Audit Office (2015) 'Exploiting the UK Brand Overseas' available at https://www.nao.org.uk/report/exploiting-the-uk-brand-overseas/.

Portland Communications (2015) 'The Soft Power 30 – A Global Ranking of Soft Power' available at http://www.portland-communications.com/the-soft-power-30/.

Royal Shakespeare Company/British Council (2012) 'Shakespeare: A Worldwide Classroom', see http://theatreanddance.britishcouncil.org/projects/2012/world-shakespeare-festival/.

9
Sponsoring Shakespeare

Susan Bennett

There is, by now, a long critical history of how Shakespeare has been appropriated and performed in advertising campaigns for a remarkable diversity of consumer products, from StarKist canned tuna to easyJet's low-cost air travel, from Red Bull energy drinks to Google+.[1] Even more commonplace is the analysis of how the Bard is deployed to promote cultural institutions and places involved directly in the production of his works. In this context, Shakespeare's role in cultural tourism has been particularly well documented, and not just in the obvious locations of Stratford-upon-Avon and London, but in festival cities such as Stratford, Ontario and Ashland, Oregon.[2] Against the backdrop of this expansive Shakespeare 'industry', Kate McLuskie and Kate Rumbold have explored whether Shakespeare can rightly be considered a 'brand', suggesting that what is at stake 'is the question of how Shakespeare's value is constructed and conferred in commercial settings'.[3] I am interested here in taking up the notion of value in practices of corporate sponsorship. In particular, I want to explore how value was assumed and attained by Shakespeare's presence in the Cultural Olympiad attached to London 2012 and, specifically, the relationship of his 'brand' to corporate sponsors for both the arts programming and the larger sporting event.

In general, then, I look to identify instrumental uses of the Shakespearean signature for multinational companies who make it part of their business to underwrite cultural performances and exhibitions. What benefits accrue to a sponsor as a result of financial investment in a Shakespeare-branded experience and how does that experience – and those who labour to produce it – depend on affiliation with the sponsoring entity? How does 'value' get created and circulated, and for whom? And, more specifically, how does Shakespeare advertise particular value (and values) for sponsors? Corporate involvement in London 2012 was, of course, especially conspicuous, but relationships between cultural producers and the companies that contribute to their costs have, in neoliberal global economies, become increasingly commonplace and, arguably, necessary. I am also interested in the emergence of counter-performances that insist on making visible the brandscapes in which Shakespeare appears, protesting not an inherent conservatism in the endless reproduction of Shakespeare's work (an argument that has been often used by theatre professionals to bemoan limited opportunities for contemporary playwrights), but instead laying bare the facts of financial and political paradigms disguised by policies of increased access, widening participation and public good. As McLuskie and Rumbold note, 'commercial organisations do not simply borrow value from Shakespeare and trade profitably on his name, but also "co-produce" new kinds of meaning and value for Shakespeare in the market'.[4] It is such acts of co-production – and their interrogation – that prompt this essay.

Shakespeare at the Olympics

As part of London's staging of the Summer Olympic Games, the city was required (as specified in Rule 39 of the IOC's Charter) to arrange 'a programme of cultural events which must cover at least the entire period during which the Olympic Village is open. Such programme shall be submitted to the IOC Executive Board for its prior approval'.[5] With this expectation, the London Organising Committee of the Olympic Games (LOCOG) set out to accomplish the largest cultural celebration in the history of the modern Olympic and Paralympic Movements,[6] a goal more than realised in the '177,717 activities and 43.4 million public engagement experiences' that Jen Harvie and Keren Zaiontz have justly described as 'a bonfire of the vanities in the face of otherwise shrinking resources for UK arts'.[7] While the full programming of the Cultural Olympiad attempted to offer something for everyone (the promotion of access and participation for all), the starring role, and substantial slice of the budget pie, accorded to Shakespeare was inescapable. Foremost in the Cultural Olympiad's ambitious calendar was no less than a cross-UK 'World Shakespeare Festival' under the artistic direction of Deborah Shaw at the Royal Shakespeare Company. As well as signature international performances in Stratford (such as the RSC-Wooster Group's collaboratively produced *Troilus and Cressida*) and London (such as Toni Morrison's, Peter Sellars' and Rokia Traoré's *Desdemona*), the 37 plays of the Globe-to-Globe Festival at Shakespeare's Globe, and regional outliers such as Mike Pearson's and Mike Brookes' *Coriolan/ us* for the National Theatre of Wales, the World Shakespeare Festival was anchored by a large-scale summer-season tourism-friendly exhibition at the British Museum – 'Shakespeare: Staging the World'. The exhibition was, in the words of British Museum director Neil MacGregor, a 'special contribution to the Cultural Olympiad, a series of events to showcase the nation's art and culture to the rest of the world'.[8] In other words, throughout the Festival, and particularly at the British Museum, Shakespeare was explicitly instrumentalised for the nation and expected to labour internationally on its behalf (as with Shakespeare's role in the GREAT campaign, discussed in Chapter 8). Thus, the Cultural Olympiad, as Paul Prescott has trenchantly observed, relied on 'Bard Branding' to convince a general public of the value (economic and entertainment) of its event programming.[9] Bard Branding was also, I suggest, important and even effective in providing value to those corporations affiliated with the production of the Games and the Cultural Olympiad.

Particularly visible among the many corporate sponsors was BP (formerly known and, I would argue, still recognised as British Petroleum).[10] The company was involved with the Games, the Cultural Olympiad and the World Shakespeare Festival and was declared by LOCOG as a 'sustainability partner' and the official 'Oil and Gas Partner' – an arrangement that immediately generated visible and vocal protest from 'environmentalists, artists, indigenous people's leaders and development groups',[11] including Greenpeace UK, the director of the Chartered Institution of Water and Environmental Management and the Polaris Institute. LOCOG defended its decision, assuring that BP had passed all the 'stringent requirements'[12] required on the part of 2012 partners, and the company enjoyed significant presence at events related to the Games and within the Cultural Olympiad. The oil and gas conglomerate had, of course, fallen far from favour in the aftermath of the Deepwater Horizon oil rig explosion and subsequent environmental disaster in the Gulf of Mexico in April 2010, when 11 workers died and the equivalent of 4.9 million barrels of oil spilled into the ocean off the coast of Louisiana. In December 2014, the US Supreme Court declined to hear a BP appeal against the Federal Court decision that BP was liable for $18 billion in civil penalties on top of $28 billion already paid out by the oil company in clean-up costs and other claims.[13] The costs to the environment in the Gulf are, as widely documented, extreme and continuing. The direct and indirect costs to local economies in the immediate vicinity have been huge. Negative press has also long followed the company for its participation in the Canadian Tar Sands extraction in Northern Alberta, where hundreds of square kilometres of boreal forest have been stripped bare and excavated, producing noxious emissions that put humans and animals at risk, as well as for its exploration activities in the Arctic.

Thus, in the Olympic year of 2012, BP was in dire need of some new messaging in service of its brand image. Bard Branding, in the form of the World Shakespeare Festival, it appeared, would be an occasion tailor-made for celebration of what the author and the company apparently shared – national identity – and what the author had and the company desired – a high level of positive brand recognition. If the inscription of 'sustainability partner' to the sports competition suggested a reformation of its environmental attitudes and practices, its role as the 'Founding Presenting Partner' of the World Shakespeare Festival refocused the public's attention on the impacts of the (once national) petroleum company for British people and British culture rather than on its environmental misadventures 5,000 miles away. But BP's sponsorship of the World Shakespeare Festival did not go unremarked. The Reclaim Shakespeare Company (the other RSC!) formed as a protest-oriented alliance, describing themselves as 'a merry troupe of players aghast that our beloved Bard's works and memory have been purloined by BP in a case of greenwash most foul. We are like a drop of water that in the ocean seeks another drop. Together, we will make a flood'.[14] Their 'flood' took the form of staged interventions at a number of participating theatrical venues as well as at the British Museum.

Their first interruption of the World Shakespeare Festival (what they called an 'anarcho-thespian performance') took place on Shakespeare's 'birthday', 23 April, before a performance of *The Tempest* at the Royal Shakespeare Company's theatre in Stratford and involved a two-minute performance delivered by two actors who had jumped up on the stage. A parody that mashed up well-known lines from Shakespeare's plays to critique BP's environmental practices, the speech encouraged spectators to join the actors in ripping the BP logo from their theatre programmes – an invitation that the video recording reveals garnered some boos from the audience, although, as a whole, the performance received rousing applause at its end. On the same day, as Reclaim Shakespeare noted on their website, a letter, signed by 28 theatre and other arts professionals and academics, was published in the *Guardian*. The writers suggested there that the launch of the World Shakespeare Festival was marred by BP's sponsorship: 'We, as individuals involved in theatre and the arts, are deeply concerned that the RSC – like other much-cherished cultural institutions – is allowing itself to be used by BP to obscure the destructive reality of its activities'.[15] In this context, Bard Branding was linked at the outset to the economic conditions of its production and to the greenwashing implicit in its reception, exposing BP's role in ways that must have horrified the company's public relations team.

Among the eight other Reclaim Shakespeare flash-mob performances that took place over the course of the World Shakespeare Festival was an intervention at the Noël Coward Theatre in London (23 October 2012). The group took over in the intermission of another Royal Shakespeare Company performance, this time of *Much Ado About Nothing*. On this occasion, their Shakespearean-styled parody involved a scene where a character 'BP' sought the help of an actor 'RSC' to remedy his sullied reputation:

> **RSC:** You seek my help in being virtuous?
>
> **BP:** Nay, I seek your help in *seeming* virtuous.
> For a thousand ducats, thou shall proclaim
> My innocence to these simple people,
> To wash away the memories of my misdeeds,
> Distract them from the destruction of the earth.
>
> **RSC:** A thousand ducats: tis a fine price! *(aside)*
>
> **BP:** By your reputation, I will mine own mend.

'BP' then pinned the company's logo onto 'RSC' and furnished her with a script that included the lines 'They sponsor us for their love of the arts, not for cheap publicity!/Sustainability is obviously at the heart of what they do/And burning fossil fuels helps improve the work for the next generation ...' – the point at which the actor broke off and declared 'I want not thy dirty ducats!' As this quotation suggests, Reclaim Shakespeare's text explicitly linked sponsorship money with the rehabilitation of BP's corporate image and instrumental purpose. According to the Reclaim Shakespeare Company report on the performance, security guards at the Noël Coward Theatre were prevented from ejecting the protestor-actors by members of the Royal Shakespeare Company cast.[16]

Since these public acts of protest contributed to the meanings generated by the Cultural Olympiad generally as well as to specific events on the World Shakespeare Festival programme, and, more importantly, initiated a robust and continuing discourse concerned with the role of corporate sponsorship in the funding of arts institutions and programming, I want to look specifically at three Reclaim Shakespeare Company performances of their 'Out Damned Logo', not only as the most significant and sustained critiques of BP's involvement but also as events that inspired a more consistent opposition to oil companies' sponsorship of the arts, particularly in a museum setting. The 'Out Damned Logo' performances took place in July, September and November 2012 in the British Museum's Great Court adjacent to the 'Shakespeare: Staging the World' exhibition.

Protesting 'Shakespeare: staging the world' and Olympic legacies

The flagship event for the World Shakespeare Festival, this exhibition featured artefacts from early modern England, an organisational principle that curator Dora Thornton and consultant Jonathan Bate claimed was 'new and distinctive': 'through a series of case studies, focused on a wide range of locations, cultures and themes, we create a dialogue between Shakespeare's imaginary worlds and the material objects of the real world of the late sixteenth and early seventeenth centuries'.[17] Both in the physical space of the Museum and in the exhibition catalogue, BP's logo was prominently displayed. In the catalogue, for example, the 'Sponsor's Foreword' precedes that of the Museum Director as well as the Editors' Preface. BP Group Chief Executive Bob Dudley stated in his Foreword that 'This BP exhibition provides an exceptional insight into the emerging role of London as a world city, seen through the innovative perspective of Shakespeare's plays'.[18] If Dudley here implies ownership of the event – it is BP's exhibition – he ends by reminding readers that 'support for *Shakespeare: staging the world* is part of the company's wider contribution to society, connecting communities with excellence in arts and culture worldwide'.[19] In other words, he makes a claim for BP's stewardship, exhibited by way of Shakespeare, on a global scale.

At 3:30 p.m. on Sunday 22 July 2012 the first, and unexpected, pop-up performance took place at the exhibition. A four-minute action, shaped as a comic adaptation of *Macbeth*, interrupted that afternoon's visitors with the opening chant: 'Double, double: oil and trouble/ Tar sands burn, as greenwash bubbles'.[20] A typical work in Reclaim Shakespeare's series of protest performances, this *Macbeth* offered an extended exposé of BP's environmental record. The actors at the British Museum translated Shakespeare's three 'weird' witches of *Macbeth* into three BP executives who 'lure a naïve museum director to his doom'. The interaction between 'executives' and 'director' was angrily interrupted by a museum visitor (in fact, another Reclaim Shakespeare actor). The visitor complained that his experience of the exhibition had been ruined, venting his frustration: 'Out, damned sponsor! Out, BP!'. By this point in the performance, British Museum security guards arrived to escort the troupe from the building while the actors chanted 'Double, double: oil is trouble/Let's reduce BP to rubble'. The actors then re-performed 'Out Damned Logo' outside the museum.

Reclaim Shakespeare returned to the British Museum and the 'Shakespeare: Staging the World' exhibition in September to interrupt a special 'Shakespeare Late' event – an evening of performances, workshops and lectures designed to enhance visitor experience. According to the Reclaim Shakespeare website, they successfully delivered three performances of 'Out Damned Logo' in the Great Court before being ejected again by security guards. In November 2012, a third performance at the British Museum was planned, described by Reclaim Shakespeare as their 'season finale'. Unlike its predecessors, the event had been widely advertised ahead of time, including in a preview article by Emily Jupp in the *Independent*, where she noted that 70 performers were anticipated at the event.[21] With this kind of media attention, the venue was amply prepared: police and additional security were called in and 'Shakespeare: Staging the World' was closed for the day as were the large iron gates outside the Museum.[22] By far the largest of the Reclaim Shakespeare interventions, the group's numbers were bolstered by participation from members of other organisations involved in the Art Not Oil Coalition and Jupp's earlier prediction of 70 actors was eclipsed by the 200 who participated.[23] One of the Reclaim Shakespeare actors who took part in the first of the museum performances summed up the purpose of their series of performances at the Museum: 'The company [BP] is trying to draw attention away from its catastrophic fossil-fuelled energy plans by sponsoring the Olympics and the World Shakespeare Festival. We're here to stop BP from using our beloved bard as a mask for its misdeeds'.[24]

I would suggest that BP's involvement in such a prestigious series of events, and particularly its role in the British Museum exhibition, functions as more than just a mask for their environmental bad practices. What BP accrues from this financial association is the appearance of commensurability with the cultural institution (museum) as the national repository of the world's treasures and with the cultural asset (Shakespeare) considered a national and, indeed, global superstar. But the affiliation advertised and promoted in the sponsorship of 'Shakespeare: Staging the World' also plays on the old name of British Petroleum, when the majority of the company was state-owned (it was privatised between 1979 and 1987). This resonance insinuates an appeal to national pride and obscures the company's behaviour elsewhere in the world; in other words, for World Shakespeare Festival audiences, BP was not to be defined by Deepwater Horizon, but was instead to be identified by its alignment with the very best of British cultural tradition. Yet, in reality, BP is today a fully global enterprise rather than a national asset, involved in 80 countries with headquarters in both London and Houston.

The mock-Shakespearean performances by Reclaim Shakespeare made visible the implicit motivations behind corporate sponsorship of the arts, and those of BP in particular, and asked museum visitors to examine their own role in this museum-corporation contract. Peter Sillitoe's review of the British Museum show noted: 'the exhibition was an excellent advert for the enduring importance of all things Shakespearean in the modern world and it hopefully surprised visitors and tourists by showing the sheer amount of material that we can link directly to Shakespeare's life and work';[25] Reclaim Shakespeare's surprise performances drew attention to another kind of 'advert' – that of the corporate sponsor – and asked why should BP be linked to the importance of Shakespeare and whether visitors tacitly endorse BP's business practices when enjoying the exhibition the company has partly funded.

While Reclaim Shakespeare's interventions received regular media attention on television and radio in the UK and in newspapers both nationally and internationally, not all critiques of 'Shakespeare: Staging the World' were so widely reported. One of the most talked-about components of this exhibition was the last artefact that visitors saw – a copy of a cheap 1970s edition of Shakespeare's complete works that had been secretly circulated among the African National Congress (ANC) leaders imprisoned on Robben Island during South African apartheid. Thornton's and Bate's exhibition catalogue explains that the inmates 'found a common bond and source of solace in Shakespeare. One of their number, Sonny Venkatrathnam, managed to get hold of a copy of Shakespeare's works, disguising the cover with Indian religious pictures. He circulated the book to all the leading prisoners, asking them to autograph their favourite passages in the margins'.[26] The book – known as the 'Robben Island Bible' – was opened to the second act of *Julius Caesar*, where the signature of Nelson Mandela, dated 16 December 1977, could be found next to the following, underlined passage:

> Cowards die many times before their deaths,
> The valiant never taste of death but once.

Of all the wonders that I yet have heard,
It seems to me most strange that men should fear,
Seeing that death, a necessary end,
Will come when it will come.
(2.2.32–38)

The catalogue also includes this extract, complete with Mandela signature and date, as a colour image on the last page of its text. Only three lines follow the quotation from Shakespeare's play: 'Shakespeare's life did not cease with the "necessary end" of his death in 1616: his plays continue to live, and to give life, four centuries on, all the way across the great theatre of the world'[27] – a reach that matches BP's global ambitions.

Collette Gordon suggests that the inclusion of the 'Robben Island Bible' was 'arguably the exhibit's major drawcard'[28] and it is certainly true that the book consistently attracted the attention of exhibition reviewers – Michael Billington, for example, wrote 'I found it deeply moving to see Nelson Mandela's signature alongside the passage from *Julius Caesar*'[29] and Richard Dorment saw the book as evidence that 'Shakespeare's voice found its way into the furthest corners of the world and deepest recesses of men's minds'.[30] But Gordon also notes that Jackson Mthembu, the ANC's spokesperson, and Ahmed Kathrada, a former prisoner and current chairperson of the Robben Island Museum, both issued 'emphatic denials' that the Shakespeare edition had been 'iconic' in the struggle for freedom.[31] Insistence on the Shakespeare text's importance in the resistance to and overthrow of South Africa's apartheid regime is fundamentally an Anglo-centric analysis of politics elsewhere in the world and, in Gordon's words, makes the book 'the ultimate fetish'.[32] Or, as Kathrada put it, 'It's iconic to those who want to make it iconic. To us, it's not'.[33] That these refusals of the narrative performed by 'Shakespeare: Staging the World' were so sparsely reported while the Reclaim Shakespeare performances received, at least by comparison, extensive media coverage is surely telling. It suggests, among other things, that pop-up performances have become familiar as a medium of protest and are thought to add to the audience's experience of the event even as it is criticised, while correction by African politicians of a British narrative about Shakespeare's importance in the world remains much more easily ignored.

Reclaim Shakespeare has maintained its repertoire of performances that draw attention to BP's sponsorship of the British Museum: a Sherlock Holmes-themed event in March 2015 staged a mock trial of the oil and gas company, charging 'BP, BP/For a tiny fee/It's here you buy/Credibility',[34] and in December they held a spoof farewell party for Neil MacGregor. The Museum Director was to leave his role at the end of 2015 and Reclaim Shakespeare offered a fake MacGregor an 'oily' farewell. The script was drawn from 19 pages of emails exchanged between the Museum's director and BP in 2014, obtained by Reclaim Shakespeare under the Freedom of Information Act as a 'celebration' of what the company calls BP's and the British Museum's 'cosy relationship'.[35] Through their ongoing programme of pop-up interventions, a debate concerned with the appropriateness of corporate sponsorship of arts and culture has stayed in the public eye as well as being addressed by those employed in the cultural domain. In May 2015 the Public and Commercial Sector Union (whose members include gallery and museum workers) passed a motion that condemned sponsorship by oil companies and called for more ethical funding policies at national institutions.[36] The most enduring legacy of 'Shakespeare: Staging the World', then, may well have been to expose the practices of the corporation that sought to benefit from affinity with the exhibition's subject.

Market messages: what Shakespeare sells

Unquestionably, Reclaim Shakespeare's adapted play texts have been vital in informing visitors, and the public at large, about the price of and motivations behind arts sponsorship in today's world. As they put it, 'action is eloquence': 'BP may need the arts, but the arts do not need BP. If people in the arts, museum and theatre world stand up for what they believe in, we can end this destructive relationship and remove the filthy stain of oil sponsorship from our beloved cultural institutions'.[37] The group has brought public attention to BP's sponsorship not just in the immediate effects of their live performances (those logos ripped from event programmes), but also through radio and television interviews and discussion, as well as in print and social media coverage.[38] But has their strategy, however popular, been effective? In November 2012, it appeared as if the Royal Shakespeare Company was re-thinking its relationship with BP as a major sponsor,[39] but in February 2013 the theatre organisation announced a new partnership with the oil company to create subsidised tickets for 16–25-year-old theatregoers.[40] At the beginning of 2015, the RSC's 'Corporate Members and Partners' page displayed the infamous logo atop a listing that showed BP as its sole corporate partner, although that page is no longer to be found on the RSC's website. The BP logo does appear at the bottom of the page for RSC Key, the programme the company sponsors for young theatregoers.[41] And, notwithstanding the efforts of Reclaim Shakespeare to challenge the appearance of the BP logo at World Shakespeare Festival events, a study by sports and entertainment market specialists Havas (reported in the UK's *Marketing Magazine*) indicated that 82% of those polled – a sample of more than 3,000 adults – recognised BP as one of the London 2012 sponsors and 38% believed that 'BP had been getting better at working towards a cleaner planet'.[42] These results suggest that Shakespeare does an excellent job in accomplishing the 'greenwash' that Reclaim Shakespeare and other critics identified as the sponsor's goal.

Importantly, the debate has continued since 2012 thanks to the work by Reclaim Shakespeare and allied groups intervening at many different cultural institutions and shows including the British Museum Viking exhibition (2014) and Indigenous Australia exhibition (2015) at Tate Britain, at the summer 'live film' performances from the Royal Opera House seen in Trafalgar Square, and at the National Portrait Gallery. Moreover, at the same time as Reclaim Shakespeare's first intervention (April 2012), a coalition known as 'Request Initiative' filed a Freedom of Information application to uncover how much money BP donated annually to London's Tate Britain. This was resolved and disclosed only in January 2015, revealing a total of £3.8 million over 17 years and in amounts that generally varied from £150,000–£330,000 per year. As Mark Brown's story in the *Guardian* recorded, the Tate considers this a 'considerable sum' while protesters suggest the amount is 'embarrassingly small'.[43] BP contributions to the Tate are estimated as representing no more than 0.5% of the gallery's annual operating budget – a bargain, for sure, in comparison to the billions it must 'donate' to Deepwater Horizon claims. Moreover, as Mel Evans has noted, BP's sponsorship money for the Tate is part of an agreement that includes other cultural institutions – the National Portrait Gallery, the British Museum and the Royal Opera House – with each at the same level of funding. She suggests that such a modest level is 'replaceable', but the 'choice of exhibits to sponsor displays the association the companies want to buy … rather than fulfilling any marginal funding need for the cultural institutions'.[44] Yet Neil MacGregor wrote in his foreword to the 'Shakespeare: Staging the World' catalogue (immediately following the one by BP Group Chief Executive Dudley): 'This BP exhibition is part of an ongoing partnership with the British Museum. We are most grateful to them for making possible this enthralling glimpse into Shakespeare's imagined worlds'.[45] But how, exactly, did BP make this signal event possible? With BP's financial commitment to the British

Museum no more than £500,000 annually (committed each year over five years, 2011–2015) and the Museum's overall budget each year currently running at about £144 million, BP's contribution is less than 1% of total operating costs. The Royal Shakespeare Company reported for 2014–15 income of £63.9 million, 25% of which came from Arts Council England. Only £3.6 million came from corporate sponsorships and donations from private individuals, trusts and foundations.[46] As a point of comparison, Evans reminds her readers that in 2004 BP 'spent over £136 million developing and rebuilding the brand of its new logo, the "helios"'.[47]

And, of course, BP is far from the only oil company hoping that arts advertising and sponsorship might clean up a tarnished brand. Shell, for example, was the co-producer with the Rijksmuseum and the National Gallery for the latter's autumn 2014 blockbuster show of Rembrandt's late paintings – the entrance to which involved navigating promotional materials that extended the partnership beyond the exhibition itself. This display suggested 'Science meets art as Shell and the National Gallery come together to preserve some of Rembrandt's finest works' and pointed out that 'Together, we are using cutting-edge laboratory techniques usually reserved for the analysis of fuel molecules to study why some red pigments found in many of Rembrandt's masterpieces are fading'. Like Shakespeare, Rembrandt functions here to co-produce Shell's message about its investment in technologies that benefit the 'best' of Western civilisation. To realise a flash-mob intervention at the Rembrandt show, actors from Reclaim Shakespeare combined with another protest group, Shell Out Sounds[48] to stage a parody of another early modern play, *Dr. Faustus*. This musical version of Marlowe's play was staged at the National Gallery on 14 October 2014; its plot had 'Museum Man' (a representation of the Gallery director) sell his soul to a Shell Executive who was dressed as the devil. Their interactions were punctuated by a repeated chorus: 'See the oil spill/Breathe the gas flare/ Taste the tar sands/The deeds of Shell'.[49] Security guards were unsuccessful in stopping the performance, and while the police were summoned to the scene, they did not arrive until the group had left the gallery.

In May 2015, it was reported that Shell had attempted to interfere in the design of a climate change exhibition at London's Science Museum for which it was a sponsor. Terry Macalister's story in the *Guardian* included quotations from emails written by a Shell employee to the museum, suggesting that the company's 'climate change advisers' be invited to help with a 'content refresh'.[50] Then, in November, the Science Museum responded to a Freedom of Information request to reveal that its sponsorship deal with Shell would not be renewed after its expiry at the end of the year. Nonetheless, the Museum's spokesperson noted: 'we have a long-term relationship with Shell, with whom we remain in open dialogue. We may or may not enter into partnership agreements with Shell in the future'.[51] Other groups in the Art Not Oil coalition bring Reclaim Shakespeare-styled interventions to other UK cultural institutions: these include Liberate Tate (campaigning against BP's sponsorship of the Tate galleries), Rising Tide UK (a climate change activist group focusing on Shell's sponsorship of the arts) and Platform London (who pursue 'projects that push for social & ecological justice, with a particular focus on the oil and gas sector').[52] In December 2015, Platform London organised a three-day unauthorised arts festival inside the Tate Modern to challenge BP's sponsorship deal with the Tate galleries, due to expire in December 2016. They reported that more than 4,000 Tate visitors engaged with the festival, with more than 1,000 actively participating in events.[53]

At the conclusion of their study of Shakespeare's cultural value in the contemporary world, McLuskie and Rumbold write: 'Shakespeare's value is not corrupted by commercial forces, but is continually co-produced by brands and institutions in an increasingly complex dance of the ultimately inseparable forces of culture and the market'.[54] So what was advertised in these various examples from the World Shakespeare Festival and for whom? These questions ask us, I think, to debate vigorously the ethical entanglements that surround the financial models of arts funding *and* our obligations as theatregoers and museum visitors as we participate in these practices. There is growing public support for fossil fuel divestment, as evidenced in the sales of oil, gas and coal company shares by more than 2,000 institutions and 400 individuals worldwide. Total withdrawals are estimated at £2.6 trillion.[55] This action suggests that visitors to theatres and museums are likely not persuaded by Bard-branded greenwashing by BP and others. But, at the same time, this shift in public opinion has not translated into a significant boycott of those cultural institutions supported by oil company funds, even if the branding strategy is exposed on site (as in the case of Reclaim Shakespeare performances). The Association of Leading Visitor Attractions figures for 2014 show the British Museum in top place (as it has been for each of the last five years), with the National Gallery and Southbank Centre in second and third – with more than six million visitors apiece.[56] Theatregoers and museum visitors might not buy the message, but they are still willing to buy the subsidised ticket.

More generally, it is the case that scholars have been rather late to this 'complex dance', and it is now more than time for us to more explicitly account for the instrumental values of Bard Branding in the market. Of course, many of the cultural institutions whose work we enthusiastically support and with which we critically engage find themselves with precarious budget conditions – sometimes of their own making, but most often as a result of government 'austerity' measures (most explicitly seen and felt in the United Kingdom, but certainly far more widespread geographically). Against this economic reality, corporate sponsorship cannot be easily refused, but the performances by Reclaim Shakespeare and other arts activists remind us that we have a responsibility to pay much more attention to the national and corporate values and goals that lie behind sponsoring Shakespeare.

Notes

1. The Charlie the Tuna example opens Michael Bristol's important 1990 book, *Shakespeare's America, America's Shakespeare* (London: Routledge); the other examples are more recent and can be found on the blog page of Christopher Mills, SEO Manager of Parallax, a digital services and content provider: https://parall.ax/blog/view/3046/how-has-shakespeare-influenced-modern-marketing, 24 April 2014, date accessed 30 December 2015.
2. See, for example, Dennis Kennedy's (1998) 'Shakespeare and Cultural Tourism', *Theatre Journal*, 50.2: 175–88; Ric Knowles's (1994) 'Shakespeare, 1993, and the Discourses of the Stratford Festival, Ontario', *Shakespeare Quarterly*, 45.2: 211–25; Sharon O'Dair's (2000) *Class, Critics and Shakespeare* (Ann Arbor, MI: University of Michigan Press); and my 'Shakespeare on Vacation' (2005) in Barbara Hodgdon and W. B. Worthen (eds) *A Companion to Shakespeare and Performance* (Oxford: Blackwell), pp. 494–508.
3. Kate McLuskie and Kate Rumbold (2014) *Cultural Value in Twenty-first Century England: The Case of Shakespeare* (Manchester: Manchester University Press), p. 213.
4. McLuskie and Rumbold, p. 213.
5. The Olympic Charter can be found at http://www.olympic.org/Documents/olympic_charter_en.pdf. This version post-dates London 2012, with revisions ratified on 9 September 2013. As far as I'm aware, Rule 39 has not been amended recently.
6. See Susan Bennett and Christie Carson (2013) 'Introduction: Shakespeare Beyond English' in Susan Bennett and Christie Carson (eds) *Shakespeare Beyond English* (Cambridge: Cambridge University Press), p. 1.
7. Jen Harvie and Keren Zaiontz (2013) 'Introduction: The Cultural Politics of London 2012', *Contemporary Theatre Review*, 23.4: 477.
8. Foreword to Jonathan Bate and Dora Thornton (2012) *Shakespeare: Staging the World* (London: British Museum Press), p. 9.
9. Paul Prescott (2015) 'Shakespeare and the Dream of Olympism' in Paul Prescott and Erin Sullivan (eds) *Shakespeare on the Global Stage: Performance and Festivity in the Olympic Year* (London: Bloomsbury Arden Shakespeare), p. 14.
10. British Petroleum started business in the early part of the twentieth century, but has since 2000 been known as BP PLC (a name adopted after a series of

mergers, making it one of the seven 'supersized' global oil and gas conglomerates). Its international headquarters remain, however, in London.

11. John Vidal (2012) 'Olympic Games Organisers Face Protests over BP Sponsorship Deal' *Guardian*, 17 February, www.theguardian.com/business/2012/feb/17/olympic-games-protest-bp-sponsorship, date accessed 30 December 2015.

12. Vidal.

13. Richard Wolf (2014) 'Supreme Court won't review oil spill settlement' *USA Today*, 8 December, www.usatoday.com/story/news/nation/2014/12/08/supreme-court-bp-oil-spill/19893851/, date accessed 30 December 2015. The documentary film *The Great Invisible* (2013) (dir. Margaret Brown) is an important record of Deepwater Horizon and its effects.

14. The quotation is taken from the 'About Us' section of their website: bp-or-not-bp.org/about/, date accessed 30 December 2015.

15. 'Oiling the Wheels of the Shakespeare Festival' *Guardian*, 22 April 2012, www.theguardian.com/stage/2012/apr/22/oiling-wheels-shakespeare-festival, date accessed 30 December 2015. Note: the letter opens 'Today, 23 April,' although the newspaper's website has the publication date as 22 April.

16. bp-or-not-bp.org/news/much-ado-about-bp-sponsorship-as-west-end-play-hit-by-protest/, date accessed 30 December 2015.

17. Thornton and Bate, p. 10.

18. Thornton and Bate, p. 7.

19. Thornton and Bate, p. 7.

20. The video and script for this intervention is available at bp-or-not-bp.org/news/museum/, date accessed 30 December 2015.

21. 'The Great Shakespearean Flash Mob Strikes Again' *Independent*, 14 November 2012, www.independent.co.uk/arts-entertainment/theatre-dance/news/the-great-shakespearean-flashmob-strikes-again-8316440.html, date accessed 30 December 2015.

22. See bp-or-not-bp.org/news/shakespearean-flashmob-hits-bp-sponsored-british-museum/, date accessed 30 December 2015.

23. Art Not Oil has been active since 2004 and currently has seven member groups including the Reclaim Shakespeare Company.

24. See bp-or-not-bp.org/news/museum/, date accessed 30 December 2015.

25. Peter Sillitoe (2014) 'Review of *"Shakespeare: Staging the World"*, British Museum, 19 July-25 November 2012', *Shakespeare*, 10.1: 110.

26. Thornton and Bate, p. 269.

27. Thornton and Bate, p. 269.

28. Collette Gordon, '"Mind the gap": Globalism, Postcolonialism and Making up Africa in the Cultural Olympiad' in Paul Prescott and Erin Sullivan (eds) *Shakespeare on the Global Stage*, p. 209.

29. 'Shakespeare: Staging the World – Review' *Guardian*, 19 July 2012, www.theguardian.com/culture/2012/jul/19/shakespeare-staging-the-world-review, date accessed 30 December 2015.

30. 'Shakespeare: Staging the World, Review' *Telegraph*, 16 July 2012, www.telegraph.co.uk/culture/theatre/william-shakespeare/9404131/Shakespeare-Staging-the-World-review.html, date accessed 30 December 2015. Dorment gives the exhibition five out of five stars.

31. See Gordon pp. 206–11 for a detailed discussion of the Robben Island Bible and its use not just in 'Shakespeare: Staging the World' but for its citation in the Royal Shakespeare Company's 'African' production of *Julius Caesar*.

32. Gordon, p. 209.
33. He is quoted in Anita Li's 'African National Congress disputes "iconic" status of Robben Island Bible displayed in British Museum' *Toronto Star*, 19 July 2012, www.thestar.com/news/world/2012/07/19/african_national_congress_disputes_iconic_status_of_robben_island_bible_displayed_in_british_museum.html, date accessed 30 December 2015. Gordon also draws on Li's article.
34. bp-or-not-bp.org/news/performers-put-bp-on-trial-for-gross-deception-at-british-museum/, date accessed 30 December 2015.
35. bp-or-not-bp.org/news/british-museum-director-given-a-bp-themed-send-off-in-museums-great-court/, date accessed 30 December 2015.
36. bp-or-not-bp.org/news/gallery-and-museum-workers-vote-to-oppose-oil-sponsorship/, date accessed 30 December 2015.
37. bp-or-not-bp.org/action-is-eloquence/, date accessed 30 December 2015.
38. The group is active on social media with both a Facebook page and a Twitter feed (@ReclaimOurBard).
39. bp-or-not-bp.org/news/rsc-backs-away-from-worlds-biggest-corporate-criminal/, date accessed 30 December 2015.
40. bp-or-not-bp.org/news/alas-the-rsc-is-back-in-the-arms-of-bp/, date accessed 30 December 2015.
41. www.rsc.org.uk/support/rsc-key/, date accessed 30 December 2015.
42. John Reynolds (2012) 'BP's Brand Image Benefits From London 2012 Sponsorship, Claims Research' *Marketing Magazine*, 17 February, www.marketing magazine.co.uk/article/1117665/bps-brand-image-benefits-london-2012-sponsorship-claims-research, date accessed 30 December 2015.
43. 'Tate's BP Sponsorship Was £150,000 to £330,000 a Year, Figures Show' *Guardian*, 26 January 2015, www.theguardian.com/artanddesign/2015/jan/26/tate-reveal-bp-sponsorship-150000-330000-platform-information-tribunal, date accessed 30 December 2015.
44. Mel Evans (2015) *Artwash: Big Oil and the Arts* (London: Pluto Press), p. 60.
45. Thornton and Bate, p. 9.
46. 'RSC: Finance and Funding', www.rsc.org.uk/about-us/facts-and-figures/finance-and-funding, date accessed 30 December 2015.
47. 'RSC: Finance and Funding', p. 37.
48. Shell Out Sounds, comprised of musicians and singers, was formed in the belief that Shell was escaping notice while Reclaim Shakespeare were focused on BP. Their focus is captured in their byline 'Voices for a Shell-free Southbank' and their pop-up performances have been concentrated on events sponsored by Shell at Southbank venues. See shelloutsounds.org/about/, date accessed 30 December 2015.
49. A video and the script is archived at bp-or-not-bp.org/news/musical-anti-oil-and-privatisation-protest-disrupts-launch-of-national-gallery-exhibition/, date accessed 30 December 2015.
50. 'Shell Sought to Influence Direction of Science Museum Climate Programme' *Guardian*, 31 May 2015, www.theguardian.com/business/2015/may/31/shell-sought-influence-direction-science-museum-climate-programme, date accessed 30 December 2015.
51. Cited in Adam Vaughan (2015) 'Science Museum Ends Sponsorship Deal with Shell' *Guardian*, 12 November, www.theguardian.com/business/2015/

nov/12/science-museum-ends-sponsorship-deal-with-shell, date accessed 30 December 2015.
52. twitter.com/PlatformLondon. Links to the other organisations participating in the Art Not Oil Coalition can be found at bp-or-not-bp.org/action-is-eloquence/, date accessed 30 December 2015.
53. The festival's press release is available at deadline.org.uk/2015/12/09/release-artists-successfully-occupy-tate-for-3-days-for-climate-festival/, date accessed 30 December 2015. The release includes a quotation from UK Green Party leader Natalie Bennett, one of the festival's speakers: 'Tate is soaking up BP's oil, and giving BP cover to keep drilling.'
54. McLuskie and Rumbold, p. 235.
55. See Emma Howard (2015) 'Ten UK Universities Divest From Fossil Fuels' *Guardian*, 10 November, www.theguardian.com/environment/2015/nov/10/ten-uk-universities-divest-from-fossil-fuels, date accessed 30 December 2015. Howard's article links to the important climate change activism organisation 350.org.
56. '2014 Visitor Figures' alva.org.uk/details.cfm?p=605, date accessed 30 December 2015.

Select Bibliography

Bate, Jonathan and Dora Thornton (2012) *Shakespeare: Staging the World* (London: British Museum Press).

Evans, Mel (2015) *Artwash: Big Oil and the Arts* (London: Pluto Press).

Goldfarb, Martin and Howard Aster (2010) *Affinity: Beyond Branding* (Toronto: MacArthur & Company).

McLuskie, Kate and Kate Rumbold (2014) *Cultural Value in Twenty-first Century England: The Case of Shakespeare* (Manchester: Manchester University Press).

Prescott, Paul and Erin Sullivan (eds) (2015) *Shakespeare on the Global Stage: Performance and Festivity in the Olympic Year* (London: Bloomsbury Arden Shakespeare).

Wu, Chin-Tao (2002) *Privatising Culture: Corporate Art Intervention since the 1980s* (London: Verso).

Index

The manufacturer's authorised representative in the EU is Springer
Nature Customer Service Centre GmbH, Europaplatz 3, 69115 Heidelberg,
Germany. If you have any concerns regarding our products, please
contact ProductSafety@springernature.com

Printed and bound by CPI Group (UK) Ltd, Croydon, CR0 4YY
23/04/2026
02095587-0015